Ripley's
BELIEVE IT
OR Not
OF AUSTRALIA
AND NEW ZEALAND

**THE MEN WHO CHIP ROCKS
WITH THEIR TEETH !**

THE **ABORIGINES**
of the Gibson Desert of Australia
ARE THE ONLY PEOPLE ON EARTH WHO
CREATE STONE TOOLS AND WEAPONS BY
SHAPING ROCKS WITH THEIR TEETH !

Ripley's BELIEVE IT OR Not

OF AUSTRALIA

AND NEW ZEALAND

Edited by
Richard Shears

VIKING O'NEIL

Viking O'Neil
Penguin Books Australia Ltd
487 Maroondah Highway, P.O. Box 257
Ringwood, Victoria 3134, Australia
Penguin Books Ltd
Harmondsworth, Middlesex, England
Viking Penguin Inc.
40 West 23rd Street, New York, N.Y. 10010, U.S.A.
Penguin Books Canada Ltd
2801 John Street, Markham, Ontario, Canada L3R 1B4
Penguin Books (N.Z.) Ltd
182-190 Wairau Road, Auckland 10, New Zealand

First published by Currey O'Neil Ross Pty Ltd 1983
as *Ripley's Believe It or Not!* ® *Book of Australia and New Zealand*
This edition published by Penguin Books Australia Ltd 1988
10 9 8 7 6 5 4 3 2
Copyright © Penguin Books Australia Ltd 1988

Produced by Viking O'Neil
56 Claremont Street, South Yarra, Victoria 3141, Australia
A division of Penguin Books Australia Ltd

Typeset in Garamond in Singapore
Printed and bound in Australia by Australian Print Group

National Library of Australia
Cataloguing-in-Publication data

Ripley, Robert L. (Robert LeRoy), 1893–1949.
    Ripley's believe it or not of Australia and New Zealand.

    ISBN 0 670 90087 7.

    1. Curiosities and wonders — Australia.
    2. Curiosities and wonders — New Zealand.
    3. Australia — Miscellanea. 4. New Zealand — Miscellanea. I.
    Title. II. Title: Believe it or not of Australia and New Zealand.

001.9'3'0994

"CRABHOLES" IS THE NAME
OF SMALL BODIES OF WATER
THAT FORM IN THE ARID
AREAS OF CENTRAL AUSTRALIA
- AND STRANGELY ASSUME
THE SHAPE OF A CRAB

Contents

Robert L. Ripley

Stranger than Fiction

The world is filled with oddities, freaks, coincidences and, yes, miracles. We hear about them from time to time and, perhaps, we dismiss them because they do not fit in with our 'logical' psyche. Nevertheless, they are there and if we could see them, witness them, we would come closer to believing. While we have a great many cynics among us, we have also a large number of believers—what is conceivable for one may be inconceivable for another.

Do we believe that some humans have been kidnapped and carried off in a spaceship, as some have claimed? Was the shooting of President Kennedy a Russian plot? Did Harold Lasseter find a fabulous reef of gold in the centre of Australia, or did he make the whole thing up? And did a Maori warrior really have amazing powers of healing, or was he the world's first tribal con man? Whether we believe that man and woman began life in the Garden of Eden or whether they evolved from the ape is a decision for the individual.

We should listen to stories and read our books with care, weighing up the facts and theories and drawing our own conclusions. It is up to us to believe or disbelieve.

Australians and New Zealanders, of course, don't really need the wisdom of Solomon to be aware that a story they hear in the local pub or at a dinner party falls into one of two categories—believable or unbelievable.

We have yarns, legends, fables and stories which are so outrageously bizarre, so coincidental, so, well, unbelievable, that it is often left to the reader or listener to decide whether they have credibility. We have all had our legs pulled by some crafty story teller who has repeated a poppycock of a tale that has been told through the decades around camp fires from Tunderallarra to Tumburumba, from Whangarei to Invercargill. In the fire of the moment it matters not whether the story is true—it is enough that it has startled us, humoured us, shocked us. That it is claimed to be factual only adds to the adrenalin flow.

Scientists and psychologists tell us that the written or spoken word can have a great effect on the 'inner man'. Our adrenalin flows faster when we read an exciting crime story and it fairly gushes when we learn that it really happened.

It was Byron who said 'Tis strange—but true; for truth is always strange; stranger than fiction'. And nobody agreed with him more than a young sports artist working for the old *New York Globe* in 1918. Robert L. Ripley had always been fascinated by odd facts of life and had kept a scrap book of news clippings about unusual sporting incidents. One day at the office he was desperate for a cartoon and turned to his scrapbook. He drew a selection of cartoons based on the strange facts he had collected, among them a story about J. M. Barnett of Australia, who jumped 11 810 times with a skipping rope over a period of 4 hours!

Ripley titled his cartoon composite 'Champs or Chumps' but, feeling that he had not done a serious day's work, crossed that out and on impulse wrote 'Believe It or Not!'. He dropped the drawing on the sports editor's desk and ambled off across the street for a cup of coffee. That seemingly uneventful day was to change Ripley's life. The sports editor loved the idea and his enthusiasm was to result in the words 'Believe It or Not!' becoming a household phrase and ending up among the classic quotations in *The Penguin Dictionary of Quotations*!

The first 'Ripley's Believe It or Not!' cartoon appeared in the *New York Globe* the day after Ripley had drawn it and was so well received by the public and his newspaper colleagues that, by popular request, he drew another. That was used a week later and, as the demands grew for more, 'Ripley's Believe It or Not!' was used twice a week and finally every day. Then other newspapers asked for permission to use the cartoons and it was not long before the feature was syndicated around the world, being used in 302 newspapers in 38 countries and in 17 languages. The total readership was 80 million!

As his fame grew Ripley travelled to 198 countries in his search for new material. Although sport still interested him, he and his many admirers wanted to read about the odd things people had got up to in all walks of life. Even Ripley himself would have made cartoon material, for he searched the corners of the world hunting the bizarre, whether it was in the jungles of Papua New Guinea, on the Great Wall of China or half-way up an Egyptian pyramid! When the Duke of Windsor heard about the unusual explorer he described him as the 'Modern Marco Polo'.

Ripley was fascinated by radio and became the first artist to use the medium to send a cartoon—transmitting it to the *New York Tribune* from London. In 1934 he became, with the help of a team of linguists, the first to broadcast to several nations at the same time.

The demand grew. The world wanted to know more about the odd events that had occurred or were still being played out. Ripley knew he was on to a winner—the world itself, he said, was a wonderful and endless source of material. In 1933 in Chicago, he introduced the first of his well-known 'odditoriums': museums where he displayed exhibitions of extraordinary curiosities and information gathered during his world travels.

His is an amazing story and, of course, absolutely true, for if it were not this book of 'Ripleyisms' would not exist. Ripley searched the world for his stories. In Australia and New Zealand alone there are a wealth of astonishing facts.

We have presented a selection to amuse and astound you. There is the Queenslander who lost his legs *twice*; the wombat that acted as a security dog by walking its two children home from school each day; the witness who caught fire while giving evidence in a New Zealand court; the woman who lived with a needle travelling through her body for 22 years then used it to continue her sewing; and the pieman who ran around Sydney with a dog on his shoulders.

They are all here. Some have played on the world stage and passed on. Others are still performing. We can only record their roles, describe their acts.

It is for you to believe. Or not.

J.M. BARNETT
of Australia—
JUMPED THE
ROPE
11,810
TIMES—
(About 4 hours)

ONE

Pioneers

Harsh, Hard Times

'Have you your pistols? Have
   you your sharp-edged axes?
Pioneers! O pioneers!'
        Walt Whitman (1819–1892)
They didn't always have to use
their weapons, but the early settlers
in Australia and New Zealand felt
much safer with them, for the
indigenous Aborigines and Maoris
were not necessarily enthusiastic
about the arrival of the white man.

Australia and New Zealand were
the lands beyond the oceans, a
mecca for the likes of Captain
James Cook (1728–1779) who
declared: 'I am one who has
ambition not only to go further
than any one has done before but
as far as is possible for a man
to go.'

In the wake of Cook, who after
spending six months charting the
New Zealand coast sailed up the
eastern edge of Australia in 1770,
came the first settlers and the
convicts—the earliest pioneers.
Explorers set off into the inland
and found areas where they could
set up camp. They were harsh,
hard times and man had no option
but to live off the land and build
homes from the raw materials
available.

The stories that emerged from
those early days were numerous
and bizarre and had Robert Ripley
been able to travel into the bush
with his drawing board and
notebook he would have had a field
day. There were incredible tales of
hardship, convict cheek, punishment
and great amusement.

The pioneers were jacks of all
trades and an example of their
lifestyle is perhaps summed up
by Alexander Tolmer, South
Australia's Police Commissioner in
1852. Tolmer rubbed himself with
emu oil to cure his rheumatism so
he could withstand the 'hand-to-
hand fights and hard knocks I have
had in capturing bushrangers and
other like ruffians'.

Step back in time, then, and read
of:

A town's first doctor who
   operated with a poultry
   knife and a tenon-saw!
The coffin that served as a
   home and transport!

A horse-shoe that resulted in a man being blown up.
The men who got on their hands and knees and barked like dogs.
The world's first full length film, made and shown in Melbourne.

Wrong Diagnosis

A young colonial widow who attempted to commit suicide at Sale (Vic.) by administering an overdose of chloroform because she thought she had a serious stomach illness, was rushed to hospital where, still unconscious, she gave birth!

First Skiers

In the 1850s, 30 years before downhill skiing began in Switzerland, goldminers in the Snowy Mountains region were gliding down the snow-covered slopes at Kiandra (NSW). Wearing skis made from fence palings, skiers sat astride a single pole which they used as a brake. By 1862 Australia's first competitive skiing was taking place in the region.

The Good Oil

Alexander Tolmer, appointed South Australia's Commissioner of Police in 1852, spoke French and Portuguese, painted a picture for Queen Victoria, played the violin in an orchestra, swam like a champion and frequently rubbed himself with emu oil because he believed it was a marvellous cure for rheumatism and without its use 'both my arms would not have stood the hand-to-hand fights and hard knocks I have had in capturing bushrangers and other like ruffians'.

Much Married Bishop

Dismayed at the Aboriginal tribal custom of marrying young girls to elders, the Catholic Vicar Apostolic of Darwin, Rev. Francis Xavier Gsell, purchased native girls from their families so that under tribal law they became his wives. He was then able to line them up for marriage to Christian men but he, in turn, until his death in 1960, was known as the Bishop With 150 wives!

Good Dog

They call it Cambewarra now, but originally the NSW town was known as Good Dog after the pet of a pioneer attacked a bull which was charging the land-owner. The dog died in its amazing rescue bid but the owner lived to exclaim 'Good Dog!'—although there was a theory around for a while that he really said 'Good God!'.

Upside-Down Land

Three convicts transported from England to Australia, which they regarded as 'upside-down land', decided to live out their fantasies while working for a Sydney man—they planted cuttings of vines upside-down and built one side of a house 18 inches higher than the other! They finally saw things the right way around after they each received a whipping!

Chinese First Around Australia

The first sailors to circumnavigate Australia are believed to be the Chinese, who discovered the continent by accident. Some historians believe their junks were blown to the coast of Western Australia in 1420 and after travelling completely around the coastline they presented to Emperor Yung Lo a porcelain map of 'The Land of the South'.

Success in Excess

Mr John Coubrough, who reached the age of 101 in Sydney, attributed his long life to the fact that he had smoked heavily since the age of 10, had drunk hundreds of gallons of beer—but had travelled in a car only three times!

Smart Spider

Mrs Joan Wallis, who ran a NSW country orchard in the early 1900s, kept an enormous pet tarantula called Peter which she allowed to roam to kill flies. In the winter she fed him cake and bread crumbs. Peter lived behind a picture frame and always emerged WHEN SHE CALLED ITS NAME!

The New Deity

Spotting a steam-powered car designed and driven by David Shearer in South Australia in 1897, four ladies in a horse-driven buggy jumped to the road, got on their hands and knees and lowered their heads, believing it was the devil!

PEDRO FERNANDEZ de QUIROS (1565-1615)
the Portuguese explorer
NAMED THE CONTINENT OF AUSTRALIA
TO HONOR HIS PATRON KING PHILIP III
OF SPAIN - A MEMBER OF THE
HOUSE OF AUSTRIA.

THE CONTINENT WAS ORIGINALLY
CALLED AUSTRIALIA

First Film

The world's first full length film was made and shown in Melbourne by the Salvation Army in 1900. Entitled *Soldiers of the Cross* it might have perturbed the censor, had there been one, for it showed martyrs being beheaded, crucified, chopped with swords and fed to lions and Stephen being brutally stoned to death!

Great Guy

George Guy, of Mathinna (Tas.), numbered among his 12 children the best footballers, cricketers, axemen and cyclists in the State. Of his three great-grandchildren, two were older than his youngest daughter (by his second wife) and his eldest son was her senior by 60 years!

Death Duties

An inquest was delayed for several days in Sydney in 1889 because of the absence of the city coroner, Mr H. T. Wilkinson—his was the body.

Special Value

Mr T. T. Kelly, of Armidale (NSW), kept five coins, the dates of which matched birthdays of his family—an English coin from George II's reign, dated 1758, to mark the birth of his great-grandfather; an Italian coin, dated 1783, for the birth of his grandfather; an 1816 English coin for his father; and 1851 English coin for his own birth; and an 1898 coin for his eldest son's birth!

303 Not Out

After a 1000 mile flight from
Auckland to Dunedin (NZ) for the
town's centennial celebrations in 1948,
101 year old Mrs O. Nielson called in
on Mrs Susan McFarlane, aged one
hundred and two. The two ladies then
drove to Waikouaiti to congratulate
Mrs George Williamson who had just
celebrated her 100th year!

Kindly Rain

At the end of his tether through lack
of water in 1884, Phillip Hiern
decided to let his 3000 sheep go free
in the morning, realising he would
never be able to continue his desert-
crossing to Port Augusta.

That night it poured with rain. He
remained in the area for a week as the
rain continued. During his sojourn he
discovered that beyond 10 miles in any
direction there had not been a drop!

Marathon Game

One of the first Australian Rules
football games was played in 1858–
and turned into a four-day marathon!

Scotch College and Melbourne
Grammar School agreed to play until
one side scored two goals. The
teams—40 on each side—were made up
of boys and masters, goal posts were
more than a mile apart and the rules
were virtually non existent!

Southern Cross

Australia's modern independence
movement carries as its flag a white
cross on a blue background—the
design of the 'Southern Cross' flag
used by rebellious miners when they
fought troopers at Ballarat (Vic.)
in 1854.

The original Southern Cross, or
what is left of it, is kept at the
Ballarat Art Gallery.

Four Corners

Ross (Tas.) was often referred to as
the place of 'recreation, temptation,
damnation and salvation' because
on the four corners of the main
intersection stood a public hall, an inn,
a military barracks and a church!

Big on Bikes

At the turn of the century when more than 8000 people were riding bicycles in the Kalgoorlie (WA) district, the machine was known as 'the ship of the desert'.

Impossible Name

A survey station on a hill in New Zealand's Wanganui district was named on Geographical Society maps as: TAUMATAWHAKATAN-GIHANGAKOAUAUATAMATEA-POKAIWHENUAKITANATAHU!

Funeral's Fine Words

When prospector Hugh Carey died near Armidale (NSW) in 1860, his mates, who were conducting the funeral service, realised that none knew an appropriate prayer. Minutes later an American miner announced he'd found a prayer and mumbled some fine-sounding words from a piece of paper. Carey was buried and the mourners walked away satisfied. The American never told them he had read the Declaration of American Independence over the dead man!

TOPS IN TOPONOMY!

LACHLAN MACQUARIE
Governor of New South Wales Australia

NAMED HUNDREDS OF TOWNS, LAKES, MOUNTAINS, RIVERS, ETC. AFTER HIMSELF AND HIS WIFE ELIZABETH — SUCH AS

LACHLAN RIVER-LACHLAN DISTRICT- MACQUARIE COUNTY- PORT MACQUARIE MACQUARIE STREET-MACQUARIE HARBOR-MACQUARIE RIVER- MACQUARIE ISLE MACQUARIE PLAINS- MACQUARIE STRAIT- MACQUARIE MARSHES- FORT MACQUARIE, ETC. ELIZABETH ST- ELIZABETH BAY- ELIZABETH POINT- ELIZABETH, ETC.

Hopes Blasted

The epitaph on a headstone of a child's grave at Buckland (Tas.) read: 'Sacred to the memory of Edward Howell, who departed this life on 9 November 1852, aged 9 months. Here lies the grief of a fond Mother And the blasted expectations of an indulgent Father'.

Bush Cricket

A group of enterprising pioneer children who were avid cricket fans played a match on the south coast of New South Wales using only bush materials. The ball was cut from a lump of fungus called the black-fellow's bread, the bats were shaped from ironbark, the stumps from a wattle tree and the pads were pieces of stringybark. The pitch was on an ant bed which was not affected by rain and which lasted for weeks without wear.

Tin Can Will

When a mine collapsed at El Dorado (Vic.) at the turn of the century, a trapped miner awaiting death wrote his will on a billycan, witnessed by two mates. Rescuers found their bodies beside the 'will' which directed that all belongings should go to the miner's wife and family.

Not in Hunt

The shortest-lived hunting club in Australia was the Avoca (Vic.) Harriers, formed in 1869. At the first fence during the first week, the gelding carrying Mr John Wise crashed and its rider remained unconscious for several days. The other members lost heart and the club was disbanded.

MATTHEW FLINDERS
(1774-1814)
Australia's most famed explorer
SPENT 11 YEARS WRITING A BOOK ON HIS TRAVELS AND DIED ON THE DAY IT WAS PUBLISHED

Gunpowder Plod

Carrying 2½ tons of gunpowder on a dray along the bumpy Bathurst road (NSW), Mr J. Gamble ended his days in a violent explosion. Police concluded that one of the kegs was leaking and that a spark from one of the horse's shoes had done the rest.

Strange Jobs

Men with the strangest jobs in Australia were the 'sheep heelers' who worked at a railway siding at Newmarket (Vic.). When sheep were about to be unloaded from wagons, the men got in behind them on their hands and knees and barked like dogs to frighten them down the ramp!

Rain-Makers

In a desperate attempt to end a drought in 1902 a group of rain-making pioneers, headed by Mr Clement Wragge, sent two rockets into the sky over Charleville (Qld), and to the delight of the large crowd of onlookers a few drops fell. However, it did not last and the crippling drought continued.

90 Years a Postman

Tom Cambridge, the postman at Windsor (NSW) from 1835 to 1862, handed his job on retirement to his son, Tom Cambridge, who passed the post to his son, Tom Cambridge who kept it until 1925.

A Dampener

When the old men of his parish objected to a damp portion of St Luke's Church cemetery, Liverpool (NSW), being set aside for paupers, Rev. J. Walker said it didn't really matter where a body was buried—and to prove it he insisted that on his death his grave should be dug in a particularly damp spot. His wish was carried out and the poor were satisfied.

Lightning Path

A strange memorial has been trodden over by hundreds of thousands of feet.

Set in the footpath in Adelaide Street, Blayney (NSW), the slab reads: 'This stone was erected in memory of Elizabeth Emily Bromfield, who was struck by lightning on this spot in her 17th year. January 20, 1888. Jacob Russet, Mayor.'

Double Coffin

After the 1870 murders of the Conns, a pioneer and his wife, on the Herbert River (Qld), a double-sized coffin was ordered for their joint burial.

But the boat bringing the casket was held up by bad weather and the funeral proceeded without it. The coffin was left at an overnight hut where it served as a bunk for several years and once, when the river flooded, it was used as a punt to ferry travellers!

Twin Burial

The two most important living things in property-owner David Constable's life were his wife Catherine and his horse. When they died in New South Wales in the late 1870s he buried them side by side on his property.

Cave Courthouse

The world's most unusual courthouse and execution chamber were located in caves at Wiseman's Ferry on the Hawkesbury River (NSW).

Seats were cut into a sandstone cave and Soloman Wiseman, Superintendent of convicts, presided. Prisoners sentenced to death were taken across the river, where, hanged from the branch of a tree, they dropped into a hole in the roof of another cave!

Doctor's Basic Tools

Sam Reynolds, the first doctor in the Victorian town of Mansfield in the 1870s, worked with a local girl, Miss Quirk, as matron and performed operations with a poultry knife borrowed from a local hotel and a tenon-saw loaned by the town saddler!

Red Ruin

A strange transformation of the passengers took place during the first coach run started in the early 1890s between Southern Cross and Coolgardie (WA). So much dust was kicked up by the horses that when the passengers alighted they all had bright red hair!

Precise Warning

When the steam railway between Adelaide and Port Adelaide was opened in 1857 warning posters read: 'BEWARE OF THE SUDDEN IMPULSE TO SPRING FROM THE CARRIAGE TO RECOVER A HAT WHICH HAS BEEN BLOWN OFF!'

Lucky Visit

A chance call by Chief Constable Midgely on his old friend Rev. Browne resulted in the arrest of robbers Henry Smart and Henry Ford who were scouring the clergyman's house for valuables in Van Diemen's Land in 1846.

Show of Loyalty

Nine years after rebelling against authority by barricading themselves against troopers at Ballarat (Vic.) to protest against mining fees in the famous Eureka Stockade incident, former prospectors were among hundreds of volunteers who went to fight 'for the Queen' in New Zealand's Maori wars. Their response, they said, helped explain they had nothing against the Empress Victoria—merely her officials and agents.

The Brothers Jagajaga

When John Batman, founder of Melbourne, purchased 600 000 acres of land from an Aboriginal tribe for mirrors, blankets and beads in the early 19th century, a lawyer drew up an official document declaring that the sale had been agreed to by the brothers Jagajaga, Jagajaga and Jagajaga.

Thozet's Green Thumb

Standing on the banks of the Fitzroy River (Qld) in the late 1800s, Monsieur A. Thozet noticed a strand of wheat floating down. He removed the grain, sowed it and produced 200 stalks, each with a full ear.

He became a recognised authority on agriculture, cultivating phenomenal crops of arrowroot, wheat, barley, oats and tobacco.

When he died and was buried in his garden, the weeds grew rapidly and overran his grave!

Runaway Gentry

Born in 1773, Samuel Jervis, son of Squire Jervis of Shenstone Park near Lichfield, England, was taken to sea by his uncle. Fearing that the relative intended to leave him on a deserted island and claim title to the estate, Sammy hid in the bush in Tasmania and was adopted by an Aboriginal tribe. Twenty-six years later he moved in with a family of white settlers and what he lost in title he gained in years. For Samuel finally died in 1891—at the age of 118!

First Steam Engine

Sydney residents did not have the chance of enjoying a ride behind Australia's first steam engine—it was used to drive a flour mill in 1815!

Tram Blockade

The first traffic jam in Adelaide, in 1924, was caused by a ship at its moorings! With her bow against the tramway bridge at Port Adelaide, the US barquentine *Kate G. Pederson* projected her bowsprit across the road, preventing trams from passing!

Body Count

The Min tribespeople in the remote areas of western Papua-New Guinea have a unique form of counting, the base of their numerals being twenty-seven. To begin their counting, they start from the smallest finger of the left hand, followed by the other fingers to the thumb, the left wrist, the left forearm, the left elbow, biceps, shoulder, side of neck, ear, eye and bridge of nose and then down the right side, ending with the little finger of the right hand!

Forgotten Heroes

Matthew Flinders, one of the pioneer world's greatest navigators, and George Bass worked together exploring the Australian coast. With their names destined for history books they were headed for great things, but Bass finished his days as a captive in the mines of Chile and Flinders died in poverty in England after being held prisoner by the French at Mauritius.

Matthew Flinders

George Bass

First Flag

Mrs Honor Bowman, a farmer's wife, put her old silk wedding dress to good use—she turned it into a flag carrying a motif of a kangaroo and an emu on each side of a shield and hoisted it over her property at Richmond (NSW) in 1806!

Australia's first flag, it is now preserved in the Mitchell Library, Sydney.

Bewhiskered

In the 1850s in Melbourne some men favoured 'mutton chop' whiskers but others preferred to remain clean-shaven. Male society was so divided that a cricket match was organised between a side calling itself the Whiskers X1 and a team known as the No Whiskers X1.

Jew's Lament

When a Jewish prospector died in the Western Australian settlement of Sandstone in 1908 another Jew stepped forward to conduct the burial service. He concluded with the words: 'There lies the body of the first Jew to die in Sandstone. Please God may he be the last, because I'm the only other one in this district and I'd hate to die in a place like this.'

Signally Apt

The first long-distance telephone conversation in Australia took place in 1878 over a range of 240 miles between Port Augusta (SA) and a place named—Semaphore!

Treed by Crocodiles

'Knobbie' Clarke, a 62-year-old prospector of Finnis River, 40 miles south of Darwin, spent 15 hours sitting in a tree besieged by an angry boar and two crocodiles. He had shot and only wounded the bore and climbed the tree in a hurry when his rifle jammed.

He planned to jump into the river and swim, but then the crocodiles appeared. Only when the boar wandered off did he dare to venture down.

All Rounder

Outback police in the early 1900s had a tough time. At Brewarrina (NSW), 60 miles from Bourke, third-class Sergeant J. A. Nightingale was Registrar of Births, Deaths and Marriages; agent for the State Savings Bank; Deputy Public Trustee; Crown Lands Bailiff; Inspector under the Explosives Act; local authority for the Board of Health; Inspector of Dairies; Inspector of Nuisances; and Sanitary Inspector.

Daily Bugle

Faced with a shortage of paper in 1875, the editor of Queensland's *Etheridge Courier* purchased hundreds of handkerchiefs and printed the latest edition of his newspaper on them!

Rum Church

Four gallons of rum could buy a man another's wife in the early days of the colony in Australia. And Rev. Richard Johnson, the first librarian, paid for part of his church with the precious drop.

Walled Bone

A doctor in the Tasmanian township of Bagdad had hated bushrangers ever since they robbed his house during his absence in the 1830s and forced his wife and daughters to wait on them. When at last the villains were shot down by a party of soldiers, the doctor made a special request—and he returned home with the thigh bone of one man which he had built into the wall of his new home!

Paper Spear

A visitor to a sawmill at Goulburn (NSW) tossed away a tightly screwed up newspaper which caught in the teeth of a circular saw. It was flung with such force that it penetrated a workman's forehead, killing him!

Class Division

When Captain Philip Gidley King became the third Governor of New South Wales he commented that the colony comprised only two classes. Those who sold rum and those who drank it!

Cinema Pioneer

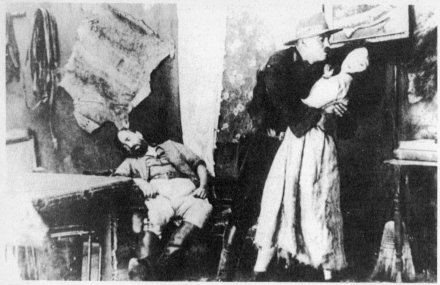

Chauvel's film Moth of Moonbi

After making several feature films when he returned to Australia from America, where he had worked in the film industry in the early 1920s, Charles Chauvel found there were no cinemas to show his work. Undeterred, he employed himself as projectionist and set up a travelling cinema, showing films in factories and shearing sheds!

Shaky Fort

A military fort which stood 15 miles from Wellington (NZ) had the distinction of being 'retired' after its first confrontation. When a cannon on the top storey was fired, once, at a passing Maori war canoe the building shook so severely it was decided never to use the premises again!

Fair Warning

'Dangerous curve just ahead. Nearest hospital, 10 miles. Nearest cemetery, 11 miles'—early road sign in South Australia.

On the Map

Although it has a small population, the Queensland outback town of Charleville has achieved a number of 'firsts'.

Established in 1888, it became an important railway centre and distribution centre for a large sheep-raising district, was developed as a centre for the Flying Doctor Service, was the take-off point for the first Qantas commercial flight—and was the location in 1902 for an unsuccessful attempt to make rain by blowing up gunpowder in the clouds!

Odd Assortment

The deed for the land on which the city of Wellington (NZ) stands shows that the following items were used for the purchase: two kegs of tobacco, three dozen red flannel nightcaps, one dozen pipes, one dozen umbrellas, two flintlock pistols, assorted muskets with powder and half a gross of Jews' Harps!

Amazing Survival

Trying to extract a cartridge wedged in his revolver in the early 1900s, a Proserpine (Qld) timber cutter jammed a metal rammer into the barrel. The weapon exploded and the rammer went in through the man's head just above the right eye, passed completely through a portion of his brain and protruded through the top of his skull for three inches.

He WALKED to get help and, without losing consciousness, was taken by coach and train to a Townsville Hospital where part of his skull cap was lifted ro remove the rammer.

Two weeks later, he left hospital to resume his wood cutting!

Shafted

Walking to inspect a Cobar (NSW) diggings hole down which a man had fallen that afternoon in 1884, a boy fell down a 93 ft shaft, but managed to drag himself through a tunnel to the river just as two of his search party dropped down another shaft 40 ft deep and sustained serious injuries! Hearing their groans, another miner went for a doctor, but he, too, fell down a shaft and when a trooper with a rope was sent for, he, too, tumbled into a hole!

Barefooted Harry

Bushman Matt Robinson, who walked the banks of the Darling River (NSW) in the early 1900s, had such hard feet, being able to walk on thorns or stand on burning cigarettes without pain, that he earned the nickname 'Barefooted Harry'.

Saved by Gold

As he was about to be strung up by the neck for spreading false stories about gold lying everywhere around Gladstone (Qld), a Cornish miner called Chapple, and known locally as 'The Magpie' because of his constant chatter, was somewhat relieved when the police commissioner rode up to the scene and urged the lynch mob to put his stories to the test. On the commissioner's instructions the men dug around the 'hanging tree' and the first pan of dirt yielded nearly half an ounce of gold. As the men went crazy their bird flew!

Good Grub

A popular food among Aborigines is the witchetty grub, a fat, white worm-like creature found among the roots of the witchetty bush. The larvae of certain moths and beetles, they are eaten baked or raw—tasting sweet when cooked, resembling butter when eaten raw!

White Tribeswoman

To gain an insight into the lives of Aborigines for the Western Australian government and to obtain material for her book *The Passing of Aboriginals*, Irish immigrant Daisy Bates (1863– 1951) lived among tribes for FORTY YEARS! If ill health had not struck, she would have continued to live with them, but she was forced to move to Adelaide where she died, aged ninety!

THE **TOWN ON WHEELS**
LAKEWOOD, in Western Australia,
A COMMUNITY IN THE HEART OF THE LUMBER AND GOLD MINING AREA
HAS ITS HOMES, SHOPS, POST OFFICE AND POLICE STATION
MOUNTED ON RAILROAD CARS

Birth of Botany Bay

Reaching an inlet swarming with stingrays, some weighing 300 lb, Captain Cook thought of calling the area Sting-rays Harbour. But two naturalists on the *Endeavour* had collected so many plants from the area they suggested Botanists' Harbour. They finally settled on a name which became famous around the world—Botany Bay.

Big Diocese

When William Broughton was appointed the first Bishop of Australia in 1836 he inherited the largest Church of England diocese in the world—the Australian mainland, Tasmania and Norfolk Island.

New Swim Stroke

Watching a young Pacific islander swimming, Arthur Cavill commented: 'It's unbelievable—he's crawling across the water!' Realising the stroke was faster than the traditional breast-stroke Cavill used it in an official competition in 1902 and it was later widely used and became known as the Australian Crawl.

Women's Rights

New Zealand was the first country in the world to recognise women's rights when in 1893 it allowed them to vote in parliamentary elections. A year later South Australian women were given similar rights.

Gruesome Solution

In the early 1890s, almost every man who committed suicide in northern Queensland placed a stick of dynamite in his mouth and blew his head off.

Ardent Churchman

When William Colenso, a pioneer missionary, arrived in New Zealand's Bay of Islands in 1834 he brought a printing press on which he produced the New Testament in Maori.

He was later dismissed from a Christian mission in the Hawke Bay area because of an 'irregular association with a Maori girl', but eight years later he was elected to the House of Representatives.

Early Imports

The first drivers to be employed in 1853 by Cobb and Co., the Australian horse-drawn coach concern, were Americans who had gained their experience from Wells Fargo.

Swagmen's Union

Among the rules of a swagmen's union that was formed in Forbes (NSW) were the conditions that no members were to be over 100 years old, they were not allowed to carry swags weighing over 10 lbs and whenever they passed a farm they had to try to obtain rations and hand-outs!

Class Distinction

When Cobb and Co.'s coaches struck a muddy patch, the driver's cry would sometimes be: 'First class, keep your seats. Second class, climb out and walk. Third class, climb out and shove!'

'Nothing Today Jack'

Realising that Mick Dougherty, a driver with Cobb and Co., had a reputation as the best yarn-spinner in Australia, passengers grinned knowingly as he told a gullible elderly passenger of a kangaroo he had trained to meet the coach, slit open the bag, sort the letters and deliver them to settlers in the district.

Rounding a bend they came across a huge kangaroo. With a crack of his whip, Dougherty sped by calling 'NOTHING TODAY JACK!'

What a Bounder

When he grabbed a huge 'old man' kangaroo in his hands in an attempt to save his dog which was faring badly in a fight between the animals, Brian Silcock's military hat, complete with strap, was knocked from his head and landed around the roo's neck. Firing his gun at the creature, Silcock hit the helmet, the bullet ricocheted and killed his dog and he stood helplessly watching as the roo bounded off into the New South Wales bush, still wearing the hat!

'Hollow Log' Jack

Swagman 'Hollow Log' Jack never slept anywhere but in the trunk of a fallen dead tree. After sending his dog in to chase out snakes and anything else which might be lurking, he sealed one end to stop draughts and settled down for the night. When old Hollow Log died of natural causes they found him, in a tree trunk of course, with a contented smile on his face!

Grown Gates

A New South Wales farmer, Mr L. Griffin, grew his own gates, bending young saplings at the desired height and forcing the trunks to grow horizontally. He then joined the two 'Ls' together into a rectangle and filled the space with branches.

Divided Town

The town of Agnew (WA) is equally divided at election time—exactly equally divided. Tommy Cock, who runs the local hotel in the old gold-mining town votes Liberal and Paddy Palmer, a prospector who lives at the hotel, votes Labor. The rest of the population? There aren't any others!

THE LIVING MEMORIAL ARCH
Adelaide, Australia

UNDER THIS GUM TREE AUSTRALIA WAS OFFICIALLY DECLARED A MEMBER OF THE BRITISH EMPIRE
-1836

Tough Training

Australian sheepdog trials were dominated in the first 20 years of the 20th century by two brothers named King and a breeder named McLeod. They trained one of their kelpie dogs to drive a chicken into a jam tin!

Bullock Cools Off

A bullock being driven through Yass (NSW) on a very hot day in 1919 broke away from the mob, ran into the bathroom of a house, caught its horn in a tap and turned on the shower which it stood under until the drover collected it!

Drilling Match

When Fred Bussey and Jim Logan of Queensland challenged one another to a rock drilling contest in 1901 they worked with hand drills into granite for 20 minutes, timed by a referee. He declared a draw—both holes were exactly 17¾ inches deep!

Nut Candle

The kernel of the quandong nut served as an excellent candle in outback Australia in the 19th century. Full of oil, it gave off a good light for hours, was smokeless and practically odourless.

Faith in Camel

In the gold-rush days of the 1850s and 1860s parish priest Father Long of Western Australia had difficulty finding a horse to do his rounds. So he bought a camel for the job.

Thrifty Squatter

Millionaire squatter James 'Hungry' Tyson was asked to hand over his only shilling to a ferry man to cross the Murrumbidgee River. 'No thanks mate', he said—and he dived in and swam across.

Gossip Sheet

The smallest newspaper in the world, published on Thursday Island, north of Australia, gathered all its news by radio and from what beachcombers and native boys heard. The *Torres Strait Daily Pilot* began in 1888 with a single woman acting as publisher, editor and reporter!

Not Riveting

The first book printed in Australia, in 1802, has NOT gone into the annals of great literary merit. It has an uninteresting start, a boring plot and a yawn-inspiring end. Its title: *New South Wales General Standing Orders*!

Stump-Jumper

One of the greatest assets to 19th-century farmers was the 'stump-jump plough', invented by brothers R. B. and C. H. Smith of South Australia. It derived its name because its shares rose automatically to pass over tree stumps or rocks when land was being cultivated.

Willow Legacy

A settler named Shanley was riding home near the town of Adaminaby (NSW) when he died after his horse fell, clutching a small willow stick he had been using as a riding whip. Because he was still gripping the stick when found, it was stuck in the ground at the head of the grave. It grew up into one of the largest willow trees in Australia!

First Tote

The 'tote', the automatic totalisator used on the racecourses of the world, was devised by George Julius of Sydney who operated the first mechanical tote in Auckland (NZ) in 1913.

Ninety the Glutton

A Tasmanian drifter, asked to tend a flock of sheep for three months in the late 1800s, was 90 head short when he brought them in for shearing. Asked where they were he replied matter-of-factly that he had eaten one a day as part of his rations. He became known as Ninety the Glutton!

Beautiful Bar

George Adams, the man behind Australia's Tatts lotteries, started life in Australia at the age of 16, working on a sheep farm. But the determined English emigrant had soon worked his way to a position where he could run a bar and later in Sydney he built an impressive bar at his Adams Hotel, a bar that included imported marble, oil paintings and stained-glass windows and which is now incorporated in the Sydney Hilton.

Escalating Pearl

An Aboriginal on a walkabout on a beach in Western Australia in 1917 was attracted by a 'white stone'. He swapped it with a local boy for a stick of tobacco but after the boy sold it for £13 it was realised it was a valuable pearl.

Under the name 'Star of the West' it was resold for many thousands of pounds and became so important that when it was exhibited at London's Wembley Exhibition armed guards had to be called in to surround it for 24 hours!

Rhyming Judge

Barron Field, who came to Australia in 1817, was known as the 'Rhyming Judge'. In addition to his role as Judge of the Supreme Court of New South Wales he was the man behind the first book of verse to be published in Australia under the appropriate title *First Fruits of Australian Poetry*. A critic described it as 'a barren field indeed'.

Laborious Press

John Pascoe Fawkner

It was no easy task producing the first newspapers in Port Phillip (later Victoria) and Western Australia—they were written by hand!

The *Melbourne Advertiser*, which came on to the streets in 1838, was written by hand by Mr J. P. Fawkner while in Western Australia Mr James Gardner was busy with pen and ink writing the *Fremantle Journal and General Advertiser*.

House Removed

Queensland cane farmer Ronald Light, returning to his house in Brisbane in the early 1950s, found that thieves had sawn through the stumps and stolen it, along with all the furniture. The house was never seen again.

Young Landlord

When land-owner Bill Feast died in the early 1950s he left his property and estate to his young friend, four-year-old Ian Webb, of Queensland, who automatically became landlord to his father, Jim! Jim's store stood on old Bill's land, which meant he then had to pay rent to his son.

School of the Air

The biggest school in the world has a class scattered over hundreds of kilometres! Australia's School of the Air brings children living in outlying areas together through a two-way radio link up. Hearing their classmates discuss problems with their tutor gives children a sense of being part of a class. There are 12 bases scattered around the country.

Wine Pioneers

Hearing about a group of Germans who were in religious conflict with the Prussian Government, George Angas, chairman of the South Australia Company—organised in England in 1836 to send settlers to Australia—lent them the money to travel to Australia.

The new immigrants settled on 11 000 ha owned by Angas in the Barossa Valley, a region that is now one of Australia's biggest wine-producing areas.

THE OLDEST BUILDING IN AUSTRALIA
THE ELIZABETH FARM IN PARRAMATTA, AUSTRALIA, WAS BUILT IN 1794

Australia—A New Gaol

Returning to England after sailing
with Captain James Cook in 1768
botanist Joseph Banks recommended
that Australia would be a good
alternative to the crowded gaols of
Britain. The British Government
finally agreed and the result was the
sailing of the First Fleet.

Giant Coach Service

Every day, the 19th-century carriage
firm Cobb and Co. harnessed some
6000 horses and covered a distance
greater than the circumference of the
earth—24 902 miles! The biggest
coach, The Leviathan, operating in
Victoria, was drawn by no less than
22 horses!

Driftwood Lighthouse

Authorities in Queensland found a use
for timber washed ashore from ships
wrecked on the Great Barrier Reef by
ordering convicts to build a lighthouse
with it!

Twenty prisoners set to work and
erected the lighthouse on Raine Islet,
which worked so well that no wood
became available for a second building
because no more ships were lost!

Fiery Fanfare

Andrew Torning, who founded
Sydney's No. 1 Volunteer Fire Company, in 1854 managed to enlist a very
important non-working member—the
Duke of Edinburgh! Torning, who
directed operations through a trumpet,
took the heat out of his life by
running the Royal Victoria Theatre,
painting and acting.

Convict's Press

One of the first things English convict
Andrew Bent did when he arrived in
Hobart (Tas.) in 1812 was publish a
privately-printed newspaper demanding
freedom of the press and protesting
against conditions in the colony!

Despite being fined and imprisoned
twice, his readers gave him much
support, although he had to continually
fight to get the paper out. In 1939 he
moved to Sydney and died in poverty.

Rump Repellant

A concoction of rum and swamp water
drunk in Bourketown (NSW) was so
powerful that it eeked through men's
pores, kept the mosquitoes at bay and
earned the name 'The Bourketown
Mosquito Net'!

Air Giant's Birth

Qantas, Australia's international airline, is the oldest in the world and has one of the highest safety records. It was registered in November, 1920, as the Queensland and Northern Territory Aerial Services and began as an air taxi service in outback Queensland.

The Same End

On the road between Boulia and Selwyn (Qld.) stood two graves—one of a traveller who died of thirst, the other of a carrier who broke into his load of spirits and drank himself to death!

Fastidious Farmer

A farmer at a South Australian dairy farm led his cows through a wind tunnel on the way to the milking shed so that all flies and dust were blown from them!

Pauper to Cattle King

Sir Sidney Kidman, who owned between 85 000 and 105 000 square miles of grazing land in central Australia, New South Wales and Queensland, began work in 1870, aged 13, with a one-eyed horse and five shillings capital! He was the biggest private land-owner in the British Empire.

Body Mislaid

A group of gold prospectors at the turn of the century started a settlement near Darwin and elected one of their own as mayor. When he died shortly afterwards they buried him, then went on a wake while awaiting a tombstone.

When it arrived, no-one could remember where the body was buried, so the headstone was left at the side of the road, the only epitaph to be erected in Australia without a body!

Sharp Reminder

Aboriginal pearl-divers went straight home if they survived a shark attack. Not because they were injured but because they believed an attack by one of the jagged-toothed creatures signified that their wives were being unfaithful!

Happy Landing

Gold prospecting at Eaglehawk (Vic.) in 1885, Peter Shirley fell off a ladder back into the 24 ft pit where he had just lit two dynamite charges. Lying injured he managed to toss one stick from the pit but could not see the other and as he lapsed into unconsciousness he was certain he would never wake in one piece again.

He need not have worried—he had landed on the second charge, putting it out!

TWO

Ratbags

An Australian Breed

They are a peculiarly Australian breed. As indigenous as kangaroos and as predictable as a bull with a thistle in its behind.

Ratbags are to Australia what eccentrics are to England. High-spirited and filled with derring-do, they live outside society's boundaries in a style all their own. Their idiosyncracies infuriate and charm us; make us laugh and cry; often leaving us sorry for ourselves... sorry that we've been duped yet strangely, perversely glad for the experience.

Dashing, flashy, conniving, selfish yet generous to a fault and both softly spoken and outspoken, they are nonetheless endearing. And often it is to a ratbag that we turn when in a tight situation for they never seem to lose their cool.

Truly a mixed bag, he's the 'nice' lodger a Sydney woman admitted to her home who then proceeded to hold a loud concert in the bath at five o'clock every morning! He's the thief who stole an old lady's bird cage but left the canary tethered to a house brick on the mantelpiece. He's the chemist who sold a customer a set of false teeth which did not fit. And he's the disguise artist who duped 500 socialites into believing he was a distinguished Swiss professor and gave them an uncomfortable lecture on face lifts. He is the gentleman who parts a rich widow from her fortune only to have her sigh wistfully: 'Ah... but he was so charming...!'

For there is always that other side to them. The bath singer moved out without a protest... the thief who stole the bird cage left a two shilling piece. And the disguise artist sent the money he had charged to a local charity.

Oddly, though ratbags abound, they are more often the male of the species! But settle back and allow yourself to be charmed by:

> The woman who attacked an umpire with a meat pie and sauce.
> The fireman who chopped up a rival's hose!
> The poet who never was.

The amazing Nunawading Messiah.
The man who drank his wife, draining her from a glass.
The dentist who filled teeth with a car number plate.

Scrappy Idea

Mr J. S. Mann, a Bundaberg (Qld) scrap dealer applied to the United Nations for a permit to salvage scrap space ship metal on the moon. His application was turned down.

Taxi Evader

For over 30 years Sydney's Bea Miles terrorised taxidrivers and the Department of Transport. She believed all public transport should be free and appeared in court on charges of fare evasion 195 times. A staunch patriot, she took taxis between Sydney, Perth, Melbourne and Broken Hill 'to view the countryside'. And on those occasions, she paid!

Big Slice

Captain de Groot, an officer of the New Guard, who brazenly rode up on his horse and sliced the ribbon on Sydney Harbour Bridge before Premier Jack Lang declared it open in March 1932, upset the crowd so much that he had to remove his uniform and put on a policeman's tunic in order to be led to safety.

Divorce and Custardy

In a case at the Sydney Divorce Court in March, 1946, engineer Thomas McDonnell was granted a decree nisi after he told how his wife would turn his wireless on full when he went to bed, sweep the room with a heavy broom and beat him with it from head to toe while he cowered under the sheets.

She had also broken every vase in the house over him, smashed a picture 2 ft square over his skull, kicked him violently in the groin, slashed his foot open with a pair of scissors, pummelled him with a block of wood and attacked him with two large knives.

When a pitying neighbour made him a custard pie, his wife grabbed it, yelled 'Cop this' and flung it all over him.

Mr McDonnell said his nerves were now quite bad!

Fancy Pansy

Sydney showgirl Pansy Montague, who loved to appear nude, got around the law by coating her body with bismuth powder and striking classic poses impersonating Greek nymphs and goddesses!

Now is the Hour

Supporting an application by her husband to have a lodger ejected from their Sydney home, Mrs Clive Jones was asked to sing in court a song sung by the lodger and which woke the house at five o'clock one morning.

'Give me five minutes more, I've got six weeks more, I've got six weeks more, I shall stay', Mrs Jones sang.

The magistrate gave the lodger his marching orders.

Trying Tenant

When Sydney landlord Jacob Aaron asked a woman tenant to stop washing dogs in the laundry, cease from drilling holes in the floor to pour dirty water into the flat below and give up playing her organ late into the night, she came at him with a Japanese sword! A magistrate ordered her to leave.

No Vacancies

When Mr Justice Dwyer arrived in Bathurst (NSW) on court business and found he could not get a bed for the night, he threatened to send the town's hotel keepers to jail for obstructing the course of justice.

'This gross affront to a Supreme Court judge going on the King's business is something I will not tolerate', he raged.

He still didn't get his bed and had to travel 35 miles a day from a hotel at Orange. Another judge joined the attack, describing New South Wales country hotels as 'bloodhouses which are a positive menace to the community'.

Something Fishy

A Brisbane man who opened a bottle of milk delivered to his doorstep found 40 FISH HOOKS of assorted sizes, three having traces attached. The top of the bottle had not been disturbed.

The Hair Affair

Joseph Ansell was imprisoned for three months with hard labour in January, 1889—for stealing the hair from his mattress at a Melbourne hospital. He gave no reason for ripping it out and packing it in his suitcase.

The Diamond Cutter

During the mid 1800s Melbourne was mesmerised by the eminent surgeon Dr James 'Diamond Jim' Beaney.

Dr Beaney, diamonds and champagne were synonymous—he never operated wearing less than £10 000 of the finest gems. For, the good doctor contended, how else could the public know of your worth as a medical practitioner unless they saw how much money you made!

Space Litter

When the United States satellite Skylab came down on the Western Australian coast, the council at Esperance served the crashdown team at NASA with an infringement notice for littering!

What a Bind

When *The Art of Rosaleen Norton*—a book of paintings by Rosaleen Norton, the Witch of Kings Cross, Sydney—was published in 1952, it was considered so 'lewd' that only an all-male team was permitted to bind it. Miss Norton had originally thought to have it bound in tanned bat skin!

Public Performance

For making love on the back seat of a bus in Perth a couple was fined $300 in February, 1982. The magistrate commented that it was an awful thing to do on public transport.

Hat Trick

While the Prime Minister of New Zealand was visiting a new limb-fitting department at Dunedin Hospital in 1920, someone stole his hat. He had to be fitted out with another at a nearby shop.

Gloom for Groom

Passing a church in Newtown (NSW) in the late 1940s, a woman recognised among a group waiting for a wedding to begin, a man who had attacked her two days earlier. She told the police—and when the groom emerged with his bride he was arrested at the church door!

PADDY, THE RAM
A CHARACTER OF SYDNEY, AUSTRALIA, IN SUMMER AND WINTER ALWAYS WORE 2 COATS, 4 SHIRTS AND 3 PAIRS OF TROUSERS

MacTart

Quong Tart, who came to Sydney from China in 1859, joined the Highland Society, became an authority on Scottish history, spoke with a Scottish accent, donned a kilt and called himself MacTart!

Sleepy Slowcoach

No-one would have taken much notice of the man sleeping in the driver's seat of a car in Sydney in 1978—if the vehicle had not been travelling along at ONE kilometre an hour! The driver was later fined $200 and lost his licence for a year for driving while asleep under the influence of alcohol!

Pudding Thief

Police in the Melbourne suburb of Hawthorn were called to investigate two items stolen from a lady's clothes-line in December 1980, they were plum puddings being hung out to dry after being steamed the previous night!

Glass Eater

A sailor, John Cunningham, who was a professional glass eater in a circus before he joined up, earned a reputation around Sydney as being a tough guy when he regularly drank his beer and then ate the glass.

A policeman called by an angry landlord was punched by Cunningham, but when he was finally arrested and brought to the police station he fainted when told he would be charged with assault!

Hard to Find

Putting out a description of a bogus doctor who was examining women in council property in the late 1940s on the excuse he wanted to find out if they were in perfect health, Melbourne police said they were looking for a very pale man, paralysed down one side and who had a distinct limp, a deformed hand and a quivering bottom lip!

What a Brick

A thief who wanted the cage but not the bird tied an elderly New South Wales woman's canary by the leg to a housebrick which was left on the mantlepiece! Beside the merrily chirping bird was a two shilling piece!

Biblical Message

Colonial cabinet-maker George Erskine, a religious fanatic with a guilty conscience about a theft, explained to Melbourne police after he had sliced off his right hand by feeding it to his firm's circular saw that he had been motivated by a passage of Scripture reading: 'If thy right hand offend thee, cut it off and cast it from thee.'

HARRY HEEMSKIRK
of Lilydale, Australia

DRINKS 90 CUPS OF TEA A DAY

Capture of Cronulla

In 1942, William Charles Wentworth, later to become a member of Parliament, embarrassed top brass by capturing the Sydney suburb of Cronulla on his own initiative, thus proving the enemy could have taken the area.

At that time a Captain in the Army, he landed a small force and in a simulated Japanese accent, used the telephone to disperse the Fire Brigade and the Police to opposite ends of Cronulla. He then reported an enemy landing and when the emergency forces arrived, bailed the lot up with bayonets. Next to be added to his bag, was the Colonel in his pyjamas, battalion headquarters, the wireless station which he blew up, the railway line which he blocked to prevent reinforcements, the signals system which he short-circuited (putting all trains out of order for 36 hours) and five Bren gun carriers. These he drove to the Ordnance Depot at Liverpool, where, eluding the sentry, he put up a sign proclaiming: 'Destroyed by W. C. Wentworth, Captain'.

It was discovered soon after that Captain Wentworth had a 'serious eye defect' and the Army retired him!

Pistol Jammed

His face a red mess after his opponent had scored a direct hit in a duel in Melbourne in 1843, Mr George Demoulin cried 'I'm killed!' while the spectators laughed. 'Show me pity, you devils!' he cried with his hand to his head. But they laughed even more after they had told him that his opponent, the Hon. Gilbert Kennedy—who had insisted they stood only a few paces from each other—had put a blank in one pistol and filled the other with raspberry jam!

Ferry King

Sydney's popular ferry services grew from a venture begun in the early 1800s by an eccentric Jamaican, Blue Billy, alias the 'Old Commodore'. He operated a one-man racket carrying passengers and produce across the harbour and when he finally left the business to his sons it expanded into a small fleet while he, dressed in an old naval officer's uniform, roamed the streets of Sydney muttering 'Still alive, never die', until his death in 1834!

Drunken Sailor

An artful wife, horrified at her husband's drunken state when he arrived home one night in June, 1831, ran from the house saying she was going to drown her baby in the local stream.

The husband stumbled to the creek and stared in disbelief at the struggling form illuminated by the moonlight in the water. Diving in, he managed to get it ashore—and discovered it was the family's pet cat!

The wife's ruse worked. He never got drunk again!

The Max Factor

Max Falstein, one of the youngest members of Parliament during the 1940s, was always getting into trouble with his blunt comments. He appalled his Parliamentary colleagues one day by saying of the House: 'This must be the only asylum in the world where the inmates are in charge.'

Silly Walk

One of the silliest races to take place in Australia was when Ararat (Vic.) resident Mr 'Duke' Jennings backed himself to walk BACKWARDS faster over 60 yards than publican Peter Danckert could run 100 yards. Mr Jennings was not backwards in coming forwards after the race to claim the £10 wager, having won by two yards!

Eye-Rate Customer

One of a few men to make artificial eyes in Australia, Mr R. Merrett, received an order from an old bushman with instructions that his new eye be sent up to him in the bush when ready. A week after its posting it was returned with a complaint from the client that it fitted alright but he couldn't see through it!

Kidnapped

Refusing to pay for a set of false teeth which did not fit, housewife Hilda Hedburg was kidnapped by William Scott, a Redfern (NSW) chemist and detained in his house for six hours in 1890. The chemist was fined £5 and Mrs Hedburg achieved satisfaction by ordering another set of teeth from a competitor.

Last Word

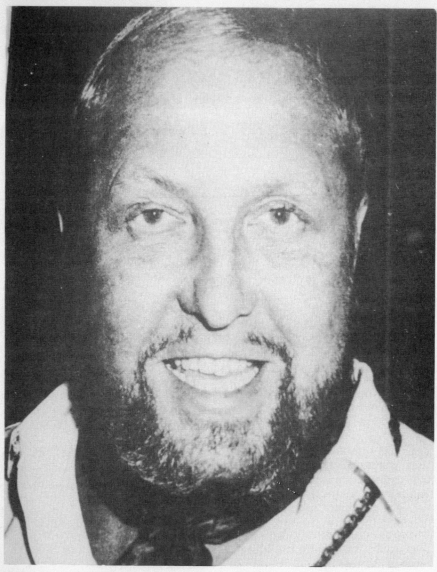

Australia's shortest and cruellest dramatic review was written by Frank Thring, a well-known star of stage and screen who doubled for a Melbourne newspaper as a critic.

He wrote: The Theatre, The Tivoli. The Show, *Jack and Jill*. The cast, Roy Barbour, Nina Cooke, John Bluthal, Ivor Bromley. The critic, THE END!

Dislodged

When it was discovered in 1980 that a masonic lodge near Auckland (NZ) had been using three 200-year-old skulls at meetings, all lodges of the Independent Order of Oddfellows were banned from using human heads in their induction ceremonies.

Slow Dancer

Police arrested a Coogee man attempting to break the world's endurance dancing record at the Oddfellows Hall, Bathurst (NSW) in 1928 and charged him with 'imposing on the public', claiming that he cheated by napping while friends kept watch. Denying the accusation, he danced all the way to the police station, kept the rhythm going while the charge was being read and continued the knees up when they slammed the cell door behind him!

Hidden Assets

South African cyclist Alan Dipple, looking for a partner in 1982 for a 'marriage of convenience' so he could remain permanently in Australia, received so many offers from women between 19 and 60—and one from a man—that he was forced to hire two security guards and go into hiding.

Pearls Before Divers

Wealthy pearl hunter Nicholas Minister was so bored one morning in the early 1900s while moored off the northern Australian coast that he gathered a handful of pearls from his cabin, cast them overboard and challenged his island divers to find them. All but one were recovered and he allowed the finders to keep them!

Water Bed

A Maori in the Tokaanu district of New Zealand spent years sleeping in a hot pool. He found a natural ledge where he could lie with the water lapping over him and declared it was just as comfortable as a bed—and a lot warmer!

Beery Bishop

A very tall churchman of Sydney's 1950s had the ungodly honour of having a long glass of beer named after him—a 'Bishop Barker'!

Annie Bags

An old woman who walked the roads of Queensland dressed in old bags and accompanied by a pack of dogs handed flowers to every lady she met. But she was remembered more for her bizarre clothing and earned the title 'Annie Bags'.

Champagne Trail

When a huge semi-trailer broke down in South Australia and blocked the road both ways in the 1950s none of the motorists held up for three days complained. For the truck contained hundreds of bottles of champagne which, although warm, were consumed for the purpose, so they all said, of relieving their boredom!

Macabre Request

She said it was lucky.

A woman walked into Melbourne police station in October, 1958, and asked permission for the hands of murderer Owen McQueeney, who had been hanged that morning, to be rubbed or stroked over her own hands. Her request was turned down, without reason.

Sex Gospel

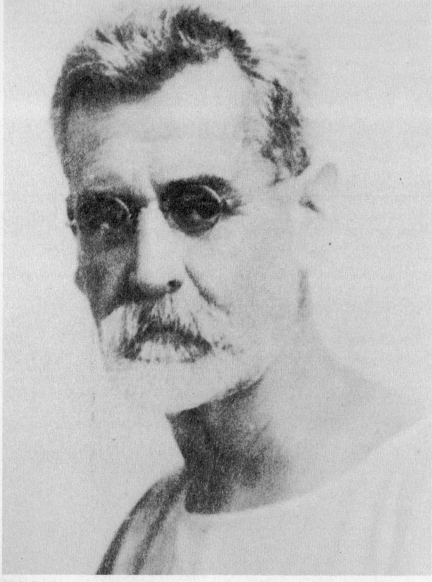

W. J. Chidley believed he had a message for the people—and he offered pamphlets for sale describing a new sex technique. He also preached his sex gospel in Sydney and Melbourne while wearing a strange silk tunic. He died in 1916 in a lunatic asylum.

Coffin Home

A swagman known as Dead Eye Jack walked the roads of Victoria in the early 1900s carrying a coffin on his back, which he used as a home. At night he would sleep in it with his swag and if it rained he stood it upright against a tree, sleeping in a standing up position, using the lid as a door. As many predicted, one day he never came out!

Tiny State

Ex-British policeman Tom Barnes, 58, is the Governor of the world's smallest State. He declared his farmland, east of Melbourne, independent because the Victorian Government would not pay compensation for flood damage to his land caused, he said, by lack of supervision of a nearby river.

Now he pays all taxes normally due to the Government to himself in his role as Treasurer, Immigration Officer and Police Minister!

Fishy Friends

Mr George Davidson, one of the biggest saddle makers in Australia in the early 1950s, entertained his friends and business associates once a week by filling a large suitcase full of fried fish, taking it down to the Tradesman's Arms Hotel, Sydney, and distributing the food among the patrons.

Marching Orders

When Mrs Jean Burke got into a Sydney bus driven by her husband, the conductress told her to get off. Mrs Burke found out later her husband was having an affair with the conductress, and when she told the story to a judge she was given her divorce ticket.

Wooden Look

A 1982 show in Warrnambool (Vic.) featured a photograph of a man posing for the camera—after he had accidentally shot himself dead. He is pictured kneeling, hat in one hand, cigarette in the other.

The caption read: 'My grand-mother's young brother, accidentally shot in 1933, aged 21.' This photo was taken shortly after his sudden death, as the family had no recent photos of him.

'Special features include: the blackened hands of those holding him upright, the cigarette drawn in his left hand and the vacant look in his eyes.'

Meaty Protest

A woman football fan who disagreed with an umpire at Sydney's Henson Park oval in the 1940s, walked to a nearby pie stand purchased a dozen pies with sauce (worth four pence each) and threw them at everyone in sight, including the umpire who was splashed with meat and ketchup!

THE WINTER MAN

FRANK P. WATSON—of MELBOURNE, Australia HAS LIVED IN **30** SUCCESSIVE WINTERS IN **15** YEARS HE TRAVELS BACK AND FORTH BETWEEN AUSTRALIA & EUROPE —SPENDING THE WINTER TIME ON EACH CONTINENT.

Fantastic Franziana

A fanfare for Madame Franziana, who kept herself cool with a fan which never left her hand, and who in 1876 introduced the 'boneshaker' bicycle to the Australian stage! She delighted audiences when she cycled onto the stage, rather wobbly at times, but those in the front rows found her so entertaining they never worried about the threat of her falling into their laps!

Water Walker

They called him the Nunawading Messiah and he moved in mysterious ways, his wonders to perform. James Cowley Morgan Fisher, a huge man with flowing white hair and a long beard, lived with three sisters as his wives in Melbourne's Box Hill and had a little band of disciples who regarded him as the true Messiah. Leading his group to Blackburn Lake in the late 1860s for the performance of a miracle he asked in his booming voice whether they had the faith to believe that he could walk on the water. They cried halleluiah and said that aye, aye, they believed so the Messiah opened his arms, looked to the heavens and declared: 'If you believe, then I have no need to do it.'

Odd Feet Club

Hands and feet have been responsible for the formation of two bizarre groups, both in South Australia!

So many people have odd feet in the state that a group was formed in 1982 to enable members to swap single shoes with other members whenever they bought a new pair.

And there's the Left Hand Club in Whyalla which has a rule stating that members can touch their drinking glasses only with their left hands, except on Wednesdays! The club was started during World War II to raise funds for charity and there is a fine of a silver coin for anyone who breaks these rules:

No asking the time, requesting cigarettes or matches or begging favours on Monday; no using the word 'yes' any similar affirmative on Tuesdays; no using the word 'no' on Fridays.

Distant Relatives

Two brothers who quarrelled became the founders of the longest town for its size in the world, Angledoon (SA). They set up house 2½ miles apart and, in between, settlers erected their homes, including a post office and store.

Only Jones

An old man with ambitions of becoming a politician put himself up for election several times under the name 'Only Jones'.

Usually he received only one vote—his own—and he was made a mockery of by local children who one day chased him into a house in Holt Street, Sydney, where he hid in the chimney. And there he remained, stuck fast, until discovered two days later.

To get him out, rescuers had to demolish the chimney stack. Only Jones took an early retirement from politics after that.

Trumpeting Volunteer

Clarence Smith, a 61-year-old pensioner who voluntarily took on the job of cleaning the streets of Sydney with a broom in 1951, was so disgusted at some residents' untidiness that he made his feelings known in a Bondi residential area at 4 o'clock in the morning and was arrested and fined £5 for using offensive language!

Soul Music

At dusk in Sydney's pre-war days an old lady would enter her late husband's vault in the local cemetery and by the light of a hurricane lamp play music on her ukelele for his soul!

Buggy Lover

The Earl of Belmore, who was Governor of New South Wales until 1872, loved his horse and buggy so much that he insisted on taking the reins himself, even on long trips into the country. When he returned to England, he stowed the buggy on his ship and took it home with him!

Screwy Name

An Adelaide resident who hasn't got on well with the Taxation Department has changed his name by deed poll to Mr Screw the Taxpayer to Support Big Government and its Parasites!

Wasted Grief

Workers at a mine near Sydney lost a total of £550 in wages in 1938 when they decided to go home as a mark of respect for a colleague reported to have died. The next day they heard he was still alive!

D. K. THOMSON Melbourne, Australia MADE A VOW TO "EAT HIS HAT" — AND DID IT!

Paper House

To avoid military service John Murdie ran off into the bush near Rangatava (NZ), built himself a hut made of newspapers which he glued together and painted to make it waterproof, and lived in it for FOUR YEARS!

Bad Night

When Mr Arthur Burrows of Kensington, Sydney, was taken to hospital he explained away his battered condition by saying he had been involved in three separate fights around town—a knife had been thrown at him in the first, a plate smashed over his head in the second and a broken bottle thrust at him in the third!

The Ern Malley Hoax

Max Harris, publisher of an Australian journal of modern poetry, received a collection of verse from an 'Ethel Malley' in 1944. In an accompanying note, she claimed that her brother Ern had written the works before his death and Harris published the lines, hailing them as great examples of Australian poetry.

Then it was revealed that James McAuley and Harold Stewart had written the poetry as deliberate nonsense—and that Ern never existed. Harris was prosecuted and fined after the police claimed the poems were obscene.

Kisses Pay Off

Ravishing 'Palmer Kate', who sold her kisses to miners at Palmer (SA) for an ounce of gold at a time, slept with her takings under her bed, which was made up of champagne cases and silk cushions, and a revolver in her hand!

Consuming Passion

In Gympie (Qld) a man consumed his wife and the authorities did nothing about it!

On her death by natural causes her husband, a Hindu, had her cremated and then dissolved the ashes in rum. He gave the concoction a good stir and swigged her down. 'It was my way of showing how much I loved her', he explained with a hiccup.

Useless Work

When eccentric Jack Dow hired men to work on his New South Wales sheep station he gave them such ridiculous jobs that many walked off without waiting for their pay. One of his favourites was to set a man turning a grindstone without having anything to sharpen on it. He just stood there and turned the wheel hour after hour...

Hard Lesson

When convict Peter Toddy, assigned to work for Sir Matthew O'Connell in Sydney, refused to lift his hat when Col. Wilson passed by in 1837, the Colonel called him a 'scoundrelly blackguard' and had him arrested and sentenced to 50 lashes. Todd lifted his hat to every man, woman and child after that.

Fiery Tempers

Because insurance companies offered rewards to the fire brigade that poured the first water on a blaze in the 1840s, competition between brigades was hot. Sometimes rival groups fought among themselves while buildings burned and one devious fellow chopped a rival brigade's hose in half to prevent them claiming 'first water'.

UNZIE

AUSTRALIAN HIRSUTE
WONDER
HIS MASS OF SNOW-WHITE
HAIR MEASURED **8** FT.
IN CIRCUMFERENCE

Journeying Juryman

A judge dismissed a jury hearing a murder trial at Melbourne's Central Criminal Court in the 1940s when he learned that a 63-year-old juryman had left the dormitory where he had been locked for the night with other jury members and, in a trance, climbed a 16 ft wall, gone for a walk, then returned to his bed.

Mr Justice Herron accepted he had had a 'sudden, temporary relapse of memory'.

Dog Fight

During a church service on the Upper Hawkesbury (NSW) in 1920, two well-known fighting dogs began such a fierce fight that the whole congregation, including the parson, came out to watch. After 10 minutes of bloody scrapping, the dogs ran off and the congregation returned to sing hymn number 90, 'All things bright and beautiful, all creatures great and small . . .'

Lucky Cat

Deciding the best thing to do with her diseased cat was to drown it, Annie, the local washerwoman of Claypan (Tas.), put the animal in a hessian bag with a lump of quartz from the yard.

On the way to the dam, the cat ate its way free and Annie was about to toss away the stone when she realised it was in the shape of a man's head with a crown on it.

When she took it home she saw it was impregnated with gold. Searching in the yard where the quartz had lain she uncovered the reef that was to become known as Annie's Lode. From the first five tons, 400 oz of gold were recovered!

All Nations

An immigrant arriving at Wellington (NZ) in 1920 told officials he was born on a Spanish ship off the Cape of Good Hope of a British mother who married a Frenchman in Italy but after his parents died in Brazil he was adopted by a Chinese whose home was in Russia!

The Time is Near

When the hands of Melbourne Town Hall clock suddenly went haywire, spinning round rapidly in 1921, many people believed the day of judgement was at hand and hurried to church!

Expensive Tastes

The wife of station owner Thomas Macqueen loved to live expensively. A bath, cut from a solid block of marble, was brought to her husband's property at Segenhoe (NSW) in the 1820s and a special herd of cows was kept on stand by—to provide milk for Mrs Macqueen to bathe in!

Not Face Value

More than 500 high society ladies paid $22 each to listen to a distinguished Swiss professor give them advice on how to retain youthful vitality. As the lecture, at the Melbourne Wentworth Hotel in October, 1982, progressed, faces grew redder.

Dr Nathan Dewring mocked the group for seeking four layers of face lifts and as his criticisms grew the ladies wriggled in their seats with embarrassed discomfort.

Finally he tore his strawberry wig and revealed himself as self-styled satirist Campbell McComas. He sent the money to a local charity.

Shy Dogs

A spinster in Coogee, Sydney, always dressed her dogs in coats before they went out and if a visitor called at the house unexpectedly and caught them in the nude they would scamper off, embarrassed and hide.

When her nephew, who inherited them on her death, couldn't get them to leave the house without something on he poisoned them all.

Dental Plate

A Sydney dentist who ran out of metal for fillings in 1920 melted down an old London car number plate and filled his patients' molars with it!

Didn't Make It

Two English girls who came to Australia in 1946 to marry airmen they had met in the war returned six weeks later—one engaged, one married, to different men! They both fell in love with officers on the ship which brought them out!

THREE

Fate

Painful Prankster

Are we instruments of fate? Is there a divine, over-all plan for each and every one of us? Or can we ultimately choose what happens to us?

Carl Jung states that 'meaningful coincidences are thinkable as pure chance. But the more they multiply and the greater and more exact the correspondence is, the more their probability sinks and their probability increases, until they can no longer be regarded as pure chance but, for lack of a causal explanation, have to be thought of as meaningful arrangements'.

In essence, of course, the great psychologist/philosopher is saying that the more strange events occur the less likely they are of being of pure coincidence. He is suggesting that something 'out there' is shaping our lives.

For some it is difficult to accept that fate holds the cards. It transcends all reason, all objective scientific inquiry—after all, do we not live in an age of science and technology?

But we are still creatures of passion, of intuition, of experiencing and 'gut' reactions. How many of us have been caught up in an event that on reflection we realise has shaped our destiny? How many of us have turned to faith healers where medicine has failed? Even those who do not like to admit it enjoy the tarot card reader, the clairvoyant who 'knows what lies in store' for us. The palmist. The astrologer. The numerologist. The nephrologist. And so on.

Daily we turn to the stars in the morning papers to find out what the forthcoming week promises. If we don't really like what is on offer, we try to manipulate the predictions to suit ourselves. But fate cannot be moulded. It always has the last laugh!

The way luck, fate, call it what you will, runs and mocks us is perhaps best summed up in the story of the 'lucky' horseshoe which was flipped from a passing cart, crashed through a shop window and hit a customer a knockout blow on the head!

Come and look into the crystal ball and see how fate has played

with us mortals. Read about:
  The fisherman who caught a
    shark—and took home corned
    beef for tea.
  The bullet that bounced from a
    man's head.

The bookmaker who used up
  all his bad luck and 'won'
  his life.
The injured footballer who
  had his leg pulled—and
  immediately recovered.

Separate Ways

Frank Gardiner

Frank Gardiner and William Dalley were school pals but when they left they went their separate ways—Gardiner to rob as 'King of the Bushrangers' and Dalley to serve his country as a statesman. The next time they met was when Dalley defended Gardiner at his 1864 trial!

Explorers Abandoned

John Longstaff Burke, Wills and King at Cooper's Creek

Weak from exhaustion and hunger, explorers Robert O'Hara Burke, William J. Wills and John King staggered into a base camp at Cooper's Creek after an incredible four month journey to the north coast and back—only to find that the main party had given them up and had left just SEVEN HOURS earlier. When at last rescuers returned to Cooper's Creek only King remained alive 'wasted to a shadow and barely to be distinguished as a civilised being'.

The Impossible

Sarah Bartlett of Marong (Vic.) turned the contents of her house upside down searching in vain for her engagement ring which had vanished from the pin tray where she had placed it to wash some clothes. Eight years later, in 1919, the large limb of a dead tree was hurled through the window during a storm tossing the missing ring, which had lain in a magpie's nest, back onto the pin tray!

Knife Returns

While serving with the 25th Battalion in the First World War in France, Mr F. Smith of Barcaldine (Qld) was made prisoner and a German relieved him of a presentation knife which had his initials on the handle.

Years later, while shearing at Terrick Station, he asked a mate for the loan of a knife. It was his own! The friend explained he had found it on the body of a dead German after a battle.

Shutter Shudder

Twin brothers Roy and Arthur Gulliver threw Melbourne into confusion when they both entered the same profession as Press photographers in the 1940s—for opposition newspapers.

When Roy took a series of pictures at a ballet school the class collapsed after an hour's strenuous work for the camera—and then the wretched man (although this time it was Arthur) came back and asked them to do it all again!

And Arthur was lucky to escape with his hide when he went to the docks and coolly started taking pictures of the workers. He didn't know that Roy had been there a few minutes before him and had had a run in with the wharfies who threatened him with violence should he show his face there again!

Devilish Team

Up to September, 1921, the Waratah football team of Goulburn (NSW) had played 13 games and won 13, the last match being played on the 13th and the team winning by 13 points!

BC 000

AUTO LICENSE NUMBER
OF CANON BARDER, Sydney, Australia

AD 000

THE MAN NEXT DOOR
TO HIM HAS THE ABOVE
NUMBER.!

Tags Return

Walking through the car park at the Oamaru trotting course (NZ) in December, 1982, Sir James Barnes, 74, a former prisoner of war, found his POW identity tags on the ground!

He had lost them 25 years earlier and found them on the 40th anniversary of the day his aircraft was shot down over France!

Wise Decision

Four seamen refused to go out on the *Indies*, claiming the sailing ship was unsafe. They were sentenced to gaol for three months—even though the ship sprang a leak after leaving Newcastle (NSW) and sank!

His Own Funeral

Walter Craig, who ran a hotel in Ballarat in the 1860s, dreamed that his horse, Nimblefoot, won the Melbourne Cup. But was puzzled as to why the jockey wore a black armband. A few days before the great race, Walter died. And Nimblefoot crossed the line first!

Flipper

Standing in a shop in Molong (NSW) Mrs G. Watts was hit on the head by a horseshoe which, lying in Bank Street, had been struck by a passing car and flipped 50 ft through the shop window!

Virgin Birth

Nine months after swimming in a public pool in Sydney, a 15-year-old virgin gave birth. Baffled doctors worked out that by a billion to one chance she had been impregnated by male sperm in the water.

Old Lady of The Swamp

Ship's carpenter Martin Wyberg was shunned by the crew because they considered he brought bad luck. He decided to strike out on his own and stole 50 000 sovereigns from the locker room, fled to Gippsland (Vic.) and hid the fortune on a block of land. Not long afterwards his own bad luck caught up with him and he drowned.

In 1912 two spinsters moved into a mansion that had been built on the land but Wyberg's curse was to hit them. The land flooded, one of the sisters, Jeanie Clement, died and the other, Margaret, found herself poverty stricken in a decaying house surrounded by water.

She became a recluse and was known as the Old Lady of the Swamp. One night, during a storm, she vanished and it was not until 1978 that what were believed to be her bones were discovered. The skull had been smashed in!

Illegal Love

When Horace Maplesden met and fell in love with a girl he knew as Ethel, they decided to get married.

In 1924 they stood trial in Adelaide on a charge of marrying while being BROTHER AND SISTER! Since childhood they had not seen each other for 13 years and did not recognise each other when they met again. It was only when officials casually checked on their backgrounds that the amazing coincidence was discovered. Ethel was freed on a bond and Horace was jailed for six months.

Rich Potato

A gold signet ring lost by a gardener at Essendon (Vic.) in 1948 was discovered a year later when a potato sprouted. Out popped the ring!

Saved by Pony

Unable to find their way out of the Mount Kembla mine after an explosion which killed 96 in 1902, three miners struck on the idea of unhitching a pit pony to see what it might accomplish. It led them through the darkness, to fresh air and survival!

White Out

In 1911 in Victoria's Glen Wills district, at a race meeting on a hot New Year's day, horses, riders and spectators were battered by a blizzard during a freak snowstorm. The winner of two races run at the height of the storm was Lily White!

THE **ROCK OF DEATH** near KANYAKA, in SOUTHERN AUSTRALIA, SO CALLED BECAUSE FOR YEARS *ABORIGINES INSISTED ON DYING WITHIN ITS SHADOW* ILL NATIVES WERE BROUGHT THERE BY RELATIVES WHO CAMPED NEARBY WHILE WAITING FOR THE PATIENT TO DIE

Hindu's Curse

When Australian tea buyer Harry Evans tossed an empty whisky bottle from a train in India in 1870 it struck a Hindu on the head. Before dying the following day, the injured man placed a curse upon Evans and all his family and descendants.

Within the span of three generations the curse of the dying man, reaching across thousands of miles to Australia, had wiped out the entire male members of the family, causes of death including a sudden blood clot on the brain, two cancers of the throat, an early childhood death and a motoring accident.

In the car crash, in September, 1923, the remaining male, Vere Evans, was driving between Tenterfield and Warwick when he rolled into a ditch, breaking his neck. Yet his passenger escaped unhurt!

Paradise 'Lovely'

A New Zealand woman whose husband had died only two days earlier fainted when, opening a telegram addressed to her, she read:

'Arrived in Paradise today, everything lovely.'

It was signed with her dead husband's initials!

Finally it was established that the telegram had been sent by a bride to her mother, telling her that she and her husband had arrived at Paradise, on Lake Wakatipu. By a strange coincidence, the telegram had been delivered to an address occupied by a woman of the same name. The bride, of course, had the same initials as the dead husband!

Going Home

A Ford motor car being driven along Sydney's Parramatta Road in 1921 lost its front tyre which did a semi-circle in the road and rolled into the garage from where it had been bought a week before!

Child's Dread

The first words little Mickie Kennedy spoke baffled his parents—'Mummy dead and Daddy gone.'

He repeated them for three years at the property in the Western District of Victoria where the family lived during the 1840s. He repeated them until one night, on his parent's ninth wedding anniversary, his father murdered his mother.

'I can't think what made me do it, unless it was the devil,' said Patrick Kennedy.

On the same day and at the same hour that he was sentenced to death, Mickie stopped the continual crooning of those first words—and suddenly and unaccountably died!

Better At Sea

Mr George Drever, who achieved international fame in the mid 1800s by sailing across the Atlantic in a six-ton yacht and crossing the English Channel on a raft became a leading authority on life-saving apparatus—yet in 1889 he drowned in a shallow mud hole in Sydney's Centennial Park!

All in Family

Before the days when a professional interest had to be declared in a court case, Mr Hubert Parker, making his first appearance as a defence attorney, at Kalgoorlie (WA) in 1906, found that the crown prosecutor was his brother Frank and the judge was his father, Sir Henry Parker!

Reef of Evil

A reef of silver ore on the coast of north Western Australia carried an evil curse which brought misfortune to all who tried to find it.

It was first found by a Malay merchant called Hadji Ibrahim who promised himself he would return to mine it. But as his ship approached the coast it was wrecked and Ibrahim and the crew drowned.

An Englishman called Lang decided to trace the ore early this century, but he, too, vanished. And in 1909 the body of a lone prospector known as Mad Jack was found dead in his cutter. His head had been split open with a tomahawk.

To this day the reef remains undiscovered. Who would dare search for it?

Brother to Rescue

During his days as a drover, Mr John Merchant of Kempsey (NSW) carved his brother's initials on a tree. Many years later when he was running a pub the former drover was surrounded by flood water and debris but the only log washed on to his verandah was the remains of the tree he had marked and which still bore the initials!

Life-Saving Rip

While Harry Freney was working for the Valley Clothing Factory, Brisbane, some 60 years ago, his shirt sleeve was caught in the belting of the machinery and he was being pulled towards the shaft when the sleeve was torn away.

He had planned that day to wear a shirt made by his company, but had put on a cheaper, flimsier garment made by a competitor—a last minute decision that had saved his arm!

Punished with Blindness

Settler John Petrie alarmed an Aboriginal tribe when he told them he was going to climb Mount Beerwah in Queensland's Glasshouse Mountains. They begged him not to make the ascent, telling him a Spirit dwelt on the mountain and it would punish with blindness anyone who looked at it.

Even when the tribe said an Aboriginal had been struck blind after coming down the mountain, Petrie insisted he was going up.

He returned in the best of health. But within months HE BECAME TOTALLY BLIND.

Shark Bait

Cutting open a shark he caught at Busselton (WA) in 1950, Mr Charles Rowe found a perfectly good can of corned beef which he took home and ate!

THE HOUSE THAT HAS WAITED 81 YEARS FOR AN OCCUPANT
THE DHURRINGHILE MANSION
near Tatura, Australia
BUILT FOR A MAN WHO DIED IN 1877 ON HIS WAY TO BUY ITS FURNITURE
HAS REMAINED EMPTY AND UNFURNISHED EVER SINCE

Kelly Connections

The hanging of Ned Kelly

When barrister Peter Conlan met Mr W. Foster, the Port Fairy (Vic.) clerk of courts, they started a discussion about old trials. Foster recalled that his father had committed Ned Kelly and he went on to mention the bravery of Sergeant Kennedy in the case. Conlan was amazed—Sergeant Kennedy was his grandfather!

Free Booter

Anxious to look after his boots, fisherman William Kennedy hid them under a bush while he went shark fishing north of Sydney in 1872. He caught a huge shark with a hook on the end of a dog chain but in the excitement couldn't remember where he had hidden his boots. On cutting open the shark, he found another pair of boots in the stomach, discovered they fitted perfectly, and went home in them!

Twist of Fate

As Ed Westcott, of Dubbo (NSW), was being carried in agony to an ambulance after a heavy rugby tackle displaced a vertebrae, one of the volunteer stretcher bearers from the crowd of spectators accidentally twisted Westcott's foot. The vertebrae snapped back into position and the player walked back to the pitch to resume play!

Long Arms of Coincidence

Standing in a Brisbane street recounting to a friend an incident of 50 years earlier when an octopus had clambered into his rowing boat clutching a bottle of beer, Cyril Hattersley looked across the road and saw the man who had been in the boat with him. He hadn't seen him for 40 years!

Deed Repaid

Hearing that a patient was in dire need of blood for a transfusion, Mr A. J. Reeve offered his at the Brisbane Hospital—and discovered that the man who received it was Mr E. Gilchrist, his old comrade from World War I who had once saved his life by shouting a warning a second before an enemy machine gun tore up the ground he had been standing on!

Triple Double Trouble

Until their retirement, the Tasmanian police force employed three sets of twins, each pair holding the same rank! There were sergeants A. J. and L. H. Rothwell and senior constables E. V. and A. A. Knowles and L. W. and L. T. Turner. What's more, the Rothwells and the Knowles were cousins!

Witchbones

An Aboriginal woman, found dead with fish bones in her throat, had been 'sung to death', according to tribal members who described how a lizard had been caught, named after the woman and had had bones inserted in its throat. A coroner decided that 'Dolly' had been murdered by her husband, Shinbone Jimmy, and sent him for trial.

Lucky Break

Graham Marsh, one of golf's biggest money winners, might never have got into the game if he had not broken his arm as a boy at his home in Perth. Graham and his now-famous wicket-keeping brother Rod built a high jump pit in the yard and when Graham broke his arm attempting a jump, the doctor suggested he drop his favourite sport, cricket, and concentrate on golf to strengthen the arm.

It was thanks to golf, too, that Rod made it to the top in cricket. He spent hours throwing a golf ball against the wall in the back yard and learned how to dive and catch it when it came back at all angles.

Bouncing Bullet

The man with the hardest head in the world was Mr T. Foley of Longreach (Qld). While trying to extract a bullet from his rifle in 1928 the weapon went off, the bullet hit Mr Foley square in the middle of his forehead— AND BOUNCED OFF!

Brooch Returned

Opening an oyster pulled from rocks off Cairns (Qld) in 1924, Mr J. Johnson found a gold brooch!

Showing it to his wife, she exclaimed 'Why, it's mine!' She had lost the brooch at the same spot many years before she was married!

Watch Back

For five years nothing was heard of a woman's watch, stolen while in transit through the Western Australian post in 1917—until it was brought in for repair to the woman's husband, a watchmaker, who was the very man who had posted it!

Blown to Safety

When Melbourne's unfinished Westgate Bridge collapsed in October, 1970, rigger Ed Halsall was saved from certain death by a freak blast of wind caused by a falling span that lifted him off the ground, blowing him clear of the tumbling debris. Thirty-five others were killed.

On the Hook

When passenger Kenneth McEwen tripped and fell into the harbour at Launceston (Tas.) while disembarking from the steamer *Port Denison*, the chief engineer threw him an umbrella which Mr Ewen hooked on the wharf and held on to until help arrived. After being hauled ashore, he realised it was his own umbrella which he had inadvertently left behind in his cabin!

Death through Shyness

The most successful jockey at a race meeting at Charleville (Qld) 60 years ago was Mr John Easton, but he was too shy to go onto the stage at the ball that evening to receive his trophy.

A number of dancers decided to carry him to the stage but John dashed out into the street where he was struck and fatally injured by a passing car!

Ungovernable Rage

It may have been a sign of his future relationship with Australian Governors-General when Gough Whitlam threw a glass of water over Paul Hasluck. Hasluck was later knighted and appointed Governor-General. Whitlam met his nemesis in Sir John Kerr!

Saved by Whale

The carcass of a whale, harpooned weeks earlier, saved two Maori women, the only survivors after a canoe sank in Cook Strait in 1834. They managed to swim to the carcass and grab the harpoon—then floated 80 miles to land!

Snore to Rocky Shore

Competing in the 1982 solo round-the-world yacht race, English skipper Desmond Hampton slept in his bunk for three quarters of an hour over his schedule—and the yacht *Gipsy Moth V*, the last vessel to be owned by Sir Francis Chichester, smashed into rocks and was wrecked.

The crash occurred within 200 m of the Gabo Island lighthouse! After Hampton scrambled ashore he told the lighthouse keeper he only slept an hour at a time. But this, the first time he had overslept, had been disastrous.

Gambler's Luck

Bookmaker Bill Munro knew he'd used up all his bad luck when he was cleaned out at the Hay (NSW) races. Returning home by car, he agreed to swap his front passenger seat with a man behind. Minutes later the vehicle overturned and the man in the front seat was killed.

Expensive Cremation

Setting alight to a dead bird near Armidale (NSW) in 1946 two woman accidently started a huge bushfire which destroyed a saw mill, burned out 15 000 acres of trees and caused more than £7000 of damage.

Dead Lines

Early deadlines can have their problems. New Zealand's TV show 'Good Morning'—recorded eight days in advance—ran a gossip item about marital problems between Princess Grace and Prince Rainier of Monaco, which went to air 48 hours after her death from injuries received in a car accident.

In the same week the national magazine the *Listener* carried an article on Lebanon including a photo of President-elect Gemayel with a caption which asked: 'Can he last?' Gamayel had been shot to death in an attack two days earlier.

A POINTING BONE
OF THE AUSTRALIAN ABORIGINES
WHEN THIS BONE IS POINTED AT A "BLACKFELLOW"
HE LIES DOWN AND DIES.

November 11

One of the most memorable events in the history of Australian politics—the sacking of Labor Prime Minister Gough Whitlam by Governor-General John Kerr—occurred on Remembrance Day, 1975! Australia's most famous folk hero, Ned Kelly, was hanged on that same day, 1880.

Kept Dangling

Early in 1940, Mrs W. Thomas of Talbot (Vic.) had a miraculous escape when earth covering an old mine shaft gave way and she was left hanging to tree roots over a 90 ft drop into 30 ft of water until her husband came to her rescue. Seven years later, while walking on the same property the same thing happened again! Once more, her husband came to her rescue!

Oops, Missed

While pushing trucks to the shaft of the Mount Finney Mine (Qld) William Ambrose delivered one when the cage was not there to receive it—and down he went. He fell 125 ft and while the truck was smashed, William escaped without a scratch!

Rebuke From Above

Ignoring rebukes from his parish priest and religious neighbours for working on Sundays, Christmas and Good Friday, Mr J. L. Rose of Brisbane built himself a four-roomed house over two years. The night before he was due to move in it was struck by lightning and burned to the ground!

Fitting End

Jack Carodini, heavily under the influence of drink, beat his pony all day and when it refused to carry him any further he began to stab it, from the saddle, with a penknife.

In its dying frenzy the pony dashed to a lagoon near the Ovens River (Vic.) and jumped in, keeping its body on top of its rider until both drowned.

Hooked by Golf

Furious at hooking a ball into a lake during a local golf tournament in 1982, Melbourne golfer Peter Marino slammed his four iron against a fence. It snapped in half and the broken part spun back and pierced his leg like an arrow! Fellow golfers gave him a piggyback to the clubhouse.

Sin Seeker

The only occupant of a long pew at Corrimal (NSW) Methodist Church in 1923, Mr Thomas Brown was struck by lightning which crashed through the window above him during a sermon on the theme 'Be Sure, Your Sins Will Find You Out'. Mr Brown survived, but he made no confessions!

Saved from the Drink

Two unconnected men both missed the passenger ship the *Koombana* sailing from Port Hedland (WA) through unchecked on-shore celebrations—and saved their own lives!

On the way to Singapore, seaman Harold Sawyer went ashore, got hopelessly drunk, was arrested for swearing and thrown into gaol, missing his ship.

Celebrating the collection of pearls he had recovered, diver Tony Ulbrecht missed the departure of the *Koombana*. He jumped into a dinghy and took a short cut across shallow water to meet the vessel, but Captain Webb refused to allow him to board. Cursing, Ulbrecht returned to shore. Hours later the *Koombana*, with 130 on board, was lost at sea.

Not Gone Yet

Mrs Noni McIntyre, of Parkside (SA) received a phone call from her brother Jack after she had mourned his death and arranged his funeral! A second Jack McIntyre had collected the wrong mail from the post office and after his death in a rail accident police found a letter from Noni among his belongings!

A BRONZE PENNY ISSUED IN ERROR BY THE AUSTRALIAN MINT IN 1930 *SOLD FOR* $400

FOUR

Builders

Playblocks of Life

'When we build, let us think that we build for ever', said John Ruskin (1819–1900).

His words may well have been the inspiration for those who put up the many fine buildings that stand in Australia and New Zealand today. But could they not also have been a stimulant for the founders of our social structure?

The early builders have to some extent shaped our destiny, for we must now live where they chose to live, endure the elements they chose to endure.

There are, of course, many other builders not involved with bricks and mortar. They are the men and women who have shaped law and order and who have created positions in government. They are our politicians and officials, our inventors and our ideas men.

They are the individuals who start with nothing and end with something—like the six-year-old boy who borrowed money from the bank to buy a suit, leaving his scooter as security.

No matter how great or small the task or the finished product, those behind the work are builders, one and all. Consider *yourself* a builder if, perhaps, you have brought about a permanent change in the office by making a simple suggestion. You have restructured a routine, added another brick to efficiency. Look how enterprising the South Australian Government was following the death of King Edward VII—they used black-edged envelopes left over from official correspondence to put the staff pay in!

In this section you will meet a wide variety of builders. They might have made a contribution to history or they might have carried out a task to better their own individual lot. They might, simply, have worked at building up friendships which, some might consider, is the most important construction job of all!

Now read about:

The men who built a hospital in exchange for barrels of rum.

The world's only nautical church.

The lighthouse built from wrecked ships.

The amateur epitaph carver.

Captain Cook's travelling cottage.

The smallest motel in the world.

THE STAR GARAGE IN SEYMOUR, AUSTRALIA, HAD SERVED FOR 51 YEARS AS A CHURCH

Boiled Up

Sir William McKell

Two men who became Governor-General of Australia had strong ties with—boilermaking!

William McKell, born in 1891, was apprenticed as a boilermaker and later became Assistant Secretary of the Boilermakers' Union. After a distinguished political career he became the second Australian-born Governor-General in 1947.

John Kerr, who made constitutional history by dismissing Labor Prime Minister Gough Whitlam in 1975, was born in Sydney in 1914, the son of a boilermaker.

Name for Fame

Sir Isaac Isaacs

Two men with the name Isaacs had remarkably similar careers in the same period, but on opposite sides of the world.

The first Australian-born Governor-General, Sir Isaac Isaacs, started as an advocate, entered parliament, became Attorney-General for his country and was subsequently knighted and appointed Chief Justice.

In England, the famous advocate Sir Rufus Isaacs followed the same course, but ultimately became Lord Reading.

Small Bills

King O'Malley, who before his death in 1953 was credited with the establishment of the Commonwealth Bank, introduced a variety of unusual bills in the South Australian Parliament which included prohibiting the employment of barmaids in hotels, legitimising children if their unwed parents marry and installing lavatories on trains!

Distilled Wisdom

Arthur Calwell

The leader of the Opposition in the Australian Parliament was entitled to one bottle of Scotch whisky per month during periods of 'short supply'. Once, a bottle was sent to Arthur Calwell, Deputy Leader of the Labor Party, by mistake. Party Leader,

Dr H. V. Evatt

Dr Evatt, who should have received it, ended up with the bill! When an annoyed Dr Evatt insisted the whisky be handed over to him, Calwell argued that 'possession was nine points of the law' and won.

Coughin' Fit for a King

Ill, and convinced that he was going to die during his 1888 voyage from San Francisco to Queensland, Mr King O'Malley brought his own lead-lined coffin aboard the steam ship for burial at sea. But he survived, lived with a group of Aborigines who fed him on kangaroo and fish and eventually became a big name in Australian politics!

Avenue of Honour

For every man and woman from Ballarat (Vic.) who served in World War I, 3900 trees form an Avenue of Honour on the main road leading into the city. Planted by girls working at a local factory, the 22.5 km line of trees forms Australia's longest war memorial.

THE BRIDGE OVER THE COAL RIVER AT RICHMOND, TASMANIA, BUILT IN 1823, IS THE OLDEST SPAN IN AUSTRALIA

THE CHURCH of CHRIST in BASSENDEAN, AUSTRALIA, WAS CONSTRUCTED IN A SINGLE DAY IT WAS BUILT BY 120 VOLUNTEERS ON JAN. 4, 1913, AND SERVICES WERE HELD IN IT THE NEXT DAY

Billy's Masseur

Australian Prime Minister during World War I Billy Hughes had a male private secretary who was also responsible for getting him mobile each day. The secretary was, by profession, a masseur!

Secretary's Terror

Veteran Australian statesman Billy Hughes was the fear of every office girl. Depending on his moods and tantrums, his secretaries lasted between 24 hours and 24 days!

A Small Loan

Anxious to have a smart suit for Sunday School, a six-year-old boy at Murwillumbah (NSW) asked a local bank for a loan of 36 shillings. The bank agreed and took the boy's scooter as security!

THE TOWERING HILLS BUILT BY MAGNETIC ANTS --SO NAMED BECAUSE THEIR SKYSCRAPER NESTS ALWAYS POINT NORTH AND SOUTH, ARE FOUND ONLY IN NORTHERN AUSTRALIA

Recipe for Success

Hans Otto Stern, a former German film comedian who arrived in Australia in 1938, brought with him his mother's recipe for pumpernickel, the black bread made from molasses and rye, and opened a pumpernickel factory in Sydney.

Mourning Money

When King Edward VII died, the South Australian Government used black-edged envelopes for all official correspondence. A large number was left over—so they were used as staff pay dockets!

Working Coffin

While working as an undertaker in Thames (NZ), Mr Bill Ainsworth made himself a coffin. But when he left the burial business to become a carpenter he decided to make his new vocation a long-time career and put the box to good use as a storage cupboard for his overalls and tools!

Cheerful Undertaker

After a flourishing year, 1834, Van Diemen's Land undertaker Mr F. Bryant put an advertisement in the local almanac stating that he offered his 'grateful acknowledgement' for the encouragement he had for some years past received 'and assures his friends that it will be his constant study to execute all orders committed to his care with neatness and despatch'.

Clock's Warning

Numbers on the dial of a warehouse clock in Melbourne in the 1920s were replaced with the letters COMEPUNCTUAL!

Prizes Galore

Joseph Lodge and his wife of Bacchus Marsh (Vic.) have won more than 2,000 prizes between them. They have entered competitions for poultry, needlework, horticulture, ploughing and shooting.

Super Net

When George Posa of Perth made a fishing net in 1950, he claimed it was the biggest in the world to be sewn by hand. Nine hundred feet long and eight feet wide, it took him just 12 days to complete.

Left Flat

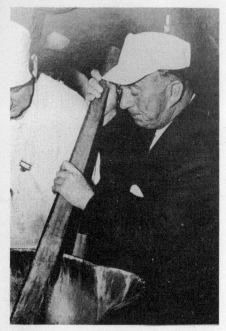

Henry Bolte, who became Premier of Victoria in 1955, was an excellent marksman and served as an artillery instructor at an Army base at Puckapunyal. But he was rejected as being of any use for his country overseas during World War II because he had flat feet!

Faint Praise

A loving husband was distraught when his slim, God-fearing wife died in Hobart (Tas.) and he felt his last duty to her would be to carve a suitable epitaph on her gravestone. He didn't do a bad job—just didn't work out the spacing properly and ran out of room. Instead of reading 'Lord, She was Thine' the epitaph read, 'Lord, She was Thin'.

Pearler's Luck

Poverty-stricken pearl hunter Nicholas Minister managed to scratch a living when he purchased a rotting boat in 1910, but gradually business went bad and to make things worse the boat was blown onto rocks in Torres Strait.

Examining the broken pieces, he found a large pearl wedged between two of the decking boards. He sold it for £300, bought himself a reliable boat and business started to boom!

Nicholas believed the pearl had been hidden in the old boat by a dishonest diver working for the previous owner and had not had a chance to retrieve it.

Durable Pastor

In 1936, Rev. V. R. Hicks married Mr and Mrs J. M. Duncan at Ballarat (Vic.). In 1957 he joined their daughter Lilian in matrimony and in 1980 he officiated at the marriage of their granddaughter, Susan!

Three Fingers

A peculiarity of Maori carvings is that all figures of men have only three fingers on each hand. It goes back to the time when the first man to carve and decorate houses had only three fingers and he perpetuated this in his carvings.

Lighthouse from Wrecks

The irony of a lighthouse built on Raine Islet, off Queensland's Great Barrier Reef, was that all the timber used in the construction came from wrecked ships!

Bridge Off Course

An iron bridge built in England for use in Russia, ended up spanning the Maribyrnong River at Keilor (Vic.). A hitch in the contract resulted in it being brought to Australia in the 1800s and among its unusual features were the solid wrought iron walls designed to keep out the bitter winds of the Russian steppes.

Second Chance

Although he was the driver of the first vehicle to be involved in a fatal motor accident in Australia, in 1907, Mr Peter Hall survived to become personal chauffeur to nine Victorian premiers!

Straight Rail

Railway lines across the Nullarbor Plain, which spans the South Australian-Western Australian border, are so straight that on a clear night train travellers can see the lights of an approaching locomotive two hours away!

Horses for Courses

Robert Menzies' Cabinet of 1956 consisted of Charles Davidson, an ex-Army colonel--Minister of the Navy; Jack Cramer, estate agent— Minister of the Army; Hugh Robertson from the agricultural district of the Riverina—Minister of Social Services; and city-bred William McMahon who lived in an apartment at Kings Cross, Sydney, kept a canary and two potted geraniums Minister for Primary Industry!

Rail Gaol

The strangest railway station in the world is at Serviceton (Vic.)—it doubles as a licensed hotel while underneath rings set in the cellar walls suggest it was also intended to be used as a temporary lock-up!

Although it's a kilometre inside Victoria, the railway station was built by the South Australian government in the 1800s because at the time there was confusion of the whereabouts of the border!

Pride of Sydney

The Sydney Harbour Bridge is the largest steel arch bridge in the world, standing 400 ft above sea level and carrying eight traffic lanes—a contrast to Australia's first bridge which was made of logs and straddled the Tank Stream in 1788!

Widest Bridge

What is thought to be the widest bridge in the world is used by thousands of people in Bendigo (Vic.) daily—yet many don't even realise they are crossing it!

Straddling Bendigo Creek, it is 200 m wide, but surrounding properties hide each side and only the main platform is visible.

Angel of Louth

When his 'angelic' wife, Mary, died, Mr I. E. Matthews, who founded the New South Wales town of Louth, wanted all to remember her and her purity. So he constructed a 1.2 m metal cross on her grave which, from certain parts of the local common, has the reflection of a halo!

Soldier's Gratitude

World War II soldier Geoff Edwards was so grateful for the way the Greeks treated him while he was a prisoner of war that when he returned home to Western Australia he built a church for the local Greek community.

Perishing Track

Australia's remote Birdsville Track, 505 km of cattle road running from South Australia to south-west Queensland, has been the demise of many motorists who have succumbed to dust storms and temperatures that reach 45 Celsius. Some stranded drivers have had to drink the water from their radiators to survive but others, who have tried to walk in search of help, have perished.

Orchids and Pearls

Mark Reuben, a rich pearl hunter, invited several residents of Broome (WA) on board the steamer *Paroo* and on arrival each was presented with a bunch of rare orchids brought from Papua packed in ice. When they lifted the covers on their dinner plates they each found a single pearl, which Reuben presented as an added gift.

Titanic Sails Again

The weathervane on the bandstand in Ballarat's (Vic.) main street, does not have a cockerel. Instead it carries a replica of the *Titanic*, in memory of the ship's bandsmen who drowned when the liner sank in 1912.

Rum Deal

Three gentlemen with a rum idea made an offer to the Government they could hardly refuse—they would build a two-storey hospital in Sydney in exchange for a monopoly of the rum trade!

Alexander Riley, D'Arcy Wentworth and Garnham Blaxcell were given the go ahead to build the hospital in Macquarie Street, the work starting in 1811 and the Government providing 20 convict labourers, 80 oxen and 20 draught bullocks.

Sydney got its hospital—and Messrs Riley, Wentworth and Blaxcell began the unhindered importation of 45 000 gallons of rum!

★★

THE CALENDAR HOUSE
MONA VALE near Ross, Australia
HAS **365** WINDOWS — ONE FOR EACH DAY OF THE YEAR
7 ENTRANCES — ONE FOR EACH DAY OF THE WEEK
12 CHIMNEYS — ONE FOR EACH MONTH
AND **52** ROOMS — ONE FOR EACH WEEK

★★

Captain Cook's Cottage

The Yorkshire cottage where Captain James Cook's parents lived after it was built in 1775, now stands under the gum-trees in Melbourne's Fitzroy Gardens! It was transported from Great Ayton to Melbourne to celebrate the 1934 centenary of the city's founding.

Big Collector

When Wellington (NZ) book collector Alexander Turnbull died in 1918 he left behind 45 000 volumes! They formed the basis for the Alexander Turnbull Library which now contains more than 250 000 books, paintings, maps and documents and the world's most comprehensive section on New Zealand.

Bad Omen

The gallows at the Old Gaol at Dubbo (NSW), last used in 1904, has 13 steps!

Massive Bar

Customers at the Working Man's Club, Mildura (Vic.) are always assured of a long drink—the bar is 90 m long and has 27 taps through which 7000 litres of beer are poured each week!

Crazy Paving

One of the world's most unusual footpaths can be seen in Melbourne's Fitzroy Gardens. It is made up of more than 1000 ceramic tiles with a variety of designs by local residents.

Naturalised

The first person to be naturalised in Australia was an American, Timothy Pitman, who changed his nationality in 1825. By the beginning of 1963 more than 350 000 migrants had been granted naturalisation.

Delayed Action

The biggest taipan—Australia's deadliest snake—ever caught was knocked out by a well-aimed clod of earth flung by builder Gordon Barton of Bri-Bri (Qld) in 1968. It measured eight feet and when Gordon took it to the local ambulance station for identification he passed out with shock on being told of the species of snake he had handled!

Water Worn

An old cafe in the Victorian township of Mount Eliza had a distinct nautical flavour—the main construction was from parts of the disused Port Melbourne pier, while the counters and doors were made from oak and mahogany salvaged from the bay steamer *Courier*.

The QUEEREST HOUSE IN AUSTRALIA AT BALLARAT

CONSTRUCTED OF AN ENDLESS MEDLEY OF MISCELLANEOUS OBJECTS IN A VAST VARIETY OF COLORS – LAMPS, JUGS, SHELLS, DISHES, PLAQUES, ROCKS, ORNAMENTS, STATUETTES, BROKEN GLASS, ETC.

THE CHURCH OF PORT ARTHUR in Australia WAS DESIGNED AND BUILT BY JAMES BLACKBURN -A PRISONER IN THE PORT ARTHUR JAIL— HE WAS GIVEN A FULL PARDON UPON ITS COMPLETION IN 1840

Fairy Bower

In 1931, artist and sculptress Ola Cohn decided the fairies of Australia needed a sanctuary. So she carved dozens of elf-like creatures and Australian animals in the trunk of a tree in Melbourne's Fitzroy Gardens and dedicated the work to 'all living creatures'.

SCULPTRESS OLA COHN HAS CARVED A 600-YEAR-OLD BLUE GUM INTO A FAIRY TREE FOR CHILDREN FROM EACH KNOB AND NOOK APPEAR WOMBATS – KOALAS – KANGAROOS – KOOKABURRAS AND OTHER CREATURES OF THE AUSTRALIAN BUSHLAND

Miniature Cathedral

Mr Frank Rusconi built a miniature cathedral using 20 948 pieces of marble which he cut and polished by hand. It took him TWENTY-EIGHT YEARS.

Mr Rusconi also sculpted the statue of the Dog on the Tuckerbox at Gundagai, Australia's most popular national monument.

The miniature cathedral is on display at the Gundagai Tourist Centre. The dog is in a garage forecourt!

Smallest Church

Because settlers had no place to pray at Australind (WA) they gathered on Sundays at a workman's cottage. In 1915 the Church of England bought the building and it was blessed by Bishop Goldsmith.

Now known as St Nicholas' Church, measuring 7 m by 4.06 m, it is the smallest in the country—and still in use!

Church of the Sea

Because it sits beside Lake Victoria, Paynesville (Vic.), St Peter's Church has a spire shaped like a lighthouse tower, a pulpit in the design of the bow of a fishing boat, a sanctuary light like a ship's riding light, while the outside cross can be seen at night by fisherman on the Gippsland lakes.

Dingo Fence

The longest fence in the world stretches for more than 5500 km around Queensland to protect sheep farms from dingoes, the wild dogs that roam the desert.

A MONUMENT TO THE EIGHT HOUR DAY!

AUSTRALIA IS THE MOTHER OF THE 8 HOUR DAY:
EIGHT HOURS FOR WORK,
EIGHT HOURS FOR RECREATION AND
EIGHT HOURS FOR SLEEP
ENACTED IN 1856
Melbourne, Australia

Suit for Air

Tuning the engine of his plane in the cold winter of 1916 while serving in England with the Royal Naval Air Service, 22-year-old Queenslander Sidney Cotton had to take off in his greasy overalls in an emergency.

On landing, other pilots complained of the biting cold, yet Cotton felt warm. He realised the grease had helped keep his body heat in.

He developed a flying suit made of one piece like his overalls and it became widely used by airmen around the world!

Big Lift

After gold was discovered at Bulolo, Papua-New Guinea, aircraft bringing dredge machinery to the district carried more freight in one month than all other airlines in the world for the whole year!

World's Largest Bottle

Some areas of Australia are so proud of their local product that they have built huge models which never cease to fascinate visitors. At Freshwater Creek (Vic.) stands the world's largest bottle, comprising 17 500 soft-drink bottles, around which a slide has been built for children.

A large cow at Yandina (Qld) is so big that tourists can walk around inside and inspect a display depicting the area's dairy industry, while on the Sunshine Coast of the state a 16-metre-high pineapple contains an observation deck and a display about tropical fruits.

Other giant models are a buffalo in the Northern Territory; a shell, a marlin, a cattle bell, Captain Cook and a cassowary and her chicks in Queensland; a banana, a rainbow trout and a codfish in New South Wales; a lobster, a rocking horse and an orange in South Australia; dinosaurs in Victoria; and, in Western Australia, a concrete-mixing company's advertising sign, READYMIX, in letters 183 m tall!

Dog, Song Co-op.

When the song 'How Much is that Doggie in the Window?' was popular in the early 1950s, a pet shop and a record shop in Sydney decided to cash in on the hit.

The music shop displayed a sign reading: 'If you want the record, come in here. If you want the dog, he's around the corner.'

The pet shop put up a similar notice, reversing the order.

There's a Small Motel

Couples only are welcome at the Landhaus Motel, Bethany (SA)—and only one couple at a time because that's all the motel can cater for! Created from an old shepherd's cottage, the Landhaus was built by German settlers in the 1850s who would never have imagined that it would become the world's tiniest accommodation for travellers!

Drummed Up

A tractor, a boat and horses all failed to pull a truck free from the mud as the tide came in at Aotea on New Zealand's North Island. Then a local Maori arrived on the scene with eight empty oil drums, fastened them to the sides of the truck, and the vehicle floated free as the water rose!

Travel Job

Applicants for the job of lighthouse keeper on Troubridge Shoal off the coast of South Australia were warned they were expected to travel—the island was gradually shifting east with the currents!

Silent Member

South Australian Parliamentarian Richard Hooper earned the nickname 'The Silent Member' in the latter part of the 19th century because in 10 years in office he made only one speech!

Carved a Career

Inia Te Wiata, a bass-baritone from Otaki (NZ) made a big name for himself in opera, musical comedy, films, television and radio in the United Kingdom, but when the new New Zealand House was built in London in 1965 he was asked not to sing but to carve the High Commission's 16-metre-high pole!

It was remembered that before he began his operatic career he had been a highly respected Maori woodcarver.

Travelling Church

Realising it would take too long to gather together materials and draw up plans for his church on arrival in Australia, Dr Charles Perry, Melbourne's first Anglican Bishop, brought one with him from England when he arrived in 1848!

It consisted of sheets of prefabricated iron, enough seats for 1000 parishioners and a 40-ft-high tower.

Town Flattened Twice

In 1942 Darwin was flattened when Japanese planes took part in the first attack on the Australian mainland by a foreign power. The town was rebuilt, but 32 years later it was completely destroyed again when Cyclone Tracy swept in at Christmas. Once more the city has been rebuilt.

FIVE

Battlers

Ready to 'have a go'

Against all odds they fight on in an effort to maintain or restore normality. Battlers win our admiration, for often they have to go it alone.

From the smouldering embers of the February, 1983, bushfires which swept through parts of South Australia and Victoria hundreds of battlers emerged. People determined to pick up the threads and start all over again, cleaning up their land, rebuilding their homes. But it was not only the physical act of restoring that which was lost which made them into battlers—it was their attitude of mind. They *believed* they could do it, they were *determined* to do it and if, in the end, they never succeeded they were battlers all the same.

We see them among the unemployed—those intent on finding work and making ends meet while they try. We see them among the handicapped, fighting on, going about life as naturally as they can.

In an effort to maintain what they consider to be their rights, battlers pit themselves against authority. They are the Davids fighting the Goliaths and if they see they cannot win they will search out another way around the problem. They are not always born cunning, but they certainly become worldly wise.

Often down on their luck, they will always 'have a go'. They back the horses, enter the lotteries, and if they win their mates wish them all the best and tackle their own problems with even more gusto.

Battlers live on the edge and the knock backs are often more frequent than the rewards. But they have the ability to pick themselves up, dust themselves off and start all over again. Can we not admire the woman who walked 600 miles in the 19th century searching for her husband among the gold-fields? Or the courage of boxer Johnny Gleeson whose dying father had said 'Go and win the fight son'—and two hours later did just that?

But here you can read about

other battlers who fought in their own individual ways. Meet:

The striking workers who kept on working.

The residents who threw away their television sets.

The injured truck driver who sucked rain from his hat.

The man who wears porpoise teeth.

The world's most unsuccessful author.

The man who died twice.

Not Trained

The most unpunctual train in the world is the 8.08 a.m. from suburban Essendon to Melbourne. In a six month survey in 1978, it was found to run late 97 per cent of the time!

Marathon Bout

James Kelly and Jonathan Smith set a world record when they fought bare-fisted at Daylesford (Vic.) for 6 hrs 15 min in November, 1855. The match ended in a draw.

Mulga Fred Model

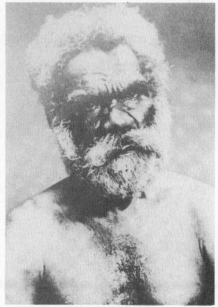

After 85-year-old Aborigine Mulga Fred was killed by a train in 1949 residents of Horsham (Vic.) subscribed to build a monument to him because they remembered him as the black model who advertised shirts for a clothing company with the words: 'Mine tink it they fit.'

No Dancing

Mr James Hull of Molong (NSW) lived to the grand old age of 109 and before his death in 1961 he attributed his long life partly to the fact that he never learned to dance. He certainly had no opportunity of taking up dancing after the age of 100—that was when he fell out of a car and broke his leg!

Itchy Trigger Finger

A duellist called Synnot was so nervous when he met his opponent, Griffin, in New South Wales in 1854 that he pressed the trigger of his pistol prematurely and set fire to his trousers. Honour, it was decided, had been satisfied and the duel was cancelled!

Safer at War

Up to 1915 jockey J. N. McGregor of Victoria had fallen off horses 127 times and broken every bone in his body—yet he was still accepted as fit for national service! Returning completely unscathed from the front, he resumed his racing career and by 1921 had brought his falls to 142 and had added many more injuries to his tally!

Tea Party

Prosper de Mestre almost brought about a new version of the Boston Tea Party in Sydney in 1844 when, after his arrival, he undersold local businessmen by buying tea direct from China at a cheap rate while Sydney-siders had, by law, to continue purchasing from the British East India Company. He eventually became the first person to be naturalised, but despite being active in business and shipping he ended his days bankrupt.

Up the Hard Way

Ex-Senator Neville Bonner, first Aboriginal elected to the Australian Parliament, was raised in poverty with virtually no education. But he worked himself into the position of head stockman on a large station and later opened his own boomerang factory before being chosen to fill a Senate vacancy. Just prior to the 1983 general election he was put to the bottom of the Senate ticket. A true battler, Bonner stood as an independent but was not re-elected.

Pippie Popper Pipped

A professionally produced pippie popper was prohibited by councillors at Byron Shire (NSW) because they thought the machine, invented to disgorge a pink and cream shellfish from sandy beaches for use as bait, would unearth too many and destroy their life cycle.

What a Drip

A night watchman at a Sydney club decided to make use of the facilities and have a shower at 4 o'clock in the morning was horrified to find the lock had jammed. He had to keep the shower running for 3 hours to stay warm, until a cleaner turned up at 7 am and let him out!

Brown Out

Police who arrived at the scene of a crash between two cars driving towards each other in 1947, found that one driver was called Mr T. Brown and so was the other! What's more, they were father and son. Neither was badly hurt but the cars were so badly damaged neither father nor son could offer the other a lift home!

Short but Sweet

Seaman Charles Brittain, of Dora Creek (NSW), returned home for only three or four days a year, yet by 1931 he and his wife were the parents of 22, the ages running from four to forty-five!

Stoic Type

After typing for 213 hours to beat the world endurance typing record in February, 1980, New Zealander Violet Burns said the effort had put her behind with personal matters—so she stayed up typing letters!

Drawing the Line

A conviction against motorist Rodney Greaves of Auckland (NZ) for failing to keep to the left of a yellow line was quashed in July, 1982, when he told an appeals court that the line was white!

Hair Care

Newlyweds Les and Lorraine Farrier decided to cancel their honeymoon because the bride had turned into a redhead after a man poured paint over her before the wedding in Adelaide in January, 1982.

Long Search

Searching for her husband from whom she had not heard for four months, a woman called Conroy made the 600 mile journey from Adelaide to the gold-fields at Mount Alexander in 1852—WALKING ALL THE WAY!

Crazy Potion

A potion guaranteed to cure drunkenness was manufactured in Sydney by the Eucrasy Co.!

Old Boots

Wagga Wagga footballer Harry Lampe played for his team for 23 consecutive seasons and on his 'retirement' in 1899 joined South Melbourne and played with them for another 14 seasons. He was well into his 50s when he finally hung up his boots!

Lamb to the Slaughter

Pugilists Bill Daniels and Bob Lee fought bare-knuckled for EIGHTY-FIVE ROUNDS in Hobart in 1817 until Daniels, who had been literally knocked blind, told Lee he could have the fight and the 60 ewes prize!

Tall Tickets

Sydney bus passengers who were more than 6 ft 3 in tall were issued with special pink tickets in 1962 allowing them to ride on the rear platforms because buses had only 5 ft 10 in of headroom!

Metal Eater

One of the most popular sideshow performers in the 1930s was Samson, a strongman from Greece. He chewed and swallowed razor blades and broke six-inch nails with his teeth. But that was really just a rehearsal for his greatest feat—eating a motor car. He got through three mudguards before his vocal chords gave out.

Student Co-operative

When a Mini Minor car broke down in Queen Street, Brisbane in 1979, police ordered it to be moved, but the student owner could not afford the towing fees. So 25 students from Queensland University PICKED IT UP and carried it away!

Postman Treed by Dogs

We've all heard of dogs that consider postmen fair game. Take John Conway Bourke, the first mailman to carry post between Melbourne and Sydney. After his horse stuck fast in the Hume River he began a long and desperate swim, reaching the far bank almost naked.

He was spotted by a pack of about 50 dogs which, he remembered, 'came on like a tornado of devils'. Bourke scrambled up a gum-tree and there he remained until a station owner came to his rescue.

Dolphin Dentures

Concerned about his worn-out dentures, Ernie Woolley had a brainwave when he came across a dead dolphin on his local beach in Queensland. He extracted the creature's teeth and for a dozen bottles of beer persuaded his dentist to make him up a new set of ivories. Now sporting a jagged-toothed grin Ernie is known as the man with the world's most porpoiseful smile!

Not So Slow

Police who set up a speed trap on a stretch of road in Stroud Shire (NSW) in January, 1961, were puzzled why every motorist was travelling well within the limit—until they found out that a group of Aborigines from a nearby camp were displaying a placard reading 'Policeman Ahead. Slow Down' and, a little further along, collecting donations from the grateful drivers!

Blind Homage

A blind man in a Brisbane asylum never missed an inmate's funeral in the 30 years he was there between 1890 and 1920. He took his stand 200 yards from the morgue and when the hearse passed, fell in behind for the mile walk to the burial ground. After listening to the service, he made his way back to his room.

He attended more than 3500 funerals!

Cutting Down

During a beer strike in Melbourne in 1980, a hotel frequented by heavy drinkers displayed a sign saying that because of union action the management was restricting draught beer to 40 glasses per person!

Six Pack Max

The fastest beer drinker in Australia is carpenter Mr Max van Dennesse of Frankston (Vic.) who guzzled six cans in 1 min 2.34 sec, beating an earlier record by 28 seconds.

Useless Catch

Fishing with a net for his missing dentures in a river near Shepparton (Vic.) a local man was delighted when he hauled in a full set. Then, with disgust, he tossed them back in.

They weren't his!

Timing

A householder in Leongatha (Vic.) waited in vain for SEVEN YEARS for a chimney sweep to call at his home. Finally he did the job himself, and as he emerged from the chimney, black from head to toe, the sweep knocked on his door!

Of Love and Death

Before leaving for her honeymoon in 1948, Mrs Ronald Broomhead of Paramatta, laid her wedding bouquet on the coffin of her grandmother who dropped dead during the marriage ceremony!

A Broad Hint

Angry about poor reception, residents of the Queensland resorts of Cannonvale and Airlie Beach gathered up 40 television sets and dumped them at the local rubbish tip in September, 1980. Authorities still didn't get the picture.

Remittance Man

Big Constable Harry Figg, a member of the Adelaide police force in 1838, had such a huge appetite that when he called at the Old Exchange Hotel the landlord always gave him half a crown to eat somewhere else!

Watery Find

In the stomach of a shark, fisherman John Fenwick of Sydney found a small wallet containing a pawn ticket which had two days left before it expired. He hurried into the city, passed it in and became the proud owner of a pocket watch!

Easy Life

While visiting a relative at a Queensland maternity hospital in 1901, Mr Robert Hargraves became ill. He was persuaded to stay in one of the wards for the night and remained for several weeks until he recovered, but by then had found life so comfortable that he stayed as a convalescent patient at a nominal rate for 15 years!

So They Said

Stepping off a ship in Melbourne in March, 1946, were four Saids from Port Said who said they were the 'advance party' of 11 other Saids, also of Port Said!

Trapped Ball

While a prisoner of war in Germany, Mr W.M. Sampson of Hobart (Tas.) made a golf ball of sewn leather.

Stuffed with a variety of materials, including feathers, it was almost identical in size and weight to a standard ball. After being hit around the camp by prisoners using sticks as clubs it was sent as a memento to St Andrew's Golf Club, Scotland.

Hooks, Lines and Sinkers

Fishing near Busselton (WA) Arthur Grocock caught on one bait one sting-ray, 16 lead sinkers, eight lines, 16 hooks—and one sting from the ray!

Any Excuse

Brisbane tram driver Norman Payne gave up smoking, sold his tobacco, roller and papers to his colleagues and bought a lottery ticket with the proceeds.

He won the £6000 first prize.

Hearing about his good fortune, Mr Payne immediately lit a cigarette to celebrate!

Dry Fishing

Deciding it was too dangerous for spectators to hold the annual fishing line casting tournament off rocks near Sydney, organisers changed the venue in 1946—and the contest was held miles inland at French's Forest, opposite the brickworks!

Stiff

A Brisbane syndicate entering a national lottery called themselves 'The Three Stiffs'. They were one short—the prize was won by 'The Four Stiffs' from Sydney!

Weighty Problem

When Les McNabb put himself up for his first boxing match in 1943 officials scratched their heads—he was so heavy the scales could not accommodate him. Finally he was weighed on a railway weighbridge!

Brick and Pipe

While working at a brick kiln at Geelong (Vic.) Mr J. Abrahams dropped his favourite pipe into the clay and despite a thorough search could not find it.

Fifty years later, while a house at Belmont, near Geelong, was being demolished, one of the bricks broke in half and the pipe fell out. The demolition men traced the original owner, who spent his last days puffing away contentedly on his verandah!

Gravest Story

While digging a spare grave at Wagga Wagga cemetery (NSW) in the early 1900s, caretaker Arthur Chaucer suddenly collapsed and died and was buried in the hole two days later.

Saved by Cap

His pelvis fractured when his truck overturned, Graham Verren, 29, kept himself alive in the desert north of Adelaide in 1979, by sucking rain water from his cloth cap after a period of drizzle. He was rescued after three days.

Thoughtful Strikers

Although on strike in February, 1980, workers on Cook Strait ferries (NZ) said they would continue work with no pay to avoid inconveniencing the public!

Burning Insult

Every day for a month the proprietor of a Kalgoorlie (WA) hotel had to replace the doily on a bedside table because it had burn marks. The occupant of the room was continually asked not to smoke in bed but he insisted he had never touched a cigarette in his life. At last, the hotel owner worked out the scorch marks were caused by the sun's rays being magnified through a water carafe!

REGINALD SPIERS of Adelaide, Australia, BROKE, AFTER FAILING TO QUALIFY IN THE JAVELIN EVENTS IN THE OLYMPIC TRYOUTS IN LONDON, ENG. (1964), HAD A FRIEND SHIP HIM HOME BY PLANE, C.O.D., IN A PACKING CRATE

Fighting Last Words

After winning a fight he was expected to lose at Sydney Stadium in 1949, Johnny Gleeson revealed he had obtained his fighting spirit from his father who had died just two hours before the bout and who, in his dying breath, had urged him to fight and win!

Big Smoker

Josephine Hickey, a cook at a Forbes (NSW) hotel like to roll her own cigarettes with pieces of newspaper wrapped around strong tobacco.

Police who broke into her room when she did not turn up for work found it piled high with cigarette butts. Medical evidence was that she died of heart failure from excessive smoking.

Basil Bones

Digging potatoes in the garden of her home at Burraneer Bay (NSW) in 1950, Mrs Errol Alcock came across a skeleton. As the house was built by convicts she presumed the bones were those of a prisoner.

The parts were wired together, he was christened Basil Bones and became a favourite playmate for the neighbourhood children!

Axeman's Error

During a woodchopping contest in north-eastern New South Wales in 1932, Stan Appleby made a terrible mistake and cut his leg off. At death's door, he was rowed across a river and rushed to hospital. After fighting for his life, he recovered to edit an axeman's magazine.

Record Failure

In 18 years, William Gold, the world's most unsuccessful author, wrote three million words, including seven novels, without having a single work published. Then he wrote a book called *One Best Seller* about the life of an unsuccessful author. It was grabbed in 1977 by a Melbourne publisher who dispatched it to the 'big timers' in America. Gold, of Canberra, commented: 'Until then my writing had made me only 50 cents when the *Canberra News* asked me to write an item for a column.'

Longlife Midwife

Nurse Edith Sloane of Adelaide acted as midwife at the births of 20 of her 24 grandchildren, then saw through the delivery of her first great-grandchild.

Rat Catchers

Although residents on Lord Howe Island lived a happy life free of taxes and rates, the man of each household was committed by law to set aside a day a week to catch rats!

Short Sentence

The shortest term of imprisonment ever handed down by an Australian court was on 17 July 1919, when newly-wed George Williams, 23, was charged with marrying a minor without parental consent and his 17-year-old bride Emily was accused of making a false registration. Justice Cussen sentenced them to 'the rising of the court', adding 'the court will now rise'!

Admitting Defeat

Longford Reserves will go down as the world's most defeated football team. The Tasmanian side rustled up only 16 players instead of the usual 18 for their Australian Rules match against Launceston Reserves.

The side was made up of school-boys, injured players or sportsmen long retired. The first half was murder. When they went to the dressing room at half-time Launceston were winning 210 points to nil. Longford then did something very unusual. They sent a message to Launceston which said:

'Blow this for a lark. We give up.' And they all went home.

Christmas High

Tinsel and Christmas cards decorating a metre-high marijuana bush in the Brisbane CIB office had to be removed because the plant was needed for evidence in a drug case.

Boot Rot Beer

New Zealand hotel employees claimed an extra two shillings a week in 1951 because they said spilt beer on bar floors rotted their boots!

Double Jeopardy

Sam Pearce of Glanville (SA) was the only man alive who was officially pronounced dead on two occasions.

Admitted to a public hospital with an illness in 1906, he was later pronounced dead and sealed in a coffin, but as he was about to be lowered into the grave he came around, shouted for release and rode back to hospital in the hearse!

Thirteen years later, Adelaide newspapers reported that he had 'dropped dead at Glanville'. Because he lived alone, a policeman was sent to his house and put in charge of the body lying in the bed, but the officer discharged himself in the morning when the 'corpse' got up and made breakfast!

Strange Stuffing

In a bizarre career Fred Psaila and his wife, both Melbourne taxidermists, have been asked to preserve a human head, a chunk of tattooed skin and a two-headed sheep. Fred decided to write a book about his occupation and one of the first titles he considered was 'How to Stuff Your Family Pet'.

Bride Price

Eighteen-stone Sam Lukhele, 28, press attaché for the Swaziland team, arrived in Brisbane for the Commonwealth Games with his heart set on winning a bride. He offered a herd of cows and up to $4000. Swaziland didn't win any medals and Sam was left out of the running in the marital stakes.

'I didn't have any takers', he said. 'I shouldn't have let on that we're allowed to keep several wives back home.'

Above Criticism

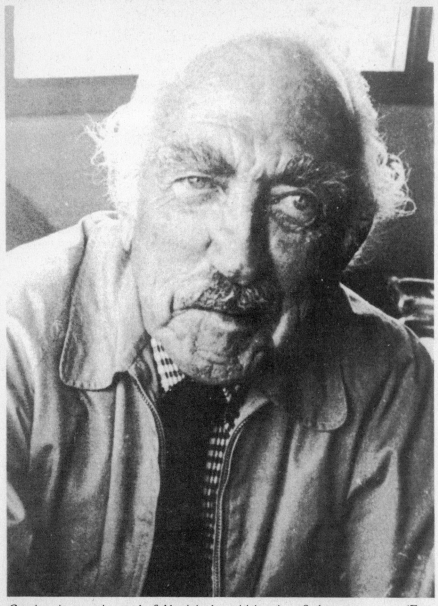

Capricornia, an epic novel of Aboriginal life by well-known Australian author Xavier Herbert, received a stinging criticism in a Sydney newspaper. 'For your Dustbin' read the headline. The novel became an Australian classic!

Clogged with Money

An old wooden shoe retrieved from Sydney Harbour in 1949 was nailed to the wall of the public bar in a Sydney pub. Locals put their loose change in it and within a year it had raised £1000 for a bus for the handicapped.

Bad Brew

Someone who did not think much of the local brew at Kissing Point penned the following words for a dead friend's gravestone:

Ye who wish to lie here
Drink Squire's Beer.

Party on Empties

Heavy drinkers in the hot and dusty South Australian township of Oodnadatta decided to give their children a special Christmas treat by rounding up all their discarded beer bottles from years of indulgence, trucking them to Adelaide for sale and throwing a big party. Afterwards everyone went around collecting the empty LEMONADE bottles.

Hot Chisel

Bricklayer 'Chisel' Ireland could carry 50 bricks in a hod from the stack and up a ladder. When another Sydney 'brickie' proved he could do it too, Chisel put an EXTRA 50 bricks on his hod, sat the challenger on top and carried the load, about a quarter of a ton, for 20 ft!

Dickens Lover

A full-blooded Queensland Aboriginal known only as Fred was an avid reader of Charles Dickens and could recite *A Christmas Carol* word for word!

Town on Wheels

When the residents of Lakewood (WA) announced they were moving house, they meant it. The town, centre of the gold-fields' timber-cutting industry in the 1930s and 1940s, consisted of shops, houses and a post office all situated on wheels on railway tracks. As trees were chopped down, the 1000 men, women and children moved their town on to the next site!

Silver Load

After fire destroyed the premises of the Overseas Film Service in Sydney in the early 1920s, chemist C. T. Counsell took 3½ tons of ash back to his laboratory and extracted from the remnants of the film 1000 oz of silver worth £162/10/–!

Unsinkable

Finding no further use for an old coal hulk because she was considered unseaworthy, the owners asked the navy to put a hole in her and sink her. HMAS *Brisbane* towed the hulk 10 miles out of Fremantle (WA) in 1917 and at a range of two miles pumped her with six-inch shells. She remained afloat and even though the *Brisbane* pummelled her with shells from various distances, not even the glass in the deckhouse was broken!

The captain decided to blow her up and 50 lb of gun cotton was exploded on board. When the smoke cleared the 'unseaworthy' hulk was still afloat!

Finding it impossible to sink her, the navy towed the vessel to a rocky shore where nature finally did the job, heavy seas breaking her up on the jagged coastline.

Blanket Billiards

The cloth of a billiard table in a pub at Poowong (Vic.) in the early 1920s was made up of a number of blankets sewn together. The pockets were old boots!

Craysy!

After hauling 317 crayfish in cages up a cliff face using block and tackle, William Harnold of Kiama (NSW) found that scores had broken free and were heading for the railway yard at Gerringong.

Grabbing a branch and releasing the rest, he herded the entire mob of crawling crays over a distance of a mile and a half to a guard's van where he signed the consignment note.

He lost only three!

Saved By Rain

Deserting soldier John Boatswain, sentenced to death, managed to hold on to his life for a rainy day—because it was too wet for his execution!

It was pouring on the day in April, 1801, when Boatswain should have been led to the gallows and the hanging was deferred. Six days later it was still lashing down and the execution was again postponed.

A few days later, because new facts came to light about his desertion, he was granted a free pardon.

Whatever the weather after that, all Boatswain saw was sunshine!

Bored with Bard

Shakespeare and theatre-going became such a craze in Sydney in the 1890s that those who could not stand it any more formed a group called 'The Society For Being Very Tired of Shakespeare'.

Rough Diamond

Inspecting the wreckage of a plane shot down by Japanese fighters in 1942, beachcomber Jack Palmer found a small package containing hundreds of diamonds! After giving handfuls away to almost everyone he met in that area, near Broome (WA), he was arrested for stealing diamonds worth £400 000 from the Royal Dutch Airlines DC3.

Many other people to whom Jack had given diamonds were pulled in, too, including a Chinese who had 460 in his pocket and who said an Aborigine had given them to him in exchange for a shirt and trousers!

Jack was finally acquitted, penniless once more, and went back to beachcombing.

Shark Lugger

Sitting in a small rowing boat, fisherman William Burns of Brisbane was towed more than two miles out to sea after harpooning a shark. Then he was tossed overboard and the last he saw of his boat as he was rescued by another fisherman was its shape growing smaller and smaller as the shark continued to tow it out to sea!

Reeling with Rice

Hit by a large handful of rice which sent her reeling at a New South Wales wedding, the bride, Mrs June Morris, grabbed an umbrella and smashed it over the head of the guest!

Lightning Recovery

While on his way home from hospital in a wheelchair in 1922, Mr Fred Seemer of Cumberland Park (Vic.) was struck by lightning. His crippled legs improved from that moment!

The FLIGHT of DEATH!

A FIGHTING PLANE-*WITH BOTH PILOT AND GUNNER DEAD* –
FLEW FOR HOURS AND THEN MADE A PERFECT LANDING
ON ITS HOME FIELD!

R.E.8, FLOWN BY 2 AUSTRALIANS
FRANCE —— 1917

Experience Counts

Mr John Ross, head gardener at
Ballarat Hospital (Vic.), had to work
without an assistant in 1922 and
single-handed kept up the supply of
vegetables for the institution, provided
for crops and kept an extensive flower
garden in order. He was 90 years old!

Tall Order

A Sydney magistrate inflicted severe
punishment on a motorist who pledged
to give up liquor for two years in
1950 when he warned the unhappy
fellow: 'Remember, this means you
must abstain from alcohol every day
and every night—even at a wake, a
wedding or on the declaration of war.'

JIM McDOWELL *A MAIL CARRIER*
on Cape York Peninsula, Australia,
WHO LED 14 PACK HORSES OVER A ROUTE OF
185 MILES, RODE HORSEBACK FOR 16 YEARS
-WITH ONLY 2 DAYS REST IN EACH MONTH

SIX

Rogues

'I'll be hanged'

They lurk in the pages of history and walk among us today, sometimes likeable, often shocking but always, always earning a grudging respect for their outrageousness.

Rogues. The very word has a gutsy, earthy ring which conjures up visions of devious deeds, rascally romps, mischievous moods. Sometimes cunning, sometimes outlandish they show little or no respect for man or woman.

We might envisage a rogue as a fat, cigar-smoking, purple-faced businessman who has no scruples; or we might see him as a swashbuckling bandit who robs the rich saying he will give to the poor but in fact pockets the bounty for himself.

The rogue feeds on cheek and a self-confidence which tells him he can get away with anything. And, of course, he always has a victim or more. For no man can be a rogue unto himself.

Yet we need our rogues to add a kind of perverted sparkle to life's routine. Their gall leaves us breathless. We need to feast upon their brashness and, indeed, their artfulness and bravery. Thieves or liars, braggarts or blackguards, the cads of society swoop like vultures, take their pickings and fly away. Yet we are drugged by their beastliness, as Falstaff observed in *King Henry IV* when, discovering that Poins had taken his horse, he remarked: '...I am bewitched with the rogue's company. If the rascal have not given me medicines to make me love him, I'll be hanged.'

The rogues you will meet here will shock you and amuse you with their disregard for the rules of life. You will be touched by their sauciness, stunned by their insolence, but you will love them all the same. Should we dare show a tinge of amusement at the English Westcountry woman immigrant who murdered her husband in the 19th century by lacing his favourite meal, a Cornish pastie, with arsenic?

Have we the audacity to grin at the skills of the convict who, transported to Sydney for stealing 400 pairs of stockings, won the heart of a rich widow and became known as the Botany Bay Rothschild?

Hundreds of thousands of rascals have found their way to Australia and New Zealand. As many have been born and raised here. Come and meet a few. There is:

The organiser of a talking contest who left the competitors speechless.

The prisoner who couldn't get to court because he was running from the police at the time.

The hangman who took a deputy sherrif to court for unpaid wages.

The football team which bent the rules and scored nearly 500 points.

The brothers who tried to assassinate a Prince and an Archbishop.

★★★★★★★

Fed Up

Complaining about prison food, a large group of convict women smashed down the gates of 'The Factory' at Parramatta, (NSW) in 1827 and headed for town to appease their hunger. Alarmed, bakers threw their bread and cakes into the streets and the women tucked in until they were full and ready for surrender.

In the Family

Prince Alfred

During the trial of Irishman H. J. O'Farrell, who tried to assassinate Prince Alfred by shooting him in the back in Sydney in 1868, it was revealed O'Farrell had a brother who had made two unsuccessful attempts to assassinate leading Catholic Archbishop Gould!

Fall from Grace

An Assistant Chief Constable called Skinner, in lone pursuit of a gang of dangerous bushrangers, ended up, as expected, seriously injured in hospital. But the desperadoes had nothing to do with it—walking along the verandah of a house near Sydney, he fell head first into an open cellar!

Sting in the Tail

The owner of a Wild West Show touring Queensland in the early 1900s put a rubber ring over a black snake's tail, tied a piece of string to the ring and attached the other end to his cash box. He was never robbed!

Hot Items

During one of the coldest nights of 1978 thieves broke into a Melbourne clothing manufacturers and stole $4000 worth of jumpers and blankets!

Raw Law

Sydney's old law courts were so cold and dilapidated in the late 1940s that judges had to sit with blankets around their legs and when it rained court orderlies had to stand by barristers' tables with mops to wipe away dripping water!

Love Locked

Pushing his head through the bars of his police station cell in Sydney to look at three passing policewomen in 1978, a 21-year-old prisoner found himself well and truly stuck. He was trapped for 90 minutes until an oxy-acetylene torch cut him free!

Up in Smoke

A soldier who was shot by a husband in the centre of Sydney while escorting the man's blonde wife, in February, 1946, staggered into a cinema and collapsed into a seat in the back row. The film being shown was *Incendiary Blonde*!

WILLIAM DAMPIER (1652-1715) THE FIRST ENGLISHMAN TO VISIT AUSTRALIA, WAS A BUCCANEER WHO COMPLAINED THAT *HE FOUND NOTHING WORTH PLUNDERING*

One-sided

The highest score in a game of Australian Rules football was recorded in 1929 by Katamatite (Vic.) which kicked 78 goals and 19 behinds for a total of 487 points!

They had to reach that figure to win the minor premiership on averages and, by arrangement, only eight of the opposition, Wattsville, turned up to play, scoring 9 points. However, the local football association declared the match null and void, despite protests from both sides!

The Dastardly Deeming

★★★★★★★★★★★★★★★

Hearth Rogue

As Messrs Bayley and Ford were buying provisions for their historic trip which was to result in their discovering gold at Coolgardie (WA), Frederick Deeming, another resident of Southern Cross, was buying cement with which he planned to bury the wife he intended murdering!

He had already murdered three men in South Africa, a wife and four children in England and a wife in Australia. He was planning to kill and bury his third wife under the hearth—his usual style—when he was arrested.

'Ripper' Confession

After Frederick Deeming was arrested in 1891 for the murder of a Melbourne woman he claimed that he was London's notorious 'Jack the Ripper'. It was thought, however, that the reason for his making that confession was to get himself declared insane. His ploy, if that is what it was, did not work—he was hanged.

Keep it Short

Having been found guilty of murder, Frederick Deeming told the judge at his Melbourne trial in 1892 not to make a long speech in passing sentence.

He complained he had been in court for four days and had arrived at 10 o'clock that morning and it was time he should go back to his cell!

★★★★★★★★★★★★★★★

The grave of Emily Mather, Deeming's last victim

Tomato Pasted

Fed up with her husband's constant nagging, 53-year-old Mrs Janet Shelley of Sydney hit him on the head with a tin of tomato soup and while he was on his way to hospital she gave herself up at the local police station. She was sent for trial on a charge of assaulting, beating and ill-treating her husband.

Swift Justice

Three-quarters of an hour before the ship *Neo Hebridais* was due to leave Sydney for Noumea in the late 1940s, custom officers found 2 oz of liquid opium behind some panelling. They carried out an investigation, arrested a man, took him to court where he was fined £25 and returned him to the ship. The vessel left on time!

Laundered Money

Members of a drug syndicate kept two garbage bags at their Sydney headquarters, one filled with money, the other containing their dirty washing. A girl took the wrong bag to the launderette. But this was not a case of illegal money being laundered—the owner of the launderette called in the police before the cash got into the wash.

Abracandlabra

The first two men to escape from a Victorian gaol, in 1838, BURNED their way out, using a long reed from the thatched roof to get a light from a warder's candle on the far side of the bars and then raising the burning reed to the roof, creating a hole to clamber through!

THE GALLOWS ROPE THAT WON A CONDEMNED MAN HIS FREEDOM JOSEPH SAMUELS SENTENCED TO DEATH FOR BURGLARY IN SYDNEY, AUSTRALIA, WAS HANGED 3 TIMES ON SEPT. 26, 1803 --BUT EACH TIME THE ROPE BROKE. AS HE WAS ABOUT TO BE HANGED A FOURTH TIME, HE WAS GRANTED A MERCY REPRIEVE IN THE BELIEF HE HAD SUFFERED ENOUGH

Bushrangers' Bungle

Crooked Robert Johnstone was heading for Sydney to join up with the bushranger Captain Thunderbolt when he met another robber on the way. They decided they could do it better than Captain Thunderbolt and formed a two-man team but were arrested on their first attempt at holding up a mail coach!

Escape for Food

Big John Caesar had an enormous appetite while in captivity in 1812 and his convict rations did nothing to ease the hunger pangs. He told his mates he was going to run off in search of food, but he ended up taking money at the point of a gun and was eventually shot dead by a Sydney settler.

Right Reward

In the early 19th century West Indian bushranger John Caesar—known as 'Black Caesar'—was caught and escaped several times until Governor Hunter offered a reward bounty hunters could not resist: five gallons of spirits. It was not long before Black Caesar was shot down.

Too Much to Ask

Sentenced to death in 1887 for the murder of a fellow worker in a mineral exploring party, Chinese cook Tim Tee had one last request as he awaited the gallows in Brisbane gaol—he wanted the authorities to send a woman in to spend his last night on earth with him! The request was refused.

Big Haul

Learning that the barque *Nelson* was planning to sail from Williamstown (Vic.) in 1852 with boxes of gold, 22 armed robbers rowed out from the beach, overcame the ship's guards and made off with the booty. Despite a widespread hunt, 18 remained free to enjoy the spoils!

Liquor is Slower

Found guilty of shooting and wounding a woman and sentenced to death in 1803, Henry Hacking received a reprieve—only to receive another death sentence within a year for theft! But he didn't die on the gallows. Reprieved once more and banished to Van Diemen's Land he took to alcohol which he drank steadily until his death from liver disease at the age of eighty-one!

FRANK McCALLUM

OF PAISLEY, SCOTLAND, IN 1850 AT THE AGE OF 18 WAS SENTENCED TO DEPORTATION TO AUSTRALIA FOR 7 YEARS FOR *SNATCHING A POTATO PIE FROM A PUSHCART*

Bad Actor

MARTIN CASH (1808-1877)
OF VAN DIEMENSLAND, AUSTRALIA,
BECAME A HIGHWAY ROBBER
IN RESENTMENT AT HAVING
BEEN SENTENCED TO **7**
YEARS IN PRISON FOR
*STEALING 6 EGGS
WORTH 24 CENTS*

Martin Cash was a successful bushranger but he was a terrible actor—and that was his downfall. When he heard that his mistress—another man's wife—was living with a new lover in Van Diemen's Land in 1845, he dressed up as a sailor in order to check up on the couple.

But Police Constable Winstanley thought the man slinking along the street didn't look like an experienced seaman and Cash was challenged. Cash drew his gun and killed the policeman.

Captured and found guilty of murder, his death sentence was later commuted.

Over-attentive

When Dr Frank Loughnan visited Dr Allan Bothamley in 1935 a fight broke out between the two medics in the surgery in Fitzroy (Vic.) during which Dr Loughnan died, despite medical attention by Dr Bothamley. Bothamley was later charged with murder.

Freedom Fight

Although tied up by bounty hunters, bushranger Michael Howe, who had a £100 price on his head, managed to snatch a knife and wound one of his captors. As the bounty hunter reeled away, Howe grabbed the man's gun and shot his companion dead. The man with the knife-wound crawled away and died. Howe got out of his ropes to rob again.

NZ's First Bushranger

New Zealand's first bushranger was Henry Garrett who had taken to highway robbery after being released from Melbourne's Pentridge Gaol in 1861. He said the authorities in Australia were too quick to give a man a chance and he decided to seek his fortune across the Tasman Sea!

Sprung by Sash

Bushranger John Foster loved the sash a Chinese coach passenger was wearing, stole it and wore it when he continued his exploits. When he was arrested at Strawberry Hills (NSW) the sash was his downfall for the Chinese happened to be in town, recognised it and put the finger on Foster for the coach robbery.

Turbulent Town

Smithfield, a small town near Cairns, was known as the Sodom and Gomorrah of Queensland after its founder, John Smith, killed a business associate in 1878 then committed suicide, sparking off a spate of 50 recorded murders and suicides in one year! After the town was destroyed in a flood, it was unanimously agreed that it should not be rebuilt.

Driven to Drink

Matthew Brady, who plundered the countryside in Van Diemen's Land, had an unusual way of dealing with belligerent or argumentative associates—he forced them at gunpoint to drink rum until they keeled over in a drunken stupor. One man drank so much he died. Brady was finally hanged in 1826.

Police Station Stolen

A policeman asked to investigate a theft in the community of Iron Range on the remote Cape York Peninsula found that it was the police station, temporarily closed, that was missing!

A gang had cut the wooden building from its stumps and carted it away. When the investigating officer made his anger known around town one of the thieves who had a conscience brought back a police badge and left it on one of the stumps!

No Notice

Pint-sized Squizzy Taylor, who ruled Melbourne's underworld in the 1920s, had the Press in his pocket, often dictating stories about himself to a couple of 'tame journalists'. After he died in a shootout the journalists wrote his obituary but although his 'friends' could have put death notices in the paper for two shillings and sixpence, nobody bothered.

Gasper Grasped

One of Australia's most daring robberies, in September, 1982, was foiled because one of the crooks ran out of air. Gang members were concealed in large crates which also contained telephone books. The crates were then hoisted into aircraft which were carrying crates of money.

The idea was for the men to get out of their boxes during the flight, swap the telephone books for the money and climb back into their boxes with their bounty. Handlers at the other end would not suspect the money was missing because the telephone books made up for the lost weight.

The 'crated' men had been 'consigned' to various addresses, but one of the thieves ran out of air, opened his box too soon and was spotted by ground staff. Australia's Great Plane Robbery was foiled.

Gunman Media Freak

Nineteen-twenties gunman Leslie (Squizzy) Taylor of Melbourne was so publicity-mad that not only did he have two pressmen 'in his pocket', he once tried to star in a film as a jockey—his boyhood ambition. But the Victorian State Government thought he was taking the authorities for a ride and clamped down on the production.

Jackanapes

When Messrs Davis, McGuinness and Connors teamed up into a bushranging gang in New South Wales in 1862 they became known by their shared Christian names—The Three Jacks!

All Talk, No Cash

The last two competitors in a talking marathon were left speechless after 91 hours of conversation in Melbourne in October 1961 when they were told that the contest organiser had vanished along with the £500 prize money.

Generous Thieves

Johnny Gilbert and his bushranger accomplice ate breakfast at a New South Wales inn in November 1863, held up all who walked or rode by, took their valuables and then offered them drinks from the bar.

Unarmed and Unashamed

Bushranger James Atterill went to great lengths to prove to police who surrounded his hut in Van Diemen's Land (Tas.) in 1838 that he was unarmed. He came out with his hands up . . . stark naked.

Hated Captain

When a hated military captain died at Richmond (NSW) in the 1800s not a soul mourned his passing for he had exerted his tyrannous influence over man and beast.

On the day of his funeral the coffin was lifted to the gun carriage, but the horses refused to pull it, despite coaxing and whipping. Bullocks also refused and when four soldiers were called forward they showed great reluctance until threatened with the death penalty.

The tyrant's influence lived on after death!

Tough but Gentle

Writer Jack Bradshaw claimed to be a friend and associate of notorious Australian bushrangers, insisting they were fine men under their tough exterior. He ought to have known—he served time himself for bank robbery!

Ride to Ruin

Margaret Catchpole of Ipswich, England, was transported to Australia after stealing a horse to ride to her lover, a smuggler on the run from police.

Hanged by a Dream

In the 1850s John Anthony arrived at Maitland (NSW) to set up home and shortly afterwards he had a vivid dream in which he saw a man being murdered and buried.

At first the police laughed at Anthony but when they finally dug the spot which he pointed out to them they found the body of farm hand Shaun Cott who had disappeared some time earlier. His employer became the only man in Australia to be hanged as the result of a dream.

Never Say Dye

On the run after a series of house and highway robberies, John Baker returned to South Australia where he asked the local barber to dye his hair. The barber refused and Baker was recognised shortly afterwards. He swore he would kill the barber for his lack of co-operation but he never had the chance. He was extradited to New South Wales and hanged in 1871.

Complete Robbery

The Eureka Gang which operated between Melbourne and Bendigo in the 1850s specialised in stripping their victims naked as well as stripping them of their valuables. They kept the garments too.

No Soap

It's a long-standing joke in Australia that the English hate to wash. Did the legend begin with George Williams, a migrant who arrived in 1862? He blackened his face and held up a mail coach then sped off with £1500. Having washed his face he booked into a hotel in Carcoar (NSW) where the coach driver was also staying. The driver recognised the black ring around Williams' neck where he had failed to wash properly. For the next 10 years the Englishman used prison soap.

Lying and Thieving

A pack horse, stolen from a paddock on the New South Wales north coast, wandered home loaded down with goods taken from a neighbour's house a week earlier. Police followed the tracks for 30 miles and found the thief lying at the roadside with a broken leg!

Incorrigible

Australia's youngest 'officially declared habitual criminal' was Arthur Brent, aged only twenty-two. His first criminal exploit was to set fire to a timber yard at the age of six; his most recent before the declaration was to burgle the residence of Mr William Ashford, former Minister for Lands.

Shrewd Chief

Maori chief Hone Heke made a small fortune in New Zealand's Bay of Islands before William Hobson's appointment as Lieutenant Governor in 1840. For every whaling ship or trading ship entering a particular bay, Hone Heke levied a tax of £10. He also leased wives for sailors during their stay!

No Hard Feelings

After bushranger Frank Gardiner held up a New South Wales sheep station in April 1862, he danced and sang with the shearers and station hands.

Final Spree

Realising that the only escape from the misery of penal servitude on Norfolk Island was death, William Westwood called a gathering of convicts and informed them he was going to send himself to the gallows. Requesting others to follow him, he charged at a policeman with a bludgeon, smashed in the head of the cookhouse overseer, clubbed another man and axed two sleeping policemen. With 13 others, Westwood's wish was granted when they were all hanged in 1846.

Model Prisoner

Prisoner Peter Degraves won time off his sentence in Hobart in the mid 1800s by designing a new gaol for the government!

Bag of Tricks

John Miles never went on a robbery in the mid 1860s without his gun and a little bag containing false moustaches, whiskers and make-up. Police were hunting for a dozen different men until he was arrested for questioning and they found his little bag of tricks.

Jacky Jacky

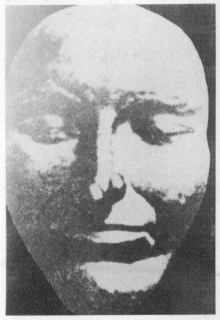

Bushranger William Westwood, who roamed New South Wales, often applied black boot polish to his face to avoid detection and earned the nickname Jacky Jacky, a colloquial name for an Aboriginal.

Pickpocket's Dictionary

James Hardy Vaux was first sent to Australia for stealing a lady's handkerchief. He was transported three times between 1801 and 1830 and chose to spend as much time as possible among prostitutes, pimps and pickpockets. It paid off for he wrote books which gave an insight into convict life in the colony. One was a dictionary of 'flash language', written in gaol and explaining the thieves argot.

First Crime

The first major crime involving Europeans on Australian territory was committed in 1629 when Dutch seamen massacred 125 castaways in Western Australia.

Burglars call Police

During a robbery in South Australia two burglars phoned the police and asked them to come and arrest them!

The peculiar circumstances arose after a night watchman at a Newton factory caught the thieves red-handed and pointed his revolver at them from the outside of a barred window. But he knew that as soon as he moved to come inside to phone the police they would flee. So he ordered them to pick up the telephone that was in the same room and phone the police. Within 15 minutes they were on their way to gaol!

Bowled Over

Two villains on the run in Queensland thought it was safe enough to wave down the motorist in the white bowling rig in 1950. Obligingly he stopped and invited them into his car, then sped to the nearest police station where the 'bowler' identified himself as Senior Constable R. N. Luxton, who had been searching for the men for days!

Mobile Lock-Up

When Russian Jack, the Samson of the gold-fields, was arrested by a trooper in Western Australia for a minor crime, he was chained to a huge log on the outskirts of a town while the trooper went to visit friends. Discovering his charge missing later, the trooper tracked him down to a pub where the log, with chain still attached to Jack, was resting on the bar. Before Jack consented to picking up his 'cell' the trooper had to buy a round of drinks.

Sale of Wife

Fed up with his nagging wife, farmer Ralph Makin put a halter around her neck and led her to a cattle auction at Windsor (NSW) in 1811.

Thomas Quire, another farmer, made the highest bid—£16—but he also had to add several rolls of cloth. He was on the point of leading Mrs Makin home when police stepped in, told Quire he could not have her, then arrested Makin and his wife!

Slave Tram

A tramway used by officials and visitors to Port Arthur (Tas.) in 1852 had carriages pushed by convicts!

Botany Bay Rothschild

Labourer Samuel Terry, who had been transported to Sydney for stealing 400 pairs of stockings, married a rich widow, became the colony's wealthiest trader and became known as the Botany Bay Rothschild.

Snake Proof

Sir Henry Brown Hayes, who fell foul of authority after abducting a Quaker heiress and forcing her into a spurious marriage, was sent as a convict to New South Wales where he finally built Vaucluse House and surrounded it with turf imported from his homeland, Ireland. The grass, he said, would keep out the snakes. It worked.

Thief to Top Cop

George Barrington, who picked the pockets of the rich and famous in London—including an attempt to deprive Prince Orlow of a diamond-studded snuff box in the front boxes at Covent Garden Theatre—was eventually freed from his convict chains by Governor Phillip in New South Wales in 1792 and became Chief Constable of Parramatta.

Akin' Heart

Before Eliza Percival was transported to Australia in 1840 for crimes in England, her lover, John Daniel, tattooed these words on her left arm:
 No pen can right
 No tongue can tell
 The akin' heart that bids farewell.

Horrific Hanging

The most horrific hanging in Australia's history took place in Adelaide in 1839 when convicted murderer Michael Magee was scheduled to meet his maker. The hangman, hidden under a mask with his clothes padded so a huge crowd of spectators who had turned the event into a picnic would not recognise him, turned out to be a hopeless amateur.

The noose slipped under Magee's chin and he was left dangling and choking. The hangman, horrified he had bungled, ran off but was caught by a mounted policeman, brought back, and told to finish the job. This he did by leaping on to the condemned man and clinging to him for 13 minutes until he died!

Walking Gaol

A drunken gang of seamen were locked in the tiny colonial gaol at Lyttleton (NZ), but a few hours later the gaoler, visiting the town centre, saw the prison walking down the street! The crew had punched holes in the floor for their legs, picked up the whole building and were making for their ship!

Fine Last View

They decided to hang murderer Francis Morgan in Sydney Harbour on Pinchgut Island, as Fort Denison was known in 1796. As the noose was about to be placed around his neck he was asked if he had any last words. Morgan replied he was not disposed to speak of death and then went on to comment about the beauty of the waters and exclaim what a fine view he had from his high vantage point!

Ladies Desist

Bushrangers John Wilson, Thomas Tracey and Richard Middleton were running a successful enterprise until the day they tried two dignified ladies in New South Wales in the late 1860s. The wives of Colonel Pitt and Colonel Campbell refused to hand over their belongings when their pony trap was held up and Mrs Pitt whacked one of them on the head with her whip. Then the ladies made off to seek help. A search by police led to the men's arrest the following day.

In the Barrel

Before a prison was built on Lord Howe Island, a military deserter named Moss who threatened to burn every house and store on the island was imprisoned in a large cask with a slot cut in the side so he could receive food and drink.

He was considered so dangerous that when a ship arrived to take him back to Sydney months later he was hoisted aboard, still in the cask. He was not let out until the barrel was taken into the confines of a gaol in Sydney!

Murder Aliases

New South Wales prospector Richard Ashe had three aliases—the names of his murder victims! After advertising for partners he accompanied them to the bush, shot them in the back and assumed their names. A fourth attempt failed and he fled by ship to America, singing songs on the way, his favourite being 'Mother Would Comfort Me'!

No Flight

After shooting dead an opponent in a duel, Dr William Bland, an aeronautical engineer, was sent to Australia as a convict. While still a prisoner he built a large flying-ship—a balloon—which was able to lift five tons. Although he had ample opportunity, he did not use the airship to perpetrate an escape from the authorities!

Up in Smoke

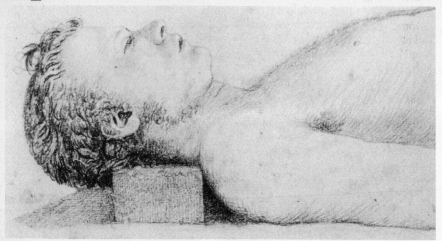

After bushranger Jack Donohue was shot by New South Wales police, a Sydney pipemaker was allowed to take a cast of his head from which he made facsimile pipes showing the scar and bleeding wound from the shot that brought the robber down.

Caught with Pants Down

Convict servant Ralph Entwhistle and a friend were bathing naked in a river during a break from leading cattle to Sydney when the State Governor and a party of dignitaries rode by. The two young men were whipped to appease the shocked party and, full of resentment, Entwhistle became a bushranger. Finally, he was rounded up and hanged.

Toil and Skin

Sentencing two prisoners at Darlinghurst Sessions, Sydney, in 1951, Judge Holden told them: 'Neither of you is any use to society. You don't toil and the only spinning you are acquainted with is the local two-up school.'

Gaol Journals

In the late 1820s Governor Darling instructed his officials to sue whenever they considered they had been libelled. As a result the editors of the *Monitor* and the *Australian* found themselves running their rival newspapers from gaol simultaneously!

Egg Hatched Police

An egg which knocked Australian Prime Minister Billy Hughes' hat off in Warwick (Qld) in 1917, hatched the Commonwealth Police Force. For Mr Hughes, having been informed twice that the young man who threw it would not be arrested by State police, decided that an 'over-riding' police force was needed.

Chest Lock-up

Before the police and a gaol arrived at Russell (NZ), offenders were stripped, tarred and feathered and locked in a large oak chest until the local Vigilance Committee saw fit to let them out.

Last Straw

When bushrangers Jefferies, Russell and Hopkins were on the run in Van Diemen's Land in the early 1820s they ran short of food. They picked straws and the loser, Russell, was killed, chopped up and eaten.

A Rosy Picture

William Buelow Gould A landlord

The first resident artist in Van Diemen's Land was William Gould, transported from England in the 1820s and such a hopeless drunk that every public house in Port Arthur possessed one of his paintings, exchanged for liquid refreshment!

Tragic Destiny

In the early 1800s the Bowers family were catapulted towards a tragic destiny when first, husband and wife were hanged in England and 14 years later their three sons, found guilty of attempted robbery, ended their lives on the end of the hangman's noose.

JOHN HARRIS

ENGLISH MILITARY SURGEON IN PARRAMATTA, AUSTRALIA, ESCAPED A COURT MARTIAL AND CHANGED THE NAME OF A LARGE SECTION OF THE CITY OF SYDNEY BY DISCOVERING IN THE MILITARY CHARGES AGAINST HIM *A ONE-WORD ERROR*— HARRIS' OFFENSE OCCURRED ON THE **19**th INSTANT (*MEANING THE 19th OF THE PRESENT MONTH*), BUT THE CHARGES ALLEGED IT TOOK PLACE ON THE **19**th ULTIMO (*THE PAST MONTH*) AND TODAY A LARGE SECTION OF SYDNEY IS NAMED "*ULTIMO*"

Living Chained to Dead

During the voyage of the second fleet of convict ships which sailed from England to New South Wales in 1789 many prisoners died from starvation, chained to their living companions. But the living said nothing about the dead in order to gain extra rations.

Moving Island

Crewmen on a navy patrol boat off the north coast were wondering if someone had spiked their rum when they spotted an island which did not appear to be on their charts. Not only that—it was moving! As they neared the palm-fringed island it picked up speed. The captain decided he'd better get alongside and investigate the phenomenon and ordered his crew to 'Catch that island!'

It was only when they were within a pebble's throw of the beach that they realised it wasn't a beach at all, but the hull of a Taiwanese fishing trawler, cleverly painted to resemble an expanse of sand. Its decks had been fitted out with trees and shrubs.

The skipper of the boat/island appeared in court later charged with fishing within Australian territorial waters and using a net with an illegally-sized mesh.

Still Lucan

British train robber Ronald Biggs
hid in Melbourne, crooked MP John
Stonehouse also came to the
Australian city after faking his
death. So when an Englishman
matching the description of runaway
peer Lord Lucan, wanted in Britain
for questioning about the murder of a
nanny, was spotted beside a burned
out car on a country road in
Queensland police yelled: 'We've got
him!'

However, it wasn't a case of
third time lucky. 'Lord Lucan' turned
out to be unemployed boilermaker
Ken Knight who had gone to the
bush to shoot pigs and had decided to
help himself to the wrecked car's horn
and alternator.

Found Out

An ancient skeleton led police to an
illegal drugs crop. While searching
for a reported skeleton near Mildura
(Vic.) in December, 1981, police
became lost in the bush—and stumbled
upon a marijuana plantation! They
also found the skeleton, which turned
out to be that of an Aboriginal and
estimated to be 2000 years old.

In Napier (NZ) two off-duty
policemen searching for a lost tennis
ball found a cannabis crop which
resulted in a man being arrested.

Cheeky Car Thieves

During a bad spate of car thefts in
Sydney in 1950, police were called in
to investigate the disappearance of
five freshly-built cars from the
assembly line at a motor factory.
While four had not clocked up
any miles, the fifth hadn't even
received its speedometer!

Not Fussy

Murdering bushranger Daniel
Morgan, who carried a reward of
£1000 on his head, stole jewels,
cash, horses—and a block of cheese
from a stable hand! He was finally
shot while robbing a sheep station in
Victoria in April, 1865.

THE PORT FAIRY JAIL - Australia
WAS BUILT BY A YORKSHIREMAN NAMED
BROADBENT WHO CELEBRATED ITS COMPLETION
SO GAILY
*THAT HE BECAME ITS
FIRST PRISONER*
1857

Thunderbolt— Gentleman Thief

Captain Thunderbolt, the fastest bushranger on a horse, was regarded as a robber with a heart because he never shot to kill, rarely loaded his pistol and sometimes returned stolen cash by post.

One of his hold-up victims was John Wirth, founder of Australia's famous circus. In the robbery at Tenterfield (NSW) Wirth begged Thunderbolt not to steal the £70 he was carrying as it was his life's savings.

'I need the money desperately', said Thunderbolt. 'But I understand your position, too. The money will be returned to you in a few weeks, care of the local post office.' Six weeks later the money duly arrived!

Captain Thunderbolt met his end in 1870 when shot and beaten to death by a constable.

Letters to the Grave

The New South Wales grave of bushranger Fred Ward, also known as Captain Thunderbolt, had a letter box attached so that mourners could write to his ghost!

Mail Must Go Through

Bushranger Captain Thunderbolt had a great respect for postmen. Holding up a rider one day and learning that he was the mailman he let him continue, saying: 'Whether it is good news or bad news you are carrying, it is your duty to deliver it.'

Long Drop

Friends of three criminals hanged at Sydney in July, 1831, were told they could take the bodies, provided they were buried at sunset. When the condition was not met a party of constables called at the house demanding that the bodies be handed over. Refusing to allow the police to enter, the friends opened a bedroom window and dropped the coffins out!

Dog, Frog and Willy-Willy

A northern Australian policeman hid a large number of bank notes recovered from a dead woman's house in a small hole in the police station yard. He was exposed when a police dog, after a frog that had jumped into the hole, began scratching the money out just as a small willy-willy blew into the compound scattering the money everywhere!

Hall of Fame

Bushranger Ben Hall took a second look at the man on the bullock wagon, then tipped his hat, offered his apologies and rode off into the bush. He had recognised the doctor who six months earlier had pulled a bullet from his leg in a pub, the medic having been told that Hall was a kangaroo shooter who had accidently shot himself!

Australia's most ambitious bushranger was Ben Hall who, in November 1864, used only two of his gang to hold up almost the whole town of Jugiong (NSW) including the local policeman.

★★★★★★★★

Nastie Pastie

The first and only woman to be hanged in South Australia was Cornishwoman Elizabeth Woolcock who, in 1873, laced her husband Thomas's Cornish pastie with arsenic!

Hangman's Noose

Thomas Ley, the New South Wales Minister of Justice, turned a deaf ear to the public pleas for mercy for a man who had murdered his mentally-ill wife and the three children he feared had inherited their mother's insanity. After repeating that the man would be executed, Ley was told by a deputation leader: 'In that case, Mr Ley, the hangman's noose hangs over all of us, including you.'

Twenty-three years later, in London in 1947, Ley, then retired from politics, was found guilty of the murder of a barman he suspected was trying to steal his mistress AND SENTENCED TO DEATH!

His appeals for mercy were granted, but he died of a heart attack three years later in a prison asylum!

End of Misery

Suffering extremely harsh treatment under detention on Norfolk Island in 1840, convicts drew straws to decide who was to kill who to put each other out of his misery. Patrick Lynch told Stephen Brennan he would like to be killed quickly, so Brennan hit him with a hammer, then stabbed him.

Brennan died, too, but not at the hands of one of his gaol mates. He was charged with Lynch's murder and hanged a few months later.

Surrender in Style

Police investigating the theft of a car in Melbourne in January, 1983, did not have to look very far—it crashed through the front of the police station at Springvale and almost ended up in the Chief Inspector's office. Police carried out what they later described as an 'on-the-spot' arrest of three youths!

Beauty and the Beast

Thomas Wainewright Mrs Wilson

Suspected of poisoning his wife and daughter, but convicted only of forgery, artist Thomas Wainewright, who exhibited at the Royal Academy, was transported to Hobart. As soon as the colony learned of the talented inmate, the Governor was petitioned and Wainewright was commissioned to paint portraits of all the colonial beauties. While he worked with the brush, an armed guard stood beside the easel!

The Most Famous Rogue

One of the smallest fees paid to a lawyer in Australia for appearing in a big criminal case was seven guineas, received by Mr Bindon for defending Ned Kelly.

Last Picture

Before he was hanged at the Melbourne Gaol, bushranger Ned Kelly asked for, and received, permission to have his photograph taken so his family would have a memory of him. They were given a very current picture—it was taken on 10 November 1880, the day before he went to the gallows!

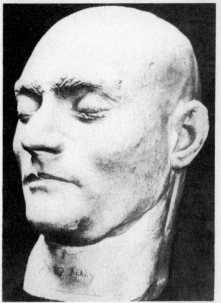

Ned Kelly, found guilty of first degree murder, said nothing when Sir Redmond Barry, the judge, said he would be hanged by the neck until he was dead. But when the judge added 'May the Lord have mercy on your soul', Kelly said: 'I will go further than that and say that when I go to the Great Beyond, I will see you there.'

Ned Kelly was hanged on 12 November 1880. Eleven days later, Judge Barry died from pneumonia which developed during treatment for a carbuncle on his neck.

How would you like to come face to face—literally—with Ned Kelly? His death mask sits in a cell at the Old Melbourne Gaol having been cast when his head was cut off following his hanging.

Hostess with the Mostest

Mrs Emma Bartley, of Moyhu (Vic.), once entertained hunted Ned Kelly and two policemen at the same time! While a wake was being held for another bushranger and two tired policemen slept in a back room, Ned Kelly called in and joined the drinking in the lounge!

Wages of Death

Demanding an unpaid fee of $95.69 for ending a man's days on the gallows in 1831, hangman Jack Ketch took the Under-Sheriff to court and was duly awarded his earnings!

Deterrent

Message on a tape recorder installed in a Melbourne car to go off when the vehicle is broken into: 'Why did you pick on my car? What have I done to you?'

Australia's Robinson Crusoe

Having escaped from a newly-formed penal settlement at Port Phillip in 1803, convict William Buckley lived with the natives for 32 years, growing his beard long and later earning the name of Australia's Robinson Crusoe. Having survived great hardship he died back in 'civilisation' in Tasmania after an accident with a cart.

Brandy Snap

Charlotte Welsh, a convict woman working as a servant in a Sydney house in the early 19th century was sent to a factory for six weeks for insolence to her mistress. She complained the Christmas pudding given to her was not good enough because it had no brandy in it!

Brazen Villains

After advertising for an electric motor to replace one stolen from his Scoresby (Vic.) property, Councillor Roland Collins was amazed when two men, answering his request, delivered the self same motor! They were arrested.

Rich Breakfast

Mr Campbell Hunter had invited several distinguished guests to breakfast at his beautiful home beside Melbourne's Yarra River in April, 1842, and they were just about to partake when three bushrangers burst in.

The guests started to reach for their watches and other valuables but robbers Ellis, Jepps, Williams and Fogarty weren't interested—they ordered the guests to move away from the table so they could tuck in!

In a gunbattle which broke out after breakfast with an armed posse, Williams was shot and the others, too full to run for it, were arrested!

First Lawyers Were Convicts

The first two lawyers to operate in Australia knew more about the wrong side of the law than the right. Crossley and Eagan were two ex-convicts who remained in business for 27 years.

Fisher's Ghost

Norman Lindsay Fisher's Ghost

After former convict Frederick Fisher vanished mysteriously from his hut at Campbelltown in 1826, a man driving his horse and trap said he saw the ghostly apparition of Fisher sitting on a rail and pointing towards a river. Police checked the rail and found blood. Then a black tracker led searchers to a pool where the decomposing body of Fisher was found. Fisher's mate, George Worrall, later confessed to the murder and was hanged.

Edible Answer

For convicts, the most unpopular recommendation by Australia's founder, Governor Phillip, was that those sentenced to death in the late 1700s should be thrown into the hands of the head-hunters of New Zealand. 'Let them be eaten', was his suggestion.

Not Quite Perfect

John Tawell, a member of the Society of Friends, was sent as a convict to Australia for forgery but within a few years of his arrival in 1814 he had made a name for himself as a wealthy chemist, built the first Quaker chapel in Sydney at his own expense and showed his worthiness by pouring 600 gallons of rum into the sea.

But Tawell's luck changed—he became the first criminal to be captured through the use of the 'new' electric telegram. After murdering his mistress (his wife's nurse), poisoning her with prussic acid, he was caught after information was passed around Australia about him. He was executed at the age of 61 in the dress of a Quaker.

Home from Home

A former gaol inmate shocked the New South Wales Government when he put in a claim in October, 1982, for compensation for items removed from his cell during a search for weapons. Among his confiscated equipment were a cocktail bar, a refrigerator and a lounge suite.

Sober Surprise

When they saw the drunk tottering towards them, bushrangers John Wilkinson and John Morgan laughed and thought he would be easy pickings. But the intoxicated man suddenly sobered up, whipped out a pistol and identified himself as Chief Constable Hildebrand. Wilkinson and Morgan were still stunned when the prison gates clanged behind them for life.

Unappealing Excuse

A prisoner, Anthony Perna, appearing at Brisbane's Appeal Court apologised for not lodging notice of appeal earlier and asked for an extension of time. The court turned down the request after Perna explained he hadn't had a chance to appeal earlier because he had been on the run after receiving his sentence!

Telling Headstone

The cemetery at St Kilda, Victoria contains an old headstone bearing a hand holding an overflowing jug of beer. The widow had carried out a threat often made to her thirsty husband!

Holy Willie

Convict women in Van Diemen's Land so despised Rev. William Bedford after he advocated cutting off their hair as punishment for misbehaviour that on one of his visits to the Female Factory—the workhouse—they tossed him in a blanket and called him 'Holy Willie'!

Macabre Photo

Following the shooting of the Kelly bushranger gang at Glenrowan in June, 1880, and the subsequent fire in the premises they were hiding in, the partly-charred body of robber Joe Byrne, 6 ft 2 in tall and the most handsome member of the gang, was strung up by rope in a standing position outside the Benalla (Vic.) gaol—so a local photographer could take his picture!

Chinese Bushranger

When a trooper challenged a bushranger in 1865 and heard the reply 'You, policeman, me shootee you' he knew he had cornered Sam Poo, the Chinese bushranger who was the only immigrant to take to highway robbery. Sam Poo was convicted of attempted murder after wounding the trooper and ended his days in the hangman's noose.

Baby Murders

After two residents digging their vegetable gardens in the Melbourne suburb of Brunswick in 1892 unearthed the bodies of three babies, police arrested and charged Mrs Frances Knorr, a baby-sitter who had tenanted both houses. As she was led to the gallows she sang 'Safe in the Arms of Jesus'.

Prison Firefighters

Bushfires were so bad in Tasmania in 1967—when 62 died and 4000 lost their homes—that prisoners were let out of Hobart Gaol to help fight the flames!

Turncoat Hanger

Thieves James Freeman and James Barrett were sentenced to death in colonial Sydney but the problem was that no hangman had been appointed in those early days. Freeman was made an offer he couldn't refuse—he would be pardoned if he agreed to become the official hangman.

He happily accepted. The first man he slipped the noose around was Barrett, his partner in crime.

'Dead Eye' Jack

Sgt Jack 'Dead Eye' Murphy of Melbourne (Vic.) captured eight criminals on the run between 1923 and his retirement in 1948 by shooting them below the waist. In five years he obtained 10 000 convictions for illegal gambling—he was smarter than the 'cockatoos', the gambling school lookouts!

Over the Traces

Richard Maddox, a convict sent to the home of a wealthy Sydney resident in 1840, was sent back to gaol and given 50 lashes for getting drunk in the absence of his master and mistress, falling over the table in the parlour when in the act of waiting on a visitor, failing to clean the visitor's boots and being seen escorting a servant girl. The girl, as punishment, had her head shaved.

Gaol Tree

Prisoners headed under escort towards Wyndham (WA) were sometimes housed in the strangest gaol in the world—a tree!

The 'cell' was carved into a 30-ft-high bottle-tree (baobab) with a hole in the side just big enough for a man to crawl through. A trooper taking the wanted man to a real gaol in Wyndham would sleep outside the tree and if another trooper arrived on the same night with an arrested man it was standing room only in the gaol!

Cannibal Convict

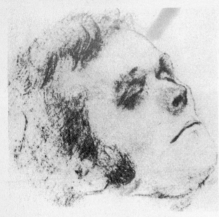

Breaking out of gaol with seven other desperadoes in Van Diemen's Land in 1822, Alexander Pierce quickly ate up the miles and then quickly ate up his companions!

After a week of running they had become tired and hungry and agreed to turn to cannibalism. Alexander Dalton, one of the escapees, was killed and eaten. Next Thomas Bodenham was murdered and roasted, followed by John Mathers and Matthew Travis. Two others had gone on ahead, which left Pierce and Robert Greenhill.

Greenhill had the axe, but when he fell asleep, he was for the chop too! When Pierce was finally captured a horrified public said hanging was too good for him, but it was the only punishment open to the law.

Paving Pinched

While nobody was looking, thieves in Rockingham (WA) stole a 3300 slab footpath worth $10 000 in January, 1980.

Charlotte and the Good Ship *Venus*

With the aid of a mate who had fallen for her and a handful of fellow convicts, temptress Charlotte Badger took over the good ship *Venus* in the early 1800s. After flogging the captain and appointing themselves skipper and pirate, they raided another vessel for food and firearms before sailing off for New Zealand. Although two of the convicts were later caught and hanged, Charlotte took to the bush and was last seen 20 years later sailing away with an American skipper who had also fallen for her . . .

Doggy Dinner

When old Salty, a monster 18 ft crocodile ate the local policeman's dog at the tip of Queensland's Cape York Peninsula it was the last straw. A team of men who had lost their dogs set out to capture the miscreant but he put up such a fight, knocking one man from the boat, that when finally captured, the only safe place to keep him for the night was the local lock up. The following day he was transferred to a Cairns nature park. No charges were laid.

Crooked Birds

Mafia boss 'Big Vinny' Teresa sang like a sparrow when two Australian detectives called at the nice little bird shop he ran in Seattle. What Vincent told the detectives in September 1979 resulted in police raiding four Sydney houses and smashing an international bird-smuggling racket.

★★★★★★★★★★★★★★

Scott Free

George Scott, the new lay reader
at the Anglican Church near
Bacchus Marsh (Vic.) became a
close friend of the local bank
manager. One evening the manager
heard Scott calling outside his
door and was amazed, on opening it,
to find a masked man there.
When the manager asked Mr Scott
if he wasn't being a bit silly,
Scott replied: 'Who's Scott? I'm
Captain Moonlite.' Then he robbed
the bank and continued a life
of plundering until he was caught
and hanged in the early 1880s.

Horse Sense

When stockman Monte Castle
escaped from Perth's Karnet Prison
in May, 1979, because he thought
his marriage was in trouble and he
wanted to see his wife, he had a
choice of two getaway conveyances—a
car and a horse. He chose the horse!

Tree Hideout

Irishman Harry Power, on the run
from gaol and wanted for robbery,
used as his hideout a tree into which
he had drilled holes so he could
watch for the police. On a branch
was a trained cockatoo which
screamed at strangers but the police
located his hideout when he and the
bird were asleep. After serving
15 years he ended his days by falling
into the Murray River and drowning.

Swift and Deadly

The swiftest punishment inflicted
in the early colonial days involved
17-year-old Jimmy Barrett. Starving
on the streets of Sydney in 1788,
he was arrested, charged, found
guilty, sentenced and hanged—all
within an hour!

SEVEN

Bushmen
Backbone of Australia

Bushmen are the backbone of Australia. White or black, they are a splinter group of civilisation, crafty in art and artful in craft.

The Aborigines were, of course, our original bushmen who knew the ways of the desert and forests. They knew how to light fires without matches, how to build shelters, how to find food where none seemed to exist.

It was the bushmen who paved the tracks through the mountains and found their way across the wastelands. From the bushmen came our story-telling traditions. The Aborigines talked of the Dreamtime...our forebears sat around camp fires and spun the yarns that are bandied about in pubs and around dinner tables today.

From this rare breed came another type of story—stories of their exploits, of the type of people they were. For man cannot live in outback areas without confronting the odd, the curious and the bizarre. And these were the amazing incidents for which Robert Ripley searched the world.

Farmers, drovers, rangers, hikers and campers...all can be considered bushmen of sorts and although often alone in their desert or forest environment, tales of their doings have filtered back to 'civilisation'. Tales of fabulous luck, tales of woe, yarns to make you laugh, stories to make you cry.

Come then, for a stroll into the world of the bushmen. Perhaps by the end of this chapter you will know what makes him tick. Or perhaps you will be even more bewildered when you encounter:

The strange story of the bushman's jumping dog.
The face that grew on a tree.
The Aboriginal medicine-man who left no footprints.
The stockman who was shot by a kangaroo!
The drover who changed from a man into a woman.
The bushman's dog which wore leather shoes.

YOUNG ABORIGINES OF CENTRAL AUSTRALIA PLAIT THE HAIRS OF THEIR BEARD AROUND *THE CURVED TAIL OF A THALGOO -- AN AUSTRALIAN MAMMAL*

Black Sheep

When a flock of 565 pure white sheep, loaded on to a train at Taihape (NZ) were brought out at their destination they had all turned jet black! When the train entered a tunnel thick fumes had brought about the amazing transformation!

One to Them

Stockman Arthur Crosbie was admitted to Darwin Hospital in October, 1946, with a bullet wound in his arm—having been shot by A KANGAROO!

He had wounded the animal and had walked up to finish it off when the kangaroo reached up, grabbed the gun, got its paw around the trigger and pulled. Then it jumped up as Crosbie fell down and, nursing only a graze, bounded off into the bush!

Given the Boot

Walking near Billinudgel (NSW) in the early 1900s, station-hand Fred Baker was struck a glancing blow by a falling tree which severed his foot above the boot and buried it 12 inches in the ground. Baker kept the boot and fitted it to a false foot!

Roving Bovines

Grass grew so high at Derrinallum (Vic.) in 1948 that farmers had to climb trees to find their cows!

Wooden Head

In 1880 an Aboriginal carved the face of a man on a young beefwood tree near Thargomindah (Qld). As the tree grew, the face became huge and the area was named 'Man's Face Flat'.

Twin Burden

How to tell whether ewes are about to give multiple births: according to a lecturer at a Gippsland (Vic.) rural conference the pregnant flock should be marched along the road and the last 30 per cent, the ones who lagged behind, would be likely to be bearing twins.

Shady Trick

For three days, drovers Tom Garner and Jim Devereaux moved a flock of 5000 sheep across 35 miles of parched desert towards Avon Downs in the Northern Territory.

On the fourth day, in sight of their destination, the sheep saw a small timbered area and rushed for the limited shade. Those behind clambered on those in front and soon they were piled feet high. Four thousand eight hundred suffocated!

Tree of Life

After their home was destroyed by a bushfire in the early 1920s, the Penny family of Gippsland—grandparents, parents and three children—lived in a large HOLLOW TREE for 18 months!

Hook Up

Telephone technicians who went to a farm at Bringelly (NSW) in 1982 were told by the owner that he was getting calls but the phone didn't ring. Asked how he knew a call was coming through he replied that the dog jumped up and down.

Examining the dog, the technicians found he was attached by a chain to a long piece of wire which gave him freedom to run up and down, but one end of the wire had been hooked to the telephone line. Every time the phone rang, the dog received 40 volts!

Clever Cakes

An early 1800s 'recipe for catching wild horses', contained in an old document passed down through a New South Wales family:

'Take two pounds of flour and six ounces of powdered ginger and half a pint of treacle; knead them in the usual way, and bake them; then sweat them well under the arm-pits, then go into the field where the wild horse is, get to windward of him, and hold the cakes in each hand. Advance towards him, and he will advance towards you, and will eat the cakes, during which operation you will have no difficulty in catching him.'

Not Much Chop

The mutton that was available in Australia's colonial days was so tough that one historical writer said it put such a terrible strain upon the molars that a diet of it 'would soon qualify anyone for pulpit, bar or stage, if muscular strength of jaw were the only qualification necessary for those professions'.

ROBERT B. DAWES, JR. - New South Wales OWNED A SHEEP FARM OF **2,242,939** ACRES! IT WAS LARGER THAN THE COMBINED AREAS OF DELAWARE AND RHODE ISLAND

Stockwoman

For years, a tough stockman worked for cattle stations in New South Wales and drove animals across the harshest land. But when seriously injured in a fall and taken to hospital 'he' was found to be a 'she'!

Miss Margaret McTavish had left home in the 1930s after a family dispute and she had taken up the life of a nomad. When she recovered from the accident she settled down, marrying a Canberra property owner.

Cow Race

One of the most unusual events held in Australia was a cow race, staged at Windsor (NSW) in 1812. Cows had to be ridden by their owners and there was a large amount of betting.

The Ancient Race

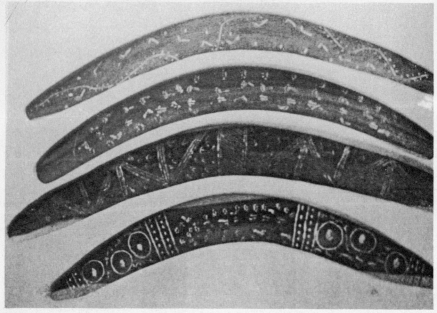

Because non-returning boomerangs—used by Aborigines along with those that do come back—were weapons in southern India some historians say this proves the Aborigines originated on the subcontinent.

Head Chewers

An old initiation ceremony among some Aboriginal tribes was head chewing! While lying face down a young man offered his head to three or four 'biters' who set to with their teeth until the blood flowed. The point of the exercise was to make the hair grow strong.

Trackless

The early Aboriginal medicine-man decreed it was against tribal tradition to leave tracks in the sand, so he wore shoes that left no imprints—made of emu feathers cemented together with human blood.

Long Lake

A lake in South Australia is known to Aborigines as Lake Cardivillawarra-ccurracurrieapparlandoo. Or, in simple language, 'the reflection of the glittering stars in the flat waters of the lake'!

FREEZING WEATHER IS CALLED A "5-DOG NIGHT" IN AUSTRALIA — BECAUSE ABORIGINES KEEP WARM *BY USING DOGS AS BLANKETS*

THE
CANOE TREE
TOMBSTONES
Australia
GIANT EUCALYPTUS
TREES MARKING THE
GRAVES OF ABORIGINES
WERE STRIPPED OF
SUFFICIENT BARK TO
MAKE ONE CANOE
*TO PROVIDE
TRANSPORTATION
FOR THE SOUL*

Sacred Objects

Oval and elongated slabs of stone and wood decorated with mythological symbols were among the most sacred objects owned by Aborigines because they were believed to contain spirits of ancestors. Sometimes they were used at initiation ceremonies, being swung around on the end of a piece of string, a hole in the 'tjuringa' producing a groaning sound!

Great Expectation

Setting off from Darwin unannounced to visit an Aboriginal community 200 miles south on the Daly River, Dr M. Miller, Northern Territory medical examiner, was amazed to find that everyone was expecting him and had even prepared him a meal!

Dark Logic

'Hangin' no blood good for blackfeller. Only good for whitefeller!' said Aboriginal convict Musquito after his death-sentence was handed down in Van Diemen's Land in 1824. When a jailer asked him why, Musquito replied: 'Whitefeller is used to it.'

Paint Sprayers

The first form of spray gun for painting was used by Aborigines—their mouths! To paint the inside of their caves they would gather yellow and red ochre from a creek, mix it to a soup-like consistency, drink it—but never swallow—and then spray it on the rock! The method was usually used to stencil an object.

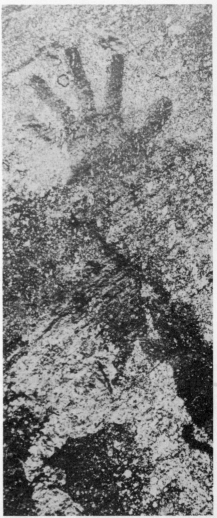

Mourning Cap

When an Aboriginal woman becomes a widow, tribal law decrees that she must cut off her hair, burn it and wear a cap made from the skin of an emu or kangaroo!

THE SKELETON BONES OF NATIVES OF GOULBURN ISLAND, AUSTRALIA, ARE ALWAYS BURIED IN *HOLLOWED-OUT TREE TRUNKS*

Big White Chief

Robert Cooper was the only white man to become king of an Aboriginal tribe, earning himself the simple title of King Joe. Before he was accepted by the tribal people of Melville Island he had to fight and conquer two warriors who also had their eyes on the throne. After his acceptance he put on a loin cloth and hunted and ate with the tribe.

Mystery Deaths

Arriving at a camp in the Northern Territory in 1885 a drover called Watts checked over his sheep and found that half were missing. Following their tracks the next morning he found them grouped around two men. One, an Australian was dead with his throat cut, the other a Chinese, had died from thirst! The mystery of the deaths was never solved.

Heady Story

Returning to a farm north of Melbourne with the head of a sheep he had just killed and hung, a labourer was set upon by a pack of wild dogs and, running for his life, fell headlong into a deep pit. The snarling animals surrounded the hole and he was forced to remain there, accompanied by the dripping head, for hours until a mounted station-hand drove the dogs away with a stock whip!

Happy Wretches

William Dampier, one of the first whites to meet Aborigines, in 1688, saw them as the 'miserablest people in the world...setting aside their human shape they differ but little from brutes'. But Captain James Cook thought that although they might 'appear to some to be the most wretched on earth...in reality they are far happier than we Europeans'.

Long Watch

John Watson, editor of the South Australian newspaper the *Border Watch* stayed in that position for one month short of SIXTY-FOUR YEARS!

Longest Stockwhip

The longest stockwhip was made by a Sydney firm who offered it as a prize to the first man who could crack it—all 55 ft! A stockman known as 'Saltbush Bill' Mills achieved the feat.

Prompt Delivery

A farmer and his wife waiting at Tasmania's Colebrook railway station for a train bringing a pair of valuable rams heard that the train had gone over an embankment.

Driving to the crash scene, the couple saw the injured crew were being helped, so they searched for their rams. Finding the animals unhurt, the farmer pulled them down the embankment, drove them through a damaged part of a fence—and let them run free!

The train had crashed right beside the farmer's back fence!

Lucky Dog

A penniless gold prospector working a claim at the Broughton River near Charters Towers (Qld) kept a large stone on his camp table to throw at a dog which had a habit of sneaking into his tent during the day and sleeping in his bed.

A passing tin buyer, examining the stone, bought it from the prospector and had it cut and polished. It was the largest and most beautiful topaz in the world and was sent to the Shepherd's Bush Exhibition in London where it was bought by Queen Alexandra!

Dietary Evidence

Leading a group of journalists who were searching for Robyn Davidson, a woman adventurer crossing central Australia with a herd of camels, black tracker Johnny Long found her by following camel droppings through the desert scrub. Asked how he had been able to distinguish her camels from the herds of wild camels that roamed the area he explained: 'Wild camels do not eat baked beans!'

Dog Shoes

Before tracks and roads in north-west Queensland were established, cattlemen made leather shoes for the station dogs to protect their feet from thorns and sharp rocks!

Watering Hole

When a water tank was blown from a settler's home during a cyclone in northern Queensland in 1909, it was carried two miles and landed in a tree with the tap within easy reach of the ground. A passing stockman put two sheets of corrugated iron over it to catch the rain and it became a recognised 'watering hole' for passing drovers!

Ada's Veil

When Mrs Ada Stevens lost her veil while crossing a creek her husband called: 'There goes Ada's veil.' The area later became known as Adavale.

Praise Too Late

Mr C. Y. O'Connor, the engineer of the incredible pipeline carrying water 300 miles from a reservoir in the Darling Ranges to Coolgardie (WA), was criticised for a project that people thought would be expensive and inefficient.

He was praised when they all saw it working in 1903, but O'Connor had not waited around to be lauded—he had committed suicide 10 months before the project was finished.

Twin Evils

After numerous quarrels over land and wives, a proverb crept into Maori life—'Women and land are the reasons why men die'!

Miserable Millionaire

James Tyson, who became Australia's first cattle millionaire from a £30 a week droving job, despised women, denied himself any pleasure, objected to trade unions, thought nothing of his workers and hated his relatives so much that when he died in 1898 leaving £2.5 million, not a penny of it went their way.

Worth the Pain

When Maoris tattooed their important tribal members they broke the skin with a chisel made from a human or albatross bone, tapping it with a wooden mallet!

The patterns were coloured with a mixture containing the juice of special berries. The process was very painful, but for the Maori chiefs the agony was not in vain for their tattooed heads were removed on death and preserved!

Big Horse-Break

Horse-breaker John Bence tamed 793 horses in eight days at Swan Hill (Vic.) in 1938.

★ ★ ★ ★ ★ ★

Toenailed

During a bush soccer match in the early 1900s between station-hands and a team of barefoot Aborigines in Queensland, the ball exploded, having been pierced through leather and bladder by a long toenail of one of the barefoots! While a new ball was rounded up, the sharp-footed kicker had his toenail attended to with a scythe!

MICHAEL **DURACK**

AND A BAND OF DROVERS HERDED 2,000 HEAD OF CATTLE FROM QUEENSLAND, AUSTRALIA TO THE KIMBERLEYS, TRAVELING 2,500 MILES ACROSS AN UNMAPPED CONTINENT

--A JOURNEY THAT STARTED JULY 29, 1883 AND ENDED SEPT. 17, 1885

EIGHT

Creatures

Paradox and Whimsy

How many times have we heard the comment: 'That dog (cat/rabbit/ guinea-pig/canary) is almost human'?

The behaviour of our four-legged/ two-legged friends has often caused astonishment but in Australia the mere appearance of some creatures is worth a double take. There's the duck-billed platypus, the lumbering wombat and a collection of marsupials that carry their young in pouches.

To the bushman these are virtually everyday friends, but for the city dweller these unusual animals are a rare and rewarding sight. Two other groups also intrigue the human race—the extinct, and the legendary monsters.

Are they *really* extinct? Are those strange monsters really legendary? Or do they roam the bush and mountains? That weird and wonderful creature, the Tasmanian Tiger ... has it really ceased to exist? Or is it running around the hills of Lang Lang, Victoria, as three men claimed a few years ago?

The United States was stunned

to hear the story of the *Incredible Journey* which told how two dogs and a cat walked across the continent to find their owners. Australia has its own versions— dogs and cats which have trudged miles through the deserts to arrive on their owners' doorsteps.

There are amazing stories, too, of the birds and the bees. There's the cockatoo which kept watch on a toll bridge, crying out a warning to the toll-keeper whenever a vehicle approached. And there are the bees which coated a dead possum in wax so their nest would not be polluted.

Should you come across a kind of Abominable Snowman while trekking in the Blue Mountains of New South Wales, you might just exclaim: 'Yow ... Eee!' which would be an accurate identification of the creature. A hairy primate from the Ice Age and known as a Yowie is said to roam the mountains.

You can read all about him and all creatures great and small here.

Read about:

The cows which loved music so much they followed the town band.

The amazing flying frog which blows up like a balloon and sails away from its enemies.

The bounding kangaroo which caused a train to run without a driver.

The two snails that spent a lifetime together.

And the swans which guard a Western Australian man's home better than a guard dog!

Colourful Hen

At a poultry show in Lismore (NSW) Mr P. Johnson won first prize with a black Orpington hen. The following year, the same bird took first prize as a WHITE Orpington!

During the year it had inexplicably changed from black to speckled to grey to white!

Given the Bird

A toll-keeper at a bridge at Indooroopilly (Qld) trained his pet cockatoo to call 'Here comes another rattle-trap' whenever traffic approached!

Fussy Eater

Michael, an Airedale dog which travelled regularly by air between Melbourne and Brisbane to be with its owners, carried this note on its collar for one flight from Queensland:

'Please give me my dinner (in the parcel) before boarding plane for Melbourne and see I have plenty of water to drink. DO NOT give me any cakes or sweets.'

Elusive Tiger

For more than 50 years the hunt has been on to spot the Tasmanian Tiger, believed to be extinct. Chris Tangey, aged 21, spent two years in the hunt and, returning to Melbourne in December, 1979, heard that three men claimed to have 'positively' sighted the animal near Lang Lang (Vic.)!

Plastered Magpie

Presented with a magpie which had its leg broken in four places after a bicycle wheel went over it in 1949, surgeons at the Royal Adelaide Hospital gave the bird a general anaesthetic and set the leg in plaster. It made a full recovery.

Runaway Train

While a six-seater steam train was travelling between Marble Bar and Port Hedland (WA) in 1946, a bounding kangaroo knocked the motor-man from his seat onto the tracks. The engine ran on for 40 miles before a passenger was able to stop it.

Laziest Sheep

The vegetable sheep of New Zealand eat no grass, produce no wool and remain in the same spot until they die—because these sheep are shrubs! The large bushes grow on the mountains and were so named because from a distance they take on the same shape and colouring as sheep!

Heavily Sedated

Seven Burmese female elephants on a sea voyage to Sydney became restless when the ship ran into a storm. The crew poured a bottle of rum into seven buckets and the voyage passed peacefully.

Best Beast

Australia's favourite monster is the Yowie, a hairy primate relic of the Ice Age which has been reportedly sighted 3000 times since 1865. Monster-hunter Rex Gilroy, of Katoomba (NSW), has plaster casts, 45 cm long and 35 cm across the toes, which were taken from prints in the Blue Mountains.

Homing Cat

Mrs June Stocker of Townsville decided there was no room in her house any more for Pinky the white cat, so she gave it to two friends who lived at Ingham, 70 miles away. Pinky went missing from Ingham the very next day and turned up, footsore and hungry five days later at Mrs Stocker's back door! 'We'll never give her away again', said her tearful owner.

High Liver

George Trigwell Johnstone, a chicken, drank a glass of draught beer every night in the early 1950s at the Ship Hotel, Busselton (WA) until he died of a soused liver.

Red Indian Fish

The Red Indian fish, which inhabits the waters west of Australia, looks very impressive with its fins which resemble a feathered head-dress, but it is such a poor swimmer it is often cast ashore in heavy storms.

Useful Appendage

A cow born on Peter Crane's dairy farm at Darbalara (NSW) had a tail behind and a tail on its forehead, which it used to keep flies from its face!

Swan Patrol

Mr Fred Edwards of Fremantle (WA) kept two pet swans in his garden because he said their hissing and wing flapping when strangers approached made them better guards than dogs!

Grateful Gull

The day after a bird was knocked out by the ball during the third Test in Adelaide in January, 1980, an advertisement appeared in a local paper signed by C. Gull, who thanked well-wishers!

Prompt Milker

The only cow allowed to graze on Sydney's Domain at the turn of the century would set off down King Street as soon as the Law Courts' clock struck three and head for her owner's shop to be milked!

Super Snake

A sea snake which inhabits the Ashmore Reef in the Timor Sea off north-west Australia has a venom ONE HUNDRED TIMES more toxic than any known land snake!

Job for Ferret

Faced with the problem of running an electrical line in a narrow tunnel, technicians in Adelaide enlisted the aid of a ferret. With a light line attached, it was lowered into a manhole while a chunk of meat was dangled from another hole further along the road.

When the ferret emerged in pursuit of the meat the electricity workers were able to pull the main cable through with the aid of the lighter line. The ferret, meanwhile, settled down with its meat.

Hard to Kill

During severe droughts which kill off cattle in central Australia tiny shrimps live on in little pools of rainwater on top of the huge monolith, Ayers Rock!

Unlucky Spot

A dog called Spot who for years followed a cow called Daisy everywhere on a property at Campbell's Creek (Vic.) moped and refused to go out after Daisy was killed by a train at a crossing. The day Spot finally went out HE WAS KILLED BY A TRAIN ON THE SAME SPOT!

THE **CROWN** OF **THORNS**, A STARFISH OF THE GREAT BARRIER REEF of AUSTRALIA WHICH MEASURES MORE THAN 18 INCHES IN DIAMETER, HAS **17** ARMS *EQUIPPED WITH POISONOUS SPINES* — IT IS SO DESTRUCTIVE TO CORAL THAT DIVERS EARN A BOUNTY FOR DESTROYING IT

Slide by Slide

Two snails found at Croydon (NSW) lived a semi-detached lifestyle. Their shells were moulded together and they slid along side by side!

Time to Eat

A post mortem on a monster shark landed at Picnic Point (NSW) in 1946 revealed a man's watch and the head of a dog!

Distant Digger

The Prince of Wales, who later became King Edward VIII, was upset when a wallaby called Digger, presented to him in Australia in 1920, died at Trinidad on the way to England. So the Prince arranged for a formal burial in the grounds of Government House, Trinidad, and a gravestone carrying an inscription to Digger's memory. It read in part 'Here lies Digger a Wallaby belonging to HRH the Prince of Wales ...'

Horse Bread

One of the strangest firms in Melbourne in the 1850s was a bakery that made bread exclusively for horses! Because they were cheaper than other breads, the 5 lb loaves sold well but when constitutional ailments were widely reported, the firm's business declined. Its 'horsy' customers were of insufficient numbers and it was forced to close.

Queen-Sized Problem

A Queen bee which got into a petrol pump at Launceston (Tas.) put it out of action for days—thousands of other bees swarmed over the pump making it impossible for mechanics to use it.

Whale Tale

A 72-ton whale caught at the entrance to Bering Strait in 1883 was found to have a harpoon bearing the inscription 'Henty, L. 1838' embedded in its flesh. Edward Henty, of Victoria, had his harpoons made in Launceston (Tas.) and whalers believed the great sea mammal had carried the harpoon around the world for 45 YEARS!

What the Herd Heard

As the Maldon (Vic.) town band made its way through the streets a herd of 20 cows and calves fell into line behind and followed the players down to the banks of the Lodden River. Undeterred by a large crowd, they then sat down in front of the band and listened to them play for the whole afternoon.

As soon as the concert was over, the herd got up and walked back to the paddock!

Flying Toad

The toad frog of Australia blows itself up when attacked by a snake and, assisted by its balloon-like gut, leaps and flies over the reeds to safety!

THE **TOAD**FROG of Australia WHEN THREATENED BY A SNAKE *PUFFS ITSELF UP LIKE A TOY BALLOON AND FLOATS SAFELY AWAY*

Possum Embalmed

A possum encased in wax was found in a hollow tree in the Adelaide Hills, (SA). Biologists worked out that the nocturnal creature had disturbed a bees' nest and had been stung to death, the bees coating it in wax to prevent pollution of their home!

Come-On Claw

'Psssst! Free tonight?' If crabs could talk that is undoubtedly what the male Beckoning Crab would be saying as it waves its one large brilliantly-coloured claw to attract the female of the species!

Stone-Fish

One of the most deadly life forms is the ugly stone-fish found in waters off northern Australia and Papua-New Guinea. Should one of its 18 spines penetrate the skin the victim is in great danger of dying in intense agony!

Rodent's Ride

Travelling on a tram in King William Street, Adelaide, Mr Brian Thompson was surprised when a rat jumped from a passing truck, ran up his trouser leg and clung to the elastic of his underpants. As Mr Thompson whipped the intruder out, another passenger rang the stop bell, called for help and the driver killed the creature with a pinch bar.

What a Boar

Nero, the biggest boar in the world, captured wild in New Zealand, stood 4 ft 3 in high, measured 7 ft 3 in around the girth and weighed 1000 lb. While on show at Rockhampton (Qld) his 'lunch' consisted of two bullocks' hearts, a score of lambs' kidneys, half a sheep and a pile of turnips and sweet potatoes, all of which was washed down with two buckets of milk!

Snakophile

THE LARGE PAPER NAUTILUS OF AUSTRALIA, HAS A SHELL 9½ INCHES LONG

Fish Tale

A vet who performed a post mortem on a horse which suddenly died on a property near the Nepean River (NSW) found a large live fish in the animal's stomach!

Mr George Cann, in charge of the reptile section of Sydney's Taronga Park Zoo in the late 1940s, was bitten more than 400 times by poisonous snakes. Yet he loved them so much he kept 50 at home as pets.

Small Prayer—Big Answer

Motorist Jack Snodgrass of Moree (NSW) claimed for years afterwards that it was a miracle....

When his car became bogged in the black soil plains between Moree and Boggabilla, he prayed for help. Along came Mr Jack McDonald in his car. But the combined efforts of the two men were futile.

Mr Snodgrass prayed once more, a little harder, and suddenly from out of the Tuncooey scrub three elephants emerged. The leader put its trunk under the car and pushed the rear with its forehead, clearing the vehicle from the bog.

Even when the rest of the travelling circus appeared to explain the elephants' presence, Mr Snodgrass still wanted to know how the big beast knew what to do!

Wary Wombat

The Harris family of Monaro (NSW) kept a pet wombat which met the children outside school each day and walked home with them like a dog. If anyone tried to interfere with the children, it tried to protect them by charging at strangers!

Climbing Fish

If you should see some movement out on the Queensland mud flats, don't worry—it's only the Mud Skipper enjoying a dance! Blessed with fins that are similar to limbs, the fish is able to frolic on the mud and even climb trees. And to help it keep a watch out for enemies, its prominent eyes can turn in all directions.

Fish Photographs

Country fishermen in the 19th century believed that fish carried inside them a 'photograph' of the place they were spawned. It was imprinted on the air bladder and when exposed the 'picture' appeared. One such picture, taken from a 46 lb cod and pickled by a fisherman from Wee Waa (NSW) showed a tree with roots on the bank of a river!

THE **FRILLED LIZARD** of Australia, FRIGHTENS OFF PREDATORS BY REARING UP AND UNFOLDING A MANTLE **9** INCHES IN DIAMETER

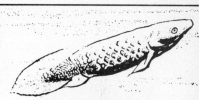

THE CERATODUS A 5-FOOT FISH WITH LUNGS, WAS CONSIDERED EXTINCT FOR MILLIONS OF YEARS—BUT IN 1868 AN AUSTRALIAN FARMER NAMED WILLIAM FOSTER *REVEALED HE HAD BEEN CATCHING THEM IN A RIVER NEAR HIS FARM*

Pebbles in Crocodiles

Aborigines believe that for every pebble found in the stomach of a crocodile, a human has been eaten.

The pebbles are, in fact, an aid to digestion, but who is to prove the belief wrong?

Dancing Brolgas

When the Brolga, a type of crane, performs a dancing ceremony, strutting and flapping its wings, Aborigines believe it is re-enacting a movement taught by a beautiful dancing girl called Brolga who was changed into a bird by witchcraft!

Mammoth Worm

Looking for sandworms for bait in 1911, Steve Dowling, Manly's champion surfboard rider, pulled from the sand a worm measuring 8 ft 6 in long and ¾ inch in diameter.

Old Monty

When Monty the draught horse died in Albury (NSW) in 1970 he was 52 years old! Having achieved the record of the oldest horse in Australia, his jaws were put on display at the School of Veterinary Science at Melbourne University.

Barking Lizard

When alarmed, a species of lizard on the Nullarbor Plain between South Australia and Western Australia lifts itself onto its toes—and barks like a dog!

Overkill

New Zealand ornithologist Sir Walter Buller, the first man to produce a comprehensive guide to the birds of his country, recommended that native birds should be protected—yet critics complained that to obtain his information he killed too many specimens!

Creature from the Past

While sinking a mine shaft at the opal town of White Cliffs (NSW) prospector Ken Harris came across a strange skeleton.

It was identified as that of a plesiosaur, which lived more than 100 million years ago. Because the Sydney Museum could not agree with Mr Harris on a price to buy the rare find, the prospector set it up as a tourist attraction at White Cliffs.

Animal Bar

A pub in Darwin (NT) has a bar completely enclosed in thick wire meshing which is known as 'The Animal Bar'. It is said to date back to when crocodiles and dogs tried to follow the patrons in, but regulars who proudly admit they drink more beer than any town in the world say its modern use is to keep the animals in!

Foiled by 'Roo

A domestic airliner was forced to circle Canberra for 30 minutes in September because a kangaroo bounced onto the runway and refused to move. At last it hopped away but as the TAA Boeing 727 came in to land it hopped onto the tarmac again. The pilot gave up and took his laughing passengers back to Sydney for more fuel. The plane finally landed safely at Canberra more than two hours late.

Massive Nest

Can you imagine a bird's nest weighing 300 tons? The Mallee Fowl builds such a home out of decaying vegetable matter, the heat of which helps the eggs to hatch. The big mound, sometimes measuring 200 ft in circumference, is built, understandably, by the male!

Shark in a Jam

Wondering what had caused a motor launch's engines to suddenly jam, maritime engineers near Christchurch (NZ) raised the vessel on a hoist and found a live eight foot shark jammed between the propeller and the rudder post! It was then killed, but releasing it took more than two hours.

Friendly Dolphins

The friendliest dolphins in the world come in to the shallow waters at Monkey Mia, near Denham (WA), to be fed and patted by bathers!

Waterless Cows

Large herds of cattle in the north of Queensland have never tasted grass or water! They live on the prickly pear, a type of cactus, from which they obtain moisture and food.

Moth Hunters

At the turn of the century, sharp-shooters went out hunting not for deer, kangaroos or wild buffalo but— moths! The largest species of moth in the world, the Atlas Giant, stretched its wings to 17 inches flying between Cairns and Cape York and made a perfect target against the moon.

Aged Tortoise

The oldest and most travelled tortoise in the world is Torty, aged 133, and resident of Bundaberg Zoo (Qld).

She was carried aboard a ship at Madagascar in the pocket of Mr John Powe while on his way to Sydney in November, 1874. Torty then lived with five generations of his family until she took up residence in the zoo.

Dinosaur Tracks

When the tide goes out at Gantheaume Point, near Broome (WA), huge dinosaur tracks, about 130 million years old, are exposed embedded in rock. Following the coast around, more fossilised dinosaur prints can be seen in South Australia at Dinosaur Point, while in Victoria, on the bed of the Genoa River, the tracks of four-footed animals dating back to 355 million years ago were discovered in 1971.

Fishing Spider

A foreleg as a rod, a silky thread as a line, a sticky globule as bait—those are the 'implements' used by the Magnificent Spider which fishes for insects. Sitting on a leaf, it lowers the line some two inches and insects are caught on the sticky bait!

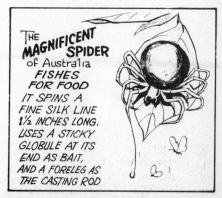

THE MAGNIFICENT SPIDER of Australia FISHES FOR FOOD IT SPINS A FINE SILK LINE 1½ INCHES LONG, USES A STICKY GLOBULE AT ITS END AS BAIT, AND A FORELEG AS THE CASTING ROD

Stuffed Hero

After the sudden death of the famous racehorse, Phar Lap, in California in 1932, his hide was worked on by taxidermists and his stuffed form now stands in Melbourne's Science Museum. His huge heart—it weighed 6.35 kilograms compared with 2.75 kilograms, the weight of an average horse heart—was put on display at the Australian Institute of Anatomy in Canberra, while his skeleton was put on show at the Dominion Museum, Wellington (NZ)!

THE MALE EMU ALWAYS HATCHES AND FEEDS ITS YOUNG

THE MOPOKE an Australian bush bird

WHEN SITTING ON A LIMB OF THE TI TREE

LOOKS LIKE A TREE BRANCH

Camel Skin Graft

One of the earliest forms of skin graft was introduced by Afghan camel drivers in central Australia—they sewed patches of goat skin over the sores of camels suffering from rubbing after carrying heavy loads of copper ore!

Shickered Sheep

An old sheep used by New South Wales abattoir workers to lead flocks across a bridge to the slaughter house on an island was always rewarded with as much beer as it could drink. One day it consumed more than it could take, staggered from the local pub, led itself hiccupping down to the wharf, toppled in and drowned.

All Dogs Out

A man's best friend is his dog—but some bullock drivers of early Australia went to such extremes to display their affection for their 'friends' that one hotel in Queensland was forced to display the notice:

'Guests are NOT allowed to take their dogs to bed with them or even keep dogs in their bedrooms. They must be tied up in the yard.'

Clever Spaniel

Mr L. G. Hodgkinson, of Burnie (Tas.), always thought his spaniel, Tim, was a smart dog and this was proved when his four-legged friend, chasing rabbits, fell through a thin layer of blackberries into a hidden well containing 13 ft of water. Unable to see the dog, Mr Hodgkinson threw a noose down, hoping to lassoo his pet and when he felt the spaniel's weight, hauled him up. Tim was grimly hanging on with his teeth!

Union Dog

Workers on a building project in Auckland were intrigued by a dog they called Spot who turned up at the site for three years, climbing ladders, walking across planks and running beside wheelbarrows. As soon as the 'knock off' whistle sounded he scampered off—and instinctively never turned up at weekends!

Heart-Broken Horse

When an old horse on the last day of his lifelong cart-pulling job at a station at Rockhampton (Qld) saw a new horse in the yard ready to take over, he walked straight to a nearby lagoon and drowned himself.

King Crab

A sand crab dabbed with red paint by a fisherman at Terwah (Qld) was immediately 'elected' king by thousands of crabs for miles around. Wherever it scuttled they all followed, like an army behind its commander!

No Allure

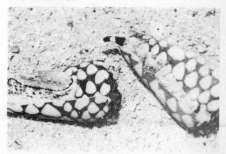

Pretty shellfish that live in the warmer waters around Papua-New Guinea and northern Australia can be fatal! A barbed tooth projecting from the narrow end of the coned shell is used to inject a deadly venom for which no antivenene is available!

Honey Pot Ant

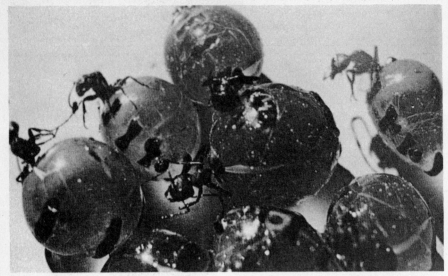

In preparation for winter, the Honey Pot Ant of Central Australia fills itself with honey until its body is the size of a small grape! They were a favourite food among nomadic Aboriginal tribes.

Ringed Rat

A gold ring, missing for years from Ballarat's George Hotel (Vic.) was recovered when a number of rats were trapped in the cellar—the ring was being worn around the neck of one and could have only fitted over its head when it was very young.

Archer Fish

The Archer fish, found in the waters of north Australia, has been known to squirt a jet of water from its mouth and extinguish an angler's cigarette!

It has been given its deadly aim by nature so it can catch its food. The water spray can hit insects hovering as much as eight feet above the water, knocking them on to the surface!

Thumpers

Scientists monitoring volcanic tremors in the New Zealand thermal region of Rotorua were convinced the town was to be hit by an earthquake. Their delicate instruments reacted strongly to tremors, particularly in the evenings. During tests a scientist wandered off into the bush and watched the wildlife, including the wallabies which bounded up, down, up, down just like the needles on the instruments.

The boffin raced back to the earthquake monitoring centre and reported his suspicions. And Dr John Latter, who led the experts, had to admit: 'It was the wallabies all the time. Still, better them than an earthquake.'

Wise 'Roos

The older a kangaroo gets, the wiser it becomes. An 'old man' kangaroo being chased by dogs makes for the nearest water hole where any persuing beast within claw-grabbing distance is dragged into the water and held under until it drowns.

Fresh Bird Food

The food in the Crested Bellbird's pantry is always fresh! The only bird to keep live creatures in storage for later consumption, the Bellbird paralyses caterpillars by squeezing them in its beak, thus preventing their deterioration or escape!

THE LOVENIA
A HEART-SHAPED SEA URCHIN, HAS EXISTED IN AUSTRALIA UNCHANGED IN 40 MILLION YEARS

Budgies' Birthplace

The budgerigar, chirpy friend of British and American families, is a native of Australia. A species of parrot, it was first exported to Britain in the early 1840s and a pair could fetch £25.

Big on Ants

Australia has some 1100 species of ant, a tenth of the world's ant population while New Zealand has only 24 species. The giant ants of Queensland can give nasty bites and some can spring up to 10 cm at a time if a nest is under danger and attack the intruder!

Patriotic Bird

A pigeon hatched in captivity at Moree (NSW) had a white head, red breast and blue tail feathers. It was named Union Jack!

THE CHINESE FISH of Australia, IS EDIBLE 9 MONTHS OF EVERY YEAR, BUT POISONOUS DURING JUNE, JULY AND AUGUST

THE GLASS EEL of Australia IS SO TRANSPARENT THAT THE PAGES OF A BOOK CAN BE READ THROUGH ITS BODY

Digestion Stones

A regular diet of the emu is a small black stone which it finds in the desert regions of South Australia! Sometimes known as emu stones because of the bird's habit of swallowing them to aid digestion, their real name is *Australites*, and despite popular opinion they are not rolled smooth in the emu's stomach—they landed on earth, round and polished, from outer space!

Pig's Edible Raft

After a flood in the Hunter Valley (NSW) a small pig was found in half a pumpkin floating down the river. It had been eating the 'meat' as it sailed!

Natural Hazards

One of the natural hazards on the golf course at Anglesea (Vic.) is kangaroos hopping along the fairway! Golfers often have to wait to putt out. So far there have been no recorded incidents of a ball landing in a kangaroo's pouch!

Crayfish Derby

Prize money for Australia's crayfish derby, a race for crustaceans held every second year at Winton (Qld) is now up to the $2000 mark. Strands of different coloured wool are tied around their bodies for identification, they are placed in the centre of a large circle, and the first to leave the circle is the winner.

Unfortunately for the crayfish, winner or loser, he often ends up in the cooking pot while his owner pockets the prize money!

THE TOOTHIEST MAMMAL
THE NUMBAT of Australia,
HAS 50 TEETH

Beer Swiller

Harry Parsons, who kept the Rising Sun Hotel in Melbourne's Little Bourke Street in the early 1900s, had a pet cockatoo that could grasp a beer bottle by the neck, nip the cap off with its beak and pour the contents into a glass!

Something Fishy

A Sydney fisherman who cut open a flathead found a piece of newspaper with the single word 'fish' on it. He compared the type with that used in a Sydney newspaper column called 'Fish Tales', wrote an article about his find and it appeared in the column.

The Dreaded Taipan

The taipan, the world's most venomous land snake, is found mainly in northern Queensland, grows to 10 ft and carries enough venom to kill 200 sheep, nearly twice as much as the Indian king cobra!

Barking Spider

A spider which attacks chickens and drags them into its burrow? Australia's biggest spider, a species of barking spider found in north Queensland, has been known to do just that. The bodies of the big members of the *Selenotypus plumipes* sometimes measure more than two inches!

'Roos Minute Young

Big oaks from little acorns grow... when born, kangaroos are about the size of a peanut! And the young koala bear is no bigger than a five cent piece!

A Rat's Tail

The tastiest food for the rats of Torres Strait islands is crab—and they catch them with their tails!

Sitting on the edge of a coral reef, the rats dangle their tails in the water like a fishing line. Unable to resist the 'bait', crabs grasp the tail and they are immediately pulled up. The angling rat's ultra-sharp teeth do the rest!

THE KOALA HAS AN APPENDIX 8 FEET LONG

Frog Mystery

A builder who removed a huge coping stone from a stone wall at Coogee, Sydney, found a full-grown live frog in a tiny cavity. Beside it was the skeleton of another large frog. The live frog hopped away leaving scientists to try to solve the mystery.

Snake's Mark

Chased by a dog, a snake took refuge in a duck house on a property at Tallangatta (Vic.) causing a panic among the birds until the owner killed the reptile. The next day a duck laid an egg—bearing a perfect design of a snake!

Follow that Bee

In order to follow the flight of a bee to its hive against a blue sky, Aborigines in outback Australia have been known to drop flour onto the back of the insect and run after it, the white 'flash' making identification easy.

Lots of Sharks

More than 110 species of shark live in the waters off Australia, New Zealand and Papua-New Guinea, several of which are man-eaters. They are prolific breeders—when fisherman Vic Hislop pulled in a 5 m tiger shark at Queensland's Moreton Bay in 1982 it was carrying FORTY young!

Bicycle Lizard

The Bicycle Lizard is believed to have got its name during the days of the Penny Farthing. It has two small legs in the front and two large legs at the back and has a peddling action when running.

Tiny Eggs

Although the Sunfish, which swims off Australia's east coast, grows to more than two tons, its eggs are no bigger than a pin-point!

Big Fish, Small Meals

The Blue Whale is the largest creature living in the waters of Australia, yet its food is plankton, the smallest form of life known to man.

Crocs' Toothbrush

The crocodile of the Northern Territory has its own personal toothbrush—the tiny trochilus bird which sits in front of the amphibian's jaws and picks food from its teeth. There have been no recorded incidents of the crocs' 'toothbrush' being converted, with a snap of jaws, into toothpaste!

Bike in Nest

Magpies are renowned for taking shiny objects back to their nests, but one went overboard—it made its nest from telegraph wire, springs and bicycle spokes, lining the top with twigs. The four kilogram nest was later displayed in the Sydney Museum.

SNAKE-NECKED TURTLE of AUSTRALIA HAS A NECK TOO LONG TO BE DRAWN INTO ITS SHELL — IT MUST BE FOLDED SIDEWAYS

Black Swans of Western Australia

When Dutch navigator Willem de Vlamingh reached the Swan River in Western Australia in 1697 he had to look twice at the long necked birds that lived there... they looked like swans, but unlike those of Europe, these were black. Later explorers were to learn that the black swan was a peculiarity of Australia and they were so abundant in the west that the bird became the emblem of the state.

Useful Bird

Islanders of Papua-New Guinea and New Britain who hunt the Cassowary, a large flightless bird, put it to good use—they eat the flesh, make knives and spears from the thigh bones and wear the feathers for decoration.

THE **NEST** OF THE RIFLE-BIRD, OF AUSTRALIA, TO FRIGHTEN AWAY PREDATORS, IS ALWAYS DECORATED WITH A *SNAKESKIN*

THE DECORATOR BIRD
THE MALE SATIN BOWER BIRD ACTUALLY PAINTS THE WALLS OF ITS BOWER NEST--*USING A FIBER BRUSH DIPPED IN CHARCOAL AND SALIVA*

KOOKABURRA

THE *LAUGHING JACKASS* IS A BIRD!

HE LAUGHS LIKE A MAN

- AND EATS SNAKES

Puffing Billy and Jerry

Whenever Jerry the stray dog heard the whistle of Puffing Billy, a steam train which worked the hills behind Melbourne, he ran to the station, jumped in a bucket of water to cool off, hopped onto the footplate and travelled with the engine. Sometimes he would run in front of the train and his tricks were known for miles around. One day, in 1934, Jerry got his timing wrong and the train ran over him, but he was remembered by a special grave and a cross bearing his name beside the line.

Deadly Ant

A species of Australian ant, the Black Bulldog, can give a lethal bite, deaths being recorded in Victoria and Tasmania just 15 minutes later!

Kangaroo Record

Chased by a pack of dogs, a kangaroo created a record for its breed by jumping over a stack of wood 10 ft 6 in high.

Biggles' Round Trip

A white cat nicknamed Biggles kept an airliner grounded for three days at Sydney while staff tried to find it in the cargo hold. When it was caught, Biggles was claimed by the Miles family of Papakura (NZ) who said they had been waiting a week for the fluffy white tom. Airline staff worked out that Biggles had got out of his crate on a flight from Brisbane to New Zealand and since then had travelled for seven days to Brisbane, Townsville, Darwin, Singapore, Perth, Brisbane, Sydney, Fiji and back to Sydney.

Dog's 2300 km Journey

Truck driver Geoff Hancock never expected to see his dog Whisky, an eight-year-old Jack Russell terrier, again when the animal was lost 180 km south of Darwin in October 1973. Yet Whisky made his way home across central Australia, covering 2300 km to turn up at Mambray Creek, 220 km north of Adelaide, eight months later.

Cattle Routes

Thanks to the cow, tourists have been able to explore wider areas of previously inaccessible parts of Australia! Realising the need to open roads to carry cattle long distances where there were no railways, the Australian and state governments decided to build or improve roads in outlying parts of Queensland, South Australia, Western Australia and the Northern Territory.

The new routes, which began in 1960 and were known as Beef Roads, opened up areas that were only accessible for tourists in four-wheel drive vehicles.

Dangling Dog

When his master, Captain Edgar Percival, a well-known Australian joy-flier of the 1920s, did a loop-the-loop for a passenger, Mick, a cross-breed dog, fell out and plunged earthwards— until a rope, tied around his neck, stopped him short. He dangled 14 ft below the plane for several minutes before Percival noticed he was missing and hauled him aboard, tail wagging!

Lizard Legend

Aborigines on the Cape York Peninsula believed that the crocodiles of the Kendall River were their blood brothers following ceremonies in which a lizard was daubed in blood taken from the arm of a youth and cast into the water. They believed the lizard grew into a crocodile!

Angry Lizards

You'll always know when you have upset the Blue Tongued Lizard of Australia and Papua-New Guinea—it will poke its tongue at you, a natural reaction when angry or alarmed!

Marsupial Lion

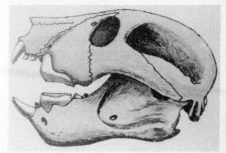

One of the earliest creatures to roam Australia was a small lion which carried its young in a pouch, just like the kangaroo.

Camels to Arabia

Australia rears such fine camels in the 'red centre' that shieks from Saudi Arabia frequently visit the country, select a number of beasts and ship them off to the sand-dunes of their country!

Mosquito Eater

Thanks to Australia's Blue Eye fish, work was able to start on the Panama Canal after worries had been expressed about the threat of malaria spreading through the work camps.

The fish, which eats the larvae of mosquitoes, was exported in shoals to the Panama Isthmus and the population of the biting insects quickly diminished!

Beetle Territory

Between them, Australia, New Zealand and Papua-New Guinea have nearly 75 000 species of beetle!

Top Layer

Te Kawau Princess, an Auckland Black Orpington hen which broke the world record by laying 361 hard-shelled eggs in 365 days, was sold to an American fancier, Mrs Waddell, for £125, while a cockerel which emerged from one of the Princess's prize-winning eggs fetched £25!

Beetle's Weapon

A beetle turned upside down at a coal colliery on the Australian south coast emitted a spark. Two ants placed near it were immediately electrocuted by a bright blue flash!

AN OAR FISH

CAUGHT BY KEITH McRAE IN SYDNEY HARBOR, AUST., MEASURED **12** FEET

Stern Measure

A rabbit hunter bitten by a tiger snake in the Victorian bush in 1948 had no knife to cut the poison out nor any string for a tourniquet—so he devised a unique way of stopping the venom. He shot half his leg off. And survived!

Decoy Tails

Black Diet

Just before the cargo ship *Thomas Stevens* sailed from Newcastle (NSW) harbour with a cargo of coal, a number of pigs were found to be missing from their pens on board. A thorough search failed to find them until, half-way to San Francisco, strange noises were heard in the coal hold. And there, fat as butter, were the missing pigs which had lived for weeks on lumps of coal—and seemingly enjoyed it.

When chased by large birds, the gecko lizard has a natural decoy—its discarded tail! The gecko is able to cast off its tail to distract an enemy and it continues to wriggle long enough for the lizard to make its getaway and start growing a new one!

NINE

Dreamers

Amazing Imaginations

Dreams are true while they last, and do we not live in dreams? Tennyson asked.

We look at a flower and see hills of buttercups. We write a letter and become lost in our thoughts. We sail along the River Nile and drift back in time to the Pharaohs. Dreams are beautiful because they take us to the stars, to a place beyond reality.

We are all dreamers. Some have visions stronger than others and so live their dreams more vividly. We are cast adrift. The real world is all around us; a radio plays, a car horn toots, someone speaks, but we hear not because we have entered another realm where there are no rules; where that which is impossible on earth proceeds with ease and simplicity.

How we wish, sometimes, that we could blend our dreams with reality! That we could have our visions and then physically step into them. Or pull them down like a fluffy cloud on a piece of string and have them encompass us and,

if it is to our advantage, others. All we need do is dream of getting away with the outrageous, step into our vision and all will be well!

Some dreamers have an ulterior motive, using their flights of fancy in the hope of 'bettering their lot'. A law-breaker may come up with an excuse to improve his chances of 'getting away with it', another will tell an outrageous tale to gain popularity. Wishful thinking, a prophesy, hopes, aspirations, call our visions what we may, they are all dreams. We want to believe in something else, something beyond our circumstances.

And if we cannot dream we can at least share the dreams of others. Read here the visions and the hopes. Read the amazing imaginations which have won fame or at least delight for those who conjured them up. Read of those who have tried to wriggle out of difficulties met in the real world by turning to the unlimited regions of the mind, to their dreaming.

Let your imagination run free as you read about:

The children who sang 'I'm Dreaming of a White Christmas' in 117 F degree heat.

The man who asked his debtors to meet him at the Pearly Gates.

The portrait of Elvis Presley which cured cataracts.

Phantom Bagpipes

A Scotsman who lived alone in the mountains between Monaro (NSW) and the coast played his bagpipes every night. A few days after the old man died and was buried, neighbours passing his property were terrified to hear the bagpipes playing on! They finally discovered the 'ghost'. A lyrebird had learned to imitate the notes exactly.

The Kingdom of Cole

Prior to the grand opening of his internationally famous Book Arcade in Melbourne in 1883, which purported to sell 'a variety of TALES', Mr E. W. Cole placed an advertisement in the *Herald* newspaper which ran for a week.

A colourful serial about tails, it began with the 'DISCOVERY of a Race of Human Beings with TAILS' and kept the city buzzing with excitement, breathlessly anticipating the next day's instalment.

As a result of the advertisement, the newspaper's circulation reached record sales!

Arcadian Fantasy

Mr Edward William Cole's famous Book Arcade—'The Palace of Intellect'—which opened in Melbourne in 1883, was the largest, the most astonishing in the world. It consisted of three storeys of trick mirrors and galleries stuffed with every conceivable delight to satiate the senses, including an elaborate refreshment parlour and a hen that laid a golden egg which, when cracked open, was found to contain a toy!

Over the entrance was an enormous rainbow under which two mechanical sailors turned the handles of a windmill-like contraption whose sails proclaimed the marvels within.

There was a veritable rainforest filled with exotic tropical birds, stuffed animals and even real animals—Mr Cole had not forgotten the trademark of all jungles, monkeys! In addition to all this, there was an orchestra that played round-the-clock and over two million books. Mr Cole encouraged people to browse. Rarely were books purchased, indeed, more often than not people tore them up, defaced them or stole them. Yet 'The Palace of Intellect' continued from strength to strength until its founder's death in 1918.

Bread that Cheers

The day before the 1982 Rugby League grand final in Sydney, two bakeries made bread in the colours of the competing teams—maroon and white loaves for Manly-Warringah, blue and gold for Parramatta supporters!

Urgent Call

Calling on his brother in a Wellington (NZ) mental hospital, a man drove his car up the steps, crashed into a patient in a wheelchair, drove along a corridor and finally parked at an untidy angle in the ward.

Poultry Offence

During an amnesty by the Campelltown Library (NSW) in 1982, an anonymous reader returned a book that was NINETY-TWO YEARS overdue! A handbook on poultry breeding, it should have been returned in 1890 and if the borrower had been asked for the amount due, the fine would have totalled $478.40.

Exercise Only

A Queensland man, Mr P. Harrison, who had courted a farm woman for 25 years, finally quarrelled with her and died a bachelor. Their homes were four miles apart and he had wooed her every Saturday and Sunday. Friends worked out that he had walked 20 000 miles after a girl he did not get!

Wrestless Love

Said by police to have been making love on a beach, a young Auckland couple were found not guilty when a court accepted their story that they were wrestling!

Stairway to Paradise

Retired Melbourne bank manager, Russell Cole, had a passion for mounting stairs, celebrating each birthday with a formidable climb. In 1959, for his 69th birthday he climbed the stairs of Melbourne's then tallest structure, the ICI building. In subsequent years he humbled the National Mutual, the Royal Insurance and the CRA buildings and, on his 82nd birthday in 1972, the AMP tower. His desire on that day had been to climb the BHP building but the company's directors put him off—they feared he might suffer a heart attack. However, the sly old gentleman managed to sneak by and that same afternoon went from the bottom to the 42nd storey in a smooth 14 minutes!

Topping Plan

In an attempt to beat an inquiry by the Sex Discrimination Board an Adelaide hotelier hired a topless waiter to join his staff of two topless waitresses!

Rowe in Cafe

Sitting in a Melbourne cafe with her husband after the war, singer Thea Rowe, whose married name was Hosking, started a conversation with two men at the same table. They discovered that they all came from Cornwall and the two men were named Rowe and Hosking!

No Surprises

To keep the 1940s records straight, Mr W.T. Hutchinson, acting Town Clerk of Metcalf (Vic.) wrote official letters to himself in his role as Shire Clerk!

Elvis Lives On

Melbourne artist John Riddell was so pleased with his portrait of Elvis, painted with the eyes looking down, that he decided to photograph it. When the picture was printed, the formerly downcast eyes were found to be looking up, straight into the camera!

'I thought they'd been up to funny business at the processors but they assured me they don't play around with customers' pictures', said John.

Since then, he claims, a friend who had a slipped disc fell while carrying the painting and his back was immediately healed.

A woman who sat in front of the portrait one day said she saw the eyes move and heard Elvis singing 'How Great Thou Art'.

A punting friend bet on horses numbered 5 and 7—the number of letters in Elvis' christian and surnames—and came back from the races with his pockets stuffed with money.

Cataracts in John's eyes started to heal.

Deliverance

When T. F. Gallagher's work *The Wild Colonial Boy*—a novel about life in the Australian bush—was being published in London, he was driving a grocer's delivery cart in Omaru (NZ). After succeeding in getting some stories published in Australian newspapers, he had tried to make a literary career in Sydney but he failed to make enough money on freelance earnings and returned to New Zealand.

Vain Promise

A Melbourne newspaper, the *Argus*, promised 'immortal fame' in 1849 to the person who could capture a bunyip, a creature said to live in the rivers and lakes of Port Phillip. The *Argus* is no more and the bunyip is still free!

Old Top Hat

Mr Lionel O'Brien, a professional remover of kinks from circular saws at a Sydney grinding firm, worked for eight hours a day wearing a top hat passed down to him by his father!

Lucky Horseshoes

Newlyweds sitting for their wedding breakfasts in Leichhardt, Sydney, used to find a pair of horseshoes placed in front of them. They were worn by Windbag when he won the Sydney Cup and were regarded as lucky.

Late Run

After running away from home at the age of 62 to marry a 70-year-old man, Olive Hildred, of Sydney, told her husband Ernest that he was too mean—so she went back home to father!

Lengthy Proposition

After meeting Helen Gray in Iowa (USA) in the early 1930s Dr Poulter, a member of an expedition to the Antarctic, proposed to her by radio from the South Pole while she was in New Zealand and married her within six hours of his stepping ashore at Dunedin!

Sea Fever

After the ship carrying him from England to Australia in 1815 was boarded by pirates, Frederick Garling took a keen interest in the sea, got a job as a customs officer in Sydney and painted every ship that entered the harbour over a 40 year period. He became recognised as Australia's first maritime artist.

Island Mixture

In Samoa it was common for girls to bear boys' names and for boys to bear girls' names. If a girl was born soon after the death of a brother or vice versa, it was believed the spirit of the deceased would live on in his or her brother or sister by the passing on of the name!

Cutting It Vine

At the end of the yam harvest on the island of Pentecost, Vanuatu, village men tie vines to their ankles and dive from towers 20 to 25 metres high, escaping death as the carefully-measured vine stops them short of hitting the ground!

The islanders believe that the spectacular land dive ensures a good yam harvest the following year. But several villagers have not survived to reap the fruits!

Cat Vision

Miss Lyn Keep, who works for the Ansett Airline, was on a trip to London when she learned that Pippin, her champion Blue Point Siamese, was missing. Friends searched in vain and in desperation Lyn went to a clairvoyant. The crystal ball gazer described the animal and said he could be found at dusk in the Blue Mountains under a pine tree surrounded by bamboo, with the Three Sisters on the left and a white picket fence to the right.

An elderly Springwood lady involved in the search knew of just such a spot. That night, in the fading light, her son found the cat.

Off His Nut

Despondent that the Government would no longer aid his struggling peanut business in the Northern Territory in the 1930s, old August Paul paid off all his debts and inserted an advertisement in a Darwin newspaper reading:

'If I've overlooked anyone, he can meet me on Friday night at 8 o'clock at the Pearly Gates.'

He shot his horses, burned down his house and at 8 p.m. on the Friday he put the muzzle of his rifle in his mouth and pulled the trigger.

A Case of Kissing

Victorian Public Works Minister Jack Simpson (Labor) caused an uproar in the State Parliament when he admitted kissing Mrs Prue Sibree, an opposition MP, in the members' dining room against her wishes in October 1982. But women who used to work for Hansard gave him their wholehearted support, describing how he had charmed them all with his humour. One recalled how she had 'waltzed up the corridor' with him. Nevertheless Mr Simpson vowed: 'From now on I'll keep to shaking hands.'

The Full Message

While repairing the courthouse at
Armidale (NSW) in 1971, workmen
found an empty cognac bottle
containing a parchment dated 26
November 1870, and signed by a
philosophical clerk of petty sessions.

In copperplate handwriting,
Mr Sydney Blythe had written: 'If
ever in ages to come this bottle is
found, I would wish to record that
Armidale is a town of about 800
inhabitants; that it has a municipal
council; that the railway has
progressed as far as Aberdeen; that
James Buchanan, Esquire, is police
magistrate; and that also I, the
undersigned, am clerk of petty
sessions, land agent and registrar of
births, deaths and marriages for the
district.

'I have also no hesitation in stating
that all the world is a stage and all
men and women merely players.

'Can the men who find this drink
their 12 glasses of grog in a day—I
doubt it. We can.'

After recording that Louis Napolean
had been kicked out of France by
the Germans and Paris was near
bombardment, Mr Blythe added: 'My
friend, whosoever you may be who
find this, rest assured that the world
has wagged before your times as it
will after your times and that nothing
is certain but death.

'For and on behalf of my numerous
creditors, Sydney Blythe.'

Good Start

Australia's 12th test-tube baby,
Matthew James Allan, was entered by
his grandmother in a Melbourne Cup
Sweep at the Queen Victoria Medical
Centre and, barely a few hours old,
won the $12 first prize!

Drone Pipe

The only wind instrument made by
Aborigines is the didgeridoo, or drone
pipe. Created from a length of wood
ranging from 1.5 m to 5 m long, the
instrument can be used to copy the
sounds of birds and animals.

Composer George Dreyfus wrote a
formal work for the didgeridoo to be
accompanied by string instruments.

THE EMPTY SHOP KEEPER

RICHARD GEORGE WILD RUNS AN EMPTY SHOP
IN BRISBANE, Australia   ALTHOUGH HE HAS NOTHING
TO SELL HE KEEPS OPEN FOR SENTIMENTAL REASONS

Kate Kelly's Bed

After bushranger Ned Kelly's sister, Kate, drowned at Forbes (NSW) in 1898, historians grabbed her most treasured possession—her bed! Kate is said to have enjoyed sleeping and now visitors to a museum at Mount Victoria (NSW) can stand at the foot of the bed and dream of those wild bushranger days!

Dressed Down

A young bride from Victoria found a man from the Fisheries and Game Department waiting for her when she returned from her honeymoon in August, 1950. Mr A. D. Butcher loved reading wedding reports in the newspapers and in one account he noticed that the bride wore osprey feathers in her dress.

Anyone found in possession of feathers of the protected bird of prey was liable to a fine of £5...

Double Dip

To spread the word, Mr and Mrs S. R. Kleinschmidt were baptised in a six-foot-long tank in busy Edward Street, Brisbane, in 1951, watched by a large crowd. Mr Kleinschmidt was dressed in a pure white shirt and trousers and his wife wore a white dress and a rubber bathing cap.

Lonesome Cowboy

Stories about the fastest guns in the West have been published by the fastest writer in the East—Sydney author Len Meares, who has written more than 500 cowboy novels!

Electronic Wizard

One of Australia's greatest modern-day adventurers is Dick Smith, a Sydney electronics millionaire who has towed a fake iceberg into Sydney Harbour on April Fools' Day, bounced across Sydney Harbour Bridge on a petrol-powered pogo stick, travelled alone around the world by helicopter and organised a flight for 439 people named Smith to Smith's Waterhole to raise money for a charity in aid of the Smith Family!

Lost Gold Reef

Since the 1930s the story of Lasseter's Reef has been an inspiration to all who dream of adventure and wealth.

Bushman Harold Lasseter, found unconscious south of Alice Springs in 1897, claimed he had found a rich reef of gold and produced rock specimens to back his story.

After several attempts over the years to get an expedition moving he set off with a team but after arguments and loss of faith by the party, Lasseter continued alone. His bones and a revolver were later found in a cave but his reef was never traced.

Did it exist? The question is still asked today!

Sad Women

Painter Charles Blackman's first exhibition, 'Schoolgirls', in 1953 was the start of a career in which most of his work portrayed women in sad poses. Many of the characters were modelled on his almost-blind wife, Barbara.

Pass the Hat

Leaning out of a train window between Leura and Katoomba (NSW) a passenger lost his hat—but it was caught by a man leaning out of a window three carriages behind. The two men turned out to be cousins who had never met before!

Price of Love

A Papuan truck driver who in 1961 fell in love with a girl he saw dancing for Lady Dunrossil, wife of the former Governor-General, offered his worldly possessions for her hand in marriage—£900 in cash and £500 worth of shells. Her family accepted!

Small Paper—Big Name

Omeo (Vic.) is one of the shortest-named towns in Australia, but its first newspaper claimed a world record for length—it was called the *North Gippsland Mountaineer, and Swift's Creek and Wombat Reporter*!

Cat-astrophic Cruise

Authorities refused to believe at first that the liner *Pericles*, carrying 300 passengers and 200 crew, was sinking off Western Australia in 1910—because it was April Fool's Day!

Despite the delays and the fact that there was only half an hour to get everyone into the lifeboats, only three lives were lost—Nelson, the one-eyed cat who jumped from a lifeboat and disappeared trying to reach her two drowning kittens.

Jack et Jules

John Feltham Archibald, who founded the *Bulletin* magazine in 1880, had such an interest in France and its people that he changed his first names to Jules Francois!

High-rise

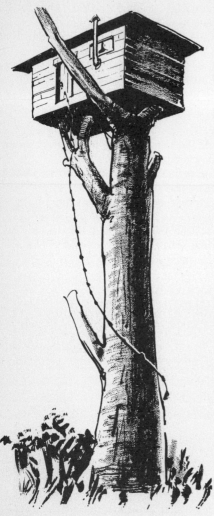

An old man in Hunter's Valley (Qld) had a bird's-eye view of the surrounding countryside from his home—he had erected it, plank by plank, at the top of a 60-ft-high gum-tree! After a stroll along the local lanes he climbed to his lounge room by means of a knotted rope!

Pebble Pledge

Two young lovers of pioneering days, miles from the nearest clergyman, threw a pebble into a river and vowed to be true and faithful until the stone floated!

Prophetic Poet

Poet Barcroft Boake, who saw life in the raw in the bush where men hungered and died of thirst, wrote a work called *Where the Dead Men Lie* and later, significantly, hanged himself with a stock whip.

Advice From Beyond

Wondering where their deceased elderly relative had left a will they knew he had made, a Penrith (NSW) family held a seance in 1921 and the words 'Pilgrim's Progress' were spelled out on a ouija board. Opening an old copy that had remained untouched on a bookshelf for years, they found £200 in notes and a receipt for repairs to the family grandfather clock. Opening the clock, they found the will!

Threepenny Prayer

During his work as engineer for Whangerei County (NZ), Mr D. C. Wilson wrote the Lord's Prayer on a piece of paper described as being 'one-fourteenth the size of a threepenny bit'.

Not to be outdone, 80-year-old Mr George Geddes, of Georgetown, North Otago (NZ) wrote the prayer on a scrap of paper measuring thirteen-sixteenths of an inch by eleven-sixteenths.

And Colonel Arthur Morrow of Auckland wrote the prayer ELEVEN times in concentric circles in an area equal to the size of a threepenny bit!

Rope Trick

A young tribal boy who saw his first movie, a Western, in Papua-New Guinea later tried his skills by tossing a lassoo at a man standing on the back of a passing truck. By a fluke, the noose went right over the man's head and caught him around the throat. He lived only because the rope was snatched from the boy's hands. A posse of police arrested the boy and he ended up in gaol for 14 days.

Grateful Bride

A young woman sitting in the public library at Wanganui (NZ) in 1924 was approached by another and asked if she would act as a witness at her marriage at a registry office. The ceremony over, the bride promised the young woman she would benefit for her assistance. Twenty-three years later she was told she was the beneficiary under the will of the girl she had helped nearly a quarter of a century earlier!

Lion Again

Police in Christchurch were called out to investigate a report of a large lion stalking through a park. They found a horse wearing a khaki rug!

No Show

Convinced that Christ was about to return, the Sydney branch of the Order of the Star of the East built a large amphitheatre at Balmoral in 1924 so that believers would watch Him appear on the water at Sydney Heads. Seats were sold at prices ranging from £5 to £1000. After allowing for miscalculations and Heavenly delays, the building was demolished.

Shuttle Service

Killarney, an Aboriginal boy from the outback, loved his first 400 mile flight in an air ambulance from Roper Valley Station to Darwin (NT) for treatment for a broken arm. He went to extremes to have another flight...

Eighteen months later he became sick with pneumonia and chicken pox and was flown back to hospital. Hardly had he returned to the station on recovery when he fell off a horse. No guesses where they took him for treatment!

Onion Head

Police constable Malcolm Pengilly of Sydney started a rush to the vegetable shops when he said he had grown hair on his bald head by regularly rubbing the pate with raw onions, salt and water before going to bed!

Sign For Divers

A road sign near a creek on Big Jack Mountain (NSW) read: 'When this sign is under water, the crossing is dangerous.'

Claustrophobic

Peter Scott of the Upper Hawkesbury River (NSW) dug and bricked in his own grave, explaining he could not bear to think of being buried in a hole that might fall on him!

Hot Christmas

When train driver Ron Ryan brought Christmas presents to a group of children in the heart of the outback in temperatures of 117 degrees, the youngsters sang 'I'm Dreaming of a White Christmas' and 'Sleigh Bells in the Snow'.

SYD DARNLEY of Sydney, Australia, BUILT A SCALE MODEL OF THE SYDNEY TOWN HALL USING 74,000 SEASHELLS

Wrong Church

The bridegroom, from Queensland, stood nervously at the altar of a church in Coogee, Sydney, as the organ struck up 'Here Comes the Bride'. When she reached his side he turned, smiled—and recoiled in horror. Wrong bride!

Accompanied by his best man, he hurried out past the vestry where the other groom, who was late, was making adjustments to his tie, and found his church and his bride a short distance away.

The bride's relatives did not realise he was the wrong groom because they had never met him.

Long-Life Bread

Just before a young man named Payne left England to try his luck in South Australia, his mother handed him a loaf of home-made bread as a token of good luck and a reminder of home.

He treasured the loaf for years and just before his death cut it into pieces and distributed it among his Adelaide friends. One of the pieces was exhibited at a meeting of master bakers in 1923 and, although 85 years old, was pronounced to be in excellent condition!

Icecream to Eskimos

During a heat wave in Brisbane in the early 1950s, British shoe salesman Robert Pierce sold every pair of his supply of fur-lined snow boots and had to travel to Sydney for a further consignment.

Although he did not sell them at a cut price, he said people thought they had to be getting a bargain because no-one would try to sell snow boots in summer time!

Golden Clue

A Melbourne clairvoyant asked professional gold prospector George Hamm whether the name James Brodie meant anything to him. It didn't, but later George found some old notes which told how a James Brodie had unearthed a 40 lb gold nugget at a spot called Guy's Rush (Vic.) more than 100 years earlier, in 1869. Digging in the area, George uncovered a 7 oz chunk of gold!

Spirit Place

On Cape Reinga, the northern peninsula of New Zealand's North Island, a lighthouse has been built in an area the Maoris believe is the 'leaping place of spirits'.

A legend says spirits of the dead travel to the Cape and descend into the sea through the roots of a Pohutukawa tree that stands there.

Although 800 years old, Maoris say the tree has never blossomed!

Another One!

Charles Bastard, lessee of the Adelaide City Baths, had to dive to the bottom in the late 1800s to rescue a man who, with iron plates attached to his feet, had claimed he had invented a contraption which would enable man to walk on water!

Novelist's Dramas

Henry Savery, Australia's first novelist, was reprieved from the death penalty in England, tried to cut his throat in Tasmania because he suspected his wife had been seduced on a ship by the Attorney General, was arrested for forging bills and died in misery in jail in 1842. His real life drama had been more exciting than anything he had dreamed up.

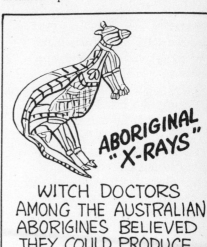

ABORIGINAL "X-RAYS"

WITCH DOCTORS AMONG THE AUSTRALIAN ABORIGINES BELIEVED THEY COULD PRODUCE RAIN BY PAINTING ON TREE BARK "X-RAY" ILLUSTRATIONS OF A KANGAROO--*CENTURIES BEFORE DR. ROENTGEN DISCOVERED X-RAYS*

TEN

Gamblers
The Fortunate Few

The world spins like a huge roulette wheel and we are the players. Fortune or disaster could fall in our lap at any moment. Without warning, events occur that can alter the rest of our lives. Do we then have the courage to step with fate? Having cast the dice, played our hand, can we assume control for the paths we can tread?

Often we court disaster—plunging headlong into situations which we know will ultimately bring problems. On the other hand, there are times when we know that nothing can go wrong. But Lady Luck's expression can change in a flash and our fate is decided with a smile or a frown.

Life, it is said, is like a huge lottery. Often no skills are necessary to win. You simply have to be in it. Consider the fortunes of the residents of the gold-mining town of Kalgoorlie earlier this century. After freak floods, nuggets were found on the roadsides. Everybody looked, but only a small percentage of townsfolk picked up any. They did not plan their search routes; they simply walked along and the finders were a random lot.

Read here of fame, of fortune and of rotten luck. Perhaps you will recognise yourself among those that follow. But can you have ever been as unlucky as the Geelong punter who went to the races and lost everything?

Place your bets, ladies and gentlemen and roll the following pages to read about:

Jockeys who have won all seven races at a meeting.

The butcher who found a gold nugget in a dead goose.

The soldier who used a coin he had lost years before to win a fortune in a two-up game.

The gold prospector who became a world famous flautist.

Stringing Them Along

As an incentive to get greyhounds into the right mood to chase the 'electronic rabbit', staff at a Gladstone (Qld) stadium showed them a dancing, stuffed wallaby, activated by strings.

Money Sandwich

Prospectors who struck it rich in the gold-rush days of the mid 1800s often held one-upmanship contests. A digger who lit a cigar with a £5 note was upstaged by another who ate a sandwich made up of bread, butter and a £10 note!

Worth a Try

Mr W. C. Wentworth almost became the biggest landlord on earth in the pioneering days when he bought 10 million acres from the Maoris of New Zealand's South Island for £200 and 200 000 acres on the North Island for £200 plus a £100 pension for the chief with whom he negotiated. Both deals were set aside by the government and Wentworth lost his deposits.

Double Trouble

Driving through Sydney in 1950, engineer Mr J. Marshall's car was hit from behind by truck driver John Tansey. In 1952, a truck ran into his car on the Harbour Bridge and a red-faced John Tansey jumped from the cab again.

Deciding that such a coincidence could only bring them luck, they bought a lottery ticket. It didn't win, but Mr Marshall ended up with £101 14s 11d—he successfully sued Mr Tansey for the two crashes.

Cup Runneth Over

Picture theatre proprietor Mr L. J McKenna backed Rainbird in the Melbourne Cup in 1945, also drew the horse in a sweep and collected £500. The following year he backed Royal Gem for the Caulfield Cup, drew THAT horse in a sweep, and won £250!

Just the Ticket

Miss Margaret Prendergast, a Newton agent who spent a day in the 1940s purchasing tickets for customers at the main lottery office in Sydney, was called to the telephone to learn that the ticket she had bought for herself while she was buying for 1000 others, had won 1st prize!

Good Odds

The sale of ale in hotels was being affected by a shortage of copper coins in the mid 1850s to such an extent that brewer Robert Tooth offered £10 000 for £5000 worth of change if it could be delivered in Sydney by a specified date!

Archie's Edict

Archie Cameron, born in Happy Valley (SA), brought an air of gloom to Parliament while in office as Speaker in 1949—he banned all betting within the precincts of Parliament House, including poker in the Press Room and ordered that photographs of racehorses in the barber shop be taken down.

Raining Gold

After heavy freak flooding in the old gold-mining town of Kalgoorlie in 1948, gold nuggets were found on the roads and footpaths! One man picked up a 13 oz nugget washed clear of the earth that had hidden it, and another found a 6 oz nugget!

Slide Ruler

The man with the most unusual job in Australia is Mr Brian Fowler, of Queensland, who is a lizard race caller!

He does the calling when the annual lizard races are held in the backyard of the Eulo Queen Hotel, 1200 km west of Brisbane.

MR. **THRIFT** OF **KEEPIT**, Australia, WON THE £**30,000** FIRST PRIZE IN A LOTTERY

Memorial Window

Bernard Holtermann, a German immigrant to Australia, was so delighted with his discovery of a huge slab of gold nearly seven feet high that he bought a home in North Sydney and had fitted a stained glass window containing a portrait of himself and part of the precious slab.

The Brush Off

Ballarat Town Council had to pass a by-law in the 1850s prohibiting men from sweeping away the roads!

The highways were made up of refuse quartz left behind as valueless by miners, but enterprising prospectors found that by sweeping up specks created by constant traffic they collected particles of gold.

So much sweeping was going on that the roads were in danger of literally being swept away until the new 'no sweeping' law was introduced.

Lean Pickings

Because goldseekers in Parkes (NSW) were having such a run of bad luck that they were forced to live on bread and dripping, the mining area later became known as Bread and Dripping Valley.

Just Hoarsing Around

Australian Mrs Susan Sangster, wife of British football pools millionaire Robert Sangster, has not been unknown to jump on a table at fashionable restaurants after a big win at the races and sing 'Waltzing Matilda'.

Welcome Stranger

Penniless Cornish miners Richard
Oates and John Deason were at the
end of their tether. They had
sailed to Australia to seek their
fortunes on the gold-fields, but
after eight years of bad luck they
decided to give up.

On their last day, Oates went
home early but Deason decided to
stay at the claim to use up the
last of their dirt-processing water,
for there was a drought on.

Three piles of dirt yielded
nothing. There was water to wash
one more pile. With a sigh,
Deason slammed his spade into the
mound and cursed the rock that
jarred his bones.

But the 'rock' turned out to be
the largest gold nugget ever found,
the 'Welcome Stranger', weighing
71 kg and worth, in 1869, the
princely sum of £9534!

Big Loser

Ernest Benson, who inherited £250 000
on his 21st birthday in 1887, came to
Australia and had such a run of bad
luck on the horses, at snooker, cards
and the stock exchange that it had all
gone by the time he was twenty-three.
Then he wrote a book entitled *How I
Lost 250 000 Pounds in Two Years*. HE
CLUNG ON GRIMLY TO THE
ROYALTIES!

Final Blow

A punter who lost a fortune at a
Geelong dog track also had his
transistor radio stolen. And when
he went to the car park he found
his car had been taken too!

Anvil Monument

The anvil on which the world's
largest nugget, 'The Welcome
Stranger', was cut up on
9 February 1869, now stands on a
monument outside the tiny museum
at Dunolly (Vic.). Historians have
since bemoaned the fact that the
71 040-gram nugget was chopped
up into lumps. Tourists have had to
make do with gold-painted replicas.

Gold Boom Business

Concerned that the commercial
system of Melbourne would collapse
because every able-bodied man was
travelling to the Blue Mountains to
hunt for gold in 1851, a group of
businessmen hit on a novel idea to
bring them all back—they offered a
£200 reward to anyone finding gold
within 250 miles of Melbourne.
Within weeks, Melbourne was
thriving once again!

Good Information

Travelling with his horse and cart to the Walhalla gold-fields in Victoria, packer Peter Clement met two gold miners who were too tired to walk on to the local store. They offered him 'valuable information' in exchange for his sacks of flour. Agreeing to the deal, Clement was advised to buy shares in the Long Tunnel mine at Walhalla and he sank all his money into it. Within a few years he was one of the richest men in Australia for the mine turned out to be one of the most profitable in the country!

Odds Go Up

Eric Conolly, one of Australia's greatest punters, learned the hard way when, at the age of 15 in 1895, he decided he could break the bookies. He sold his pony to the local butcher for £8, borrowed another £8 and by the end of the day walked off the Flemington racecourse with winnings totalling £700.

He paid back the borrowed £8 and headed for the butcher with another eight to buy back his pony.

'No go,' said the butcher. 'I've heard what you've done to the bookies and I want more than £8 for the pony.' Connolly got the animal back for £10.

Cup Tie

Mr W. A. Blacker, a well-known South Australian racing man, used to wear a necktie made from the skin of a horse that once won the Melbourne Cup!

No Takers

Jockey Johnny Higgerson made himself an easy £50 at Windsor (NSW) in 1810. The money was handed to him before a race as a bribe to lose, but Johnny won. Holding the money up to the crowd afterwards he revealed its purpose then asked: 'Would the owner please step forward and claim it?'

Mug Punter

Two horses, Wheat Ear and Su Warrow, fell and Wheat Ear's jockey was killed during the running of the 1881 Melbourne Cup after a dog ran onto the track. The dog was owned by a punter who had backed both horses!

Fair Trial

Trevor Eyden was visiting a relative in the outback town of Cue (WA) in 1979 when he decided to try out the controls of his new metal detector in the caravan park. It 'beeped' over a stone, which turned out to be a 171 gram (5½ oz) nugget of solid gold!

Quick Chop

Shearer Jack Harvey of Queensland won a bet and earned himself a plate of Fast Food when, in the space of eight minutes, he sheared a sheep, killed it, sliced it up, cut out a nice chop, grilled and consumed it!

Memorable Day

When prospector Edward Hammond Hargraves discovered gold at Ophir (NSW) on 17 April 1851, he told his guide:

'This is a memorable day. I shall be a baronet, you will be knighted and my old horse will be stuffed, put into a glass case and sent to the British Museum!'

Sunset Rum

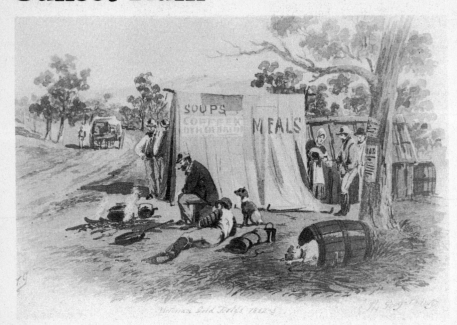

S. T. Gill Sly Grog Shanty

Although the gold-fields of Victoria were vastly overcrowded in the 1850s, a brew known as 'Sunset Rum' helped keep down the numbers. After drinking the concoction of methylated spirits, kerosene, Worcestershire sauce, ginger and sugar several prospectors wandered half crazed into the bush, never to be seen again!

Scratched

Punter W. T. Moore died after scratching a forehead pimple at the races near Singleton (NSW). Perspiration caused dye in his hat to run down into the scratch and he passed away the next morning from blood poisoning!

Small Wedding

During a wedding in Sydney, in November, 1946, guests stood on pews to watch the ceremony. The groom was well-known jockey A. Mulley.

Found His Quarry

Hearing that a schoolgirl had stubbed her toe on a gold nugget lying on a gravel road, 62-year-old pensioner Merv Webb of Wedderburn (Vic.) found out which quarry the gravel had come from, then ran his metal detector over other roads coated with stones from the quarry. He found a 9 oz (280 gram) nugget, his mate discovered a 4 oz nugget and his nephew turned up one weighing 2 oz!

Five-Legged Winner

Donald Duck the racehorse was born with five legs. The extra one was removed and Donald Duck went on to win a race at Ipswich (Qld) in the early 1940s.

Race Fight

After two jockeys crossed the finishing line in the A.J.C. Doncaster Handicap in 1869, each claimed he had won—the fight, not the horse race. During the running they had become involved in a wild argument, lashing at each other with fists and whips. Although one crossed the line first, the other third, they were both disqualified.

Number Up

Deciding to have a flutter in the state lottery, Mr Arthur Bielby of Norseman (WA) asked the Lottery Commission in 1951 if he could buy ticket no. 7598, his old Army number, but the request was refused because of the work that would be involved. The winning number drawn from the barrel was 7598.

Barrow Load

Wandering prospector Russian Jack became famous for the record load he carried on his wheelbarrow as he moved from gold-field to gold-field in the 1860s.

Making his way to Perth he carried a 22-litre drum of water, a bag of flour, baking powder, tinned meat, sugar, tea, clothes and mining equipment.

Then he picked up the loads of two distressed miners and when he met a sick man he popped him on the barrow, too!

Growth Industry

After spending 11 uncertain years on the gold-fields of Australia, Mr Chew Chong of China, found 'gold' of a different type—fungus!

Travelling to New Zealand's North Island he found that a fungus growing on decayed logs was similar to one used in China as a 'gourmet' food and medicine.

His exports to China between 1872 and 1882 were worth £75 000!

Miners' Clock

Every hour of the day, two animated figures move into life on the town hall clock at Stawell (Vic.). The gold prospectors, operating a gold-sifting cradle, are a reminder of the gold rush days of the mid 1800s and are believed to be the largest models on a clock in Australia.

Golden Goose

While cutting up a goose, Roy Stewart, a Warooka (SA) butcher found a gold nugget in the giblet bag. He bought dozens of others from the same source hoping to repeat the find but he never again found the goose that laid the golden egg!

THE STRANGEST TREASURE MAP IN HISTORY
A CIRCLE OF STONES near Dongarra, Australia, HAS HELD THE CLUE TO A BURIED TREASURE OF $30,400 IN DUTCH GUILDERS FOR 300 YEARS. THE MONEY WAS SALVAGED FROM THE DUTCH SHIP "GILT DRAGON" BY SURVIVORS OF ITS CREW, BUT THEY DIED WITHOUT RECLAIMING IT OR REVEALING THE SECRET OF THE STONE TREASURE MAP

Dragged to Win

Thrown from the leading horse, Hot Chestnut, 20 m from the finishing line at Kembla Grange (NSW) in 1973, jockey Ray Selkrig clung to the reins and was literally dragged the last few paces. After an hour-long inquiry he was awarded the win, stewards deciding the horse had carried its weight!

On the Spot

Butcher John Aggiss and his wife Francess were disappointed to find someone was hunting for gold nuggets with a metal detector in their favourite spot near Kalgoorlie (WA) in 1979. Returning to their car, Francess, who had inadvertently left her metal detector switched on, shrieked 'I've got a beep!'

They dug up a 4510 gram (145 oz) nugget!

Pool for Short

Poolparracooratharraminna was the name given to a racehorse after an Aboriginal tribe. Bookmakers who could not pronounce it called it Pool.

Cup Fly-in

It's a safe bet the mutton birds which migrate from Port Fairy (Vic.) to Siberia every year will return on the second Tuesday in November, Melbourne Cup Day!

Parting Gift

As a 'thank you' for giving him accommodation in 1951, a British sailor departing for London bought Mrs A. Tricker of Wellington (NZ) a lottery ticket in the name of 'Homeward Bound'.

It won her a first prize of £10 000 and she used it to go home, too, on a visit to her sister in England!

Like a Bad Penny

Surprised that a mean friend repaid a borrowed half crown, Syd Jones of Melbourne decided to keep it as a memento and punched his initials and the date on one side. Later, at a two-up school at a military camp at Broadmeadows in 1915, he went broke and was forced to play the coin, which he lost.

Two years later in England, at Wareham Camp, Syd was returning to his hut after losing again at two-up when he noticed a coin on the ground. To his astonishment he saw his initials and the date on his old half crown!

He returned to the game, used the long-lost memento to start a run of luck and collected £33!

Golden Secret

Convict James Daley produced a stone impregnated with gold and refused to tell the authorities where he had found it until threatened with the lash. Then he confessed that he had filed down a metal buckle and mixed the filings with particles of gold scraped from a guinea piece before baking them into clay. But some still wondered—had Daley made the story up to keep the whereabouts of a gold-bearing area to himself?

Clean Sweep

Winning all seven events at a race meeting is a rare achievement—but three Australian jockeys have done just that!

At the Elwick Racecourse, Hobart, in January, 1972, jockey Geoffrey Prouse took seven winners across the line. Charles Eaton had done the same at Cunnamulla (Qld) in 1961 and back in 1929 Bill Thomas had a clean sweep at Townsville.

WILLIAM THOMAS famed Australian jockey RODE THE WINNER IN ALL SEVEN RACES! Townsville, Queensland July 29.1929

Rough Justice

A storekeeper on the Victorian gold-fields of the 1850s never had any trouble with thieves after swift action with his axe. Seeing a hand creeping under his tent one night, he chopped it off and the next day nailed it to his counter beside a sign reading: 'Hands off!'

Crowning Shot

Stuart Donaldson (centre)—Australia's last duellist

The last duel to be fought in Australia, in 1851, could have changed the face of New South Wales politics if one of the participants, Sir Thomas Mitchell, Surveyor General, had been a better shot. For he challenged Stuart Donaldson, later to become New South Wales' first Prime Minister, after Donaldson complained of extravagance in Sir Thomas's department.

The duellists met in what is now Centennial Park but the only damage was to Donaldson's top hat which was hit by the last of three shots fired!

★★★★★★★★★★★★★★★★★★★★★★★★★★★★★★★★★★★★★★

False Boom

During a series of nickel strikes in Western Australia the stock exchange sensation of Poseidon was pegged in 1969, resulting in typists, cab drivers, doctors and professional punters pushing shares to more than $250 each within weeks. But in 1976, after losing millions of dollars, Poseidon was forced to go into receivership.

Flogged for Find

One of the first men to discover gold in Australia was a convict who picked up a nugget while on an outside working party in 1820. While other successful prospectors were rewarded or praised later, the unfortunate prisoner was flogged because it was thought he had stolen gold jewellery and melted it down to a nugget-sized lump!

Dizzy Pace

One of the most popular events for big bets at Windsor (NSW) in the 19th century was rolling people down a hill. The man who won the most money for his backers was a local Aborigine called 'Black Bobby' who tumbled head over heels for more than five minutes!

Paved with Gold

Dick Whittington missed out—it was the streets of Kalgoorlie (WA) not London, that were paved with gold!

Road builders used telluride for the pavements in the early days before miners caught on to the fact that the ore could contain gold. They considered the cost of digging up the roads and pavements to extract the gold would not be viable.

Welcome Speck

Arthur Deason, 42, grandson of John Deason, who discovered the world's biggest gold nugget, 'The Welcome Stranger', lives close to where the huge specimen was found, at Moliagul (Vic.).

'I've found gold, too', says Arthur. But his speck is so small he thinks it's the world's *tiniest* piece of gold!

Sitting On It

Jack Flett, curator of the tiny museum at Dunolly (Vic.), had a premonition in the 1970s that he would find a gold nugget just on the outskirts of town. Octogenarian Jack wandered into the bush and there, sitting on a pile of rubble, was a lump of gold washed clean by a recent rainfall!

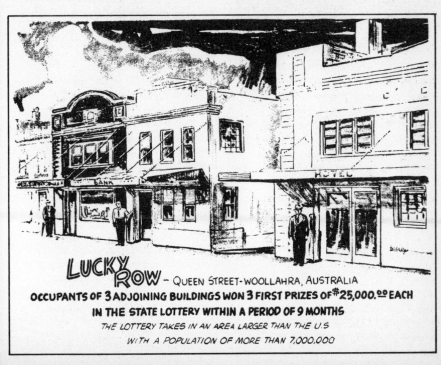

LUCKY ROW - QUEEN STREET-WOOLLAHRA, AUSTRALIA
OCCUPANTS OF 3 ADJOINING BUILDINGS WON 3 FIRST PRIZES OF $25,000.00 EACH IN THE STATE LOTTERY WITHIN A PERIOD OF 9 MONTHS
THE LOTTERY TAKES IN AN AREA LARGER THAN THE U.S WITH A POPULATION OF MORE THAN 7,000,000

Sticky Fingers

S. T. Gill Gold Buyer, Forest Creek

Unscrupulous gold buyers used novel methods to rob early prospectors of their fine gold. Among their tricks were rubbing a zinc pan with grease so that when gold was brought in for weighing many particles stuck; and growing their fingernails long in order to retain several grains while scooping the prospector's pile together!

Loser in the End

'Betting Billy' Tindall had such an uncanny horse-sense that he won a fortune at the race tracks. But when he died in 1953 it was said he did not leave enough assets to cover the cost of his funeral.

Bookie's Task

A Melbourne bookmaker was excused jury service in 1930 after he explained to a judge that he had to pay out £5000 to punters who had backed the wonder racehorse Phar Lap.

Pillar of Gold

Fossickers who removed a wooden pillar from a disused digging hole on a Bendigo gold-field in 1861 found a solid gold nugget measuring 12 inches by 6 inches—the exact shape of the pillar under which it lay!

Glittering Career

The first thing John Lemmone of Ballarat (Vic.) did when he gathered gold from a creek near his home was to buy a flute. It was the start of a glittering career, for Lemmone became a world-famous flautist.

Weighted Down

Eighty miners on board the steamer *Gothenberg* when it was wrecked off the coast of north Queensland in 1875 refused to take off their heavy money belts saying the gold they contained was their life's savings. They were all dragged to the bottom of the sea and drowned.

Black Trackers

When a horse called Leveller was stolen from his Queensland stable, owner Mr F. Hammond thought he would never see him again. But Aboriginal trackers said they would get him back and after following a misshapen hoofprint across wasteland for six days they found the horse and the thief.

Too Early

Two elated prospectors walked into Dalgety (NSW) in the mid 1850s loaded down with gold and claiming they had found the biggest nugget ever seen. They had marked the spot with a pick and shovel because it was too big for them to carry and asked for volunteers to go back with them the following day.

Meanwhile, they bought drinks all round. Then they bought more drinks all round, followed by more drinks all round. One of the prospectors died from the effects of the party and when his partner set out he couldn't find the pick and spade marking the nugget.

He searched for months and finally died of a broken heart.

Sticking Together

Three Melbourne policewomen known as 'The Inseparables' vowed in 1951 that whatever life's fortunes, they would stick together.

One by one they married and, remembering their vow, all decided to enter a raffle, believing they would bring each other luck. That raffle, in 1957, resulted in one of the women, Mrs Phyllis Robbins, winning a £1300 car.

The following year a second member of the trio, Mrs Jean Pawson also won a car. And in 1961 the third ex-policewoman, Mrs Nina Finlayson, won first prize in a competition and picked up £2000!

A TRIPLE DEAD HEAT

WAS RE-RUN IN NEW SOUTH WALES, AUSTRALIA

AND ENDED IN ANOTHER TRIPLE DEAD HEAT

THE HORSES WERE 'HIGH FLYER' - 'LOCH LOCHIE' AND 'BARDINI'   Moorefield, Sydney - Oct. 10, 1903

ELEVEN

Heroes

Meteors of Life

'See, the conquering hero
    comes!
Sound the trumpets, beat the
    drums!'
    ... Thomas Morell (1703–1784)

Where would we be without our
heroes and heroines? The course of
history would have been changed.

Generals have been rescued by
privates; presidents have been
saved by bodyguards; future
generations have been preserved
by the saving of husbands and
wives in disasters at sea, on land
and in the air.

The pages of history are steeped
with stories of outstanding
courage and endurance. But in
these modern times one does not
have to be a Florence Nightingale
or an Admiral Nelson to join the
list of heroes. For there are heroes
in sport among those who show
determination and courage without
always winning; heroes in business
among those who take enormous
gambles on the strength of their
convictions; heroes in every walk of
life who have the courage to maintain their beliefs against over-
whelming odds. There are even
animal heroes—dogs that have
alerted families to danger ... horses
which have galloped for miles at
the behest of their riders.

Heroes are our idols. In Australia
and New Zealand, two great
sporting nations, there are
gladiators on every oval, on every
pitch. Politicians who have
introduced great reforms have
become heroes of the people. The
courageous are all around us, as
the following stories portray. Some
are steeped in humour like the tale
of the brave dog that ran up and
bit the Minister for Police on the
leg; other stories make us shudder,
like that of the man who rode into
the sea on horseback and pulled a
swimmer from the jaws of a shark.

And there's the story of the
adventurer who determinedly drove
a sun-powered car across Australia
only to find he had to pay to
cross the Sydney Harbour Bridge.
It goes to show, perhaps, in
this section on heroes, that none
but the brave deserve the fare!

Pluck up courage, then, to meet the heroes of the Southern Hemisphere. Meet.

- The man who carried a pony on his shoulders.
- The pilot who saved a jumbo jet full of passengers.
- The gritty granny in navy boots.
- The one-armed pianist who played with a stick.
- The man who was shot 11 times—and lived!

Eight Sons Lost in War

Wangaratta (Vic.) residents Mr and Mrs Charles Handcock lost EIGHT sons during the First World War—a British Empire record—but the townspeople were determined the boys should be remembered.

As a result a marble clock was presented to the grief-stricken couple to commemorate their great loss. The clock is now on display at the North East Historical Society Museum, Wangaratta.

Flying Heroines

Amy Johnson

Although she had never flown more than 200 miles in a straight line, Amy Johnson achieved instant fame in 1930 when she became the first woman to fly solo from England to Australia, a flight which took 19½ days, earned her a CBE and won her a prize of £10 000. She was killed 11 years later on a short flight when her plane crashed into London's River Thames.

New Zealand's greatest woman aviator was Jane 'Jean' Batten, who

Jean Batten

achieved recognition in the early 1930s by flying an old Gypsy Moth from England to Sydney in 14 days 22½ hours, reducing Amy Johnson's record by more than four days!

In 1935 she became the first woman to fly in both directions between Australia and England and two years later, after a string of other records, she lowered the flying time between England and Australia to five days, 18 hours and 25 minutes.

Convict Makes Good

William Bede Dalley, son of a Dorset wool comber, was sentenced to life transportation for robbery. He later became Attorney-General of New South Wales, Acting Premier and, although he refused a knighthood, a Privy Councillor.

Saved for Another Day

Of the 122 people on board the wrecked ship *Dunbar* off Sydney in 1857 only James Johnson, a young seaman, survived. Nine years later, while employed at the Newcastle lighthouse, he helped rescue the only survivor of the steamer *Cawarra*.

Blind Vicar

Rev. C. M. Rogerson, Rector of Erskineville, Sydney, who lost his sight when a German shell splintered in World War I, prepared his sermons in Braille and greeted his parishioners by name when he toured the parish because he trained himself to recognise all their voices.

Crutches no Handicap

Bowler G. Hazleton, playing on crutches at a cricket match in Brisbane in 1918, took four wickets!

Sea Rescuer

Aided by her faithful horse, 16-year-old Grace Bussell of Busselton (WA) saved 48 people from the wrecked passenger steamer *Georgette*. For four hours she led the animal into the raging surf and then swam it back to shore with survivors clinging to the stirrups.

Shower Power

English migrant Michael Speed tried to destroy the myth that Poms never wash by staying under a shower for 8 days, 10 hours in 1977. The 35-year-old panel beater, living at Harbord (NSW) used a seat for some periods during his long shower and the water was kept lukewarm by a special boiler. He had hoped to clean up $10 000 for charity, but the public obviously washed their hands of the event, contributing only $1500.

14-year-old Designed Flag

Thirty-thousand people entered a competition organised by the Federal Government to design a flag for the nation in 1901. The joint winner, among all the experienced designers and artists, was Ivor Evans—aged fourteen!

THE **FLAG** OF AUSTRALIA WAS DESIGNED BY IVOR EVANS—— A 14-YEAR-OLD SCHOOLBOY—— WHOSE SUGGESTION WON OVER **30,000** COMPETITORS!

In the Know

from G. D. Giles Last stand made by the Boers

During the Boer War, the captain of a Queensland unit, rebuked by a senior British officer for allowing his men to call him by his Christian name and for telling them in advance about a planned attack, replied: 'I don't regard my men as private soldiers—they're my mates. And I want them to know why I'm asking them to risk their lives.'

Chasing Father

George Barnes, son of Eric Barnes, an Australian middleweight boxing champion, resolved to become the first son of a national champion to win a big title in his own right.

This followed taunts that he was the son of the great Eric—in boxing circles Eric was known as Frank Byrnes—and when George had his first fight, completely untrained, he was beaten.

Receiving coaching from his father, George avenged his defeat a few weeks later and went on to become welterweight champion of Australia in 1953.

After being knocked out for the first time in his career, in 1962, George retired to grow pineapples!

Iron Man

Fred Gallagher of Townsville (Qld) had such strong teeth that he could pull out 10-inch nails driven up to their heads in a beam. When disbelieving circus owner Tom Fitzgerald called to see the amazing man at work, Fred showed he could do more than pull nails out—and thumped a dozen into the beam with a handkerchief wrapped around his fist!

All in Family

A cricket team in the Goulburn (NSW) district in the late 1800s was made up entirely of the 13 Henderson brothers—11 players, a scorer and an umpire!

PATRICK HANNAN

WHO DISCOVERED THE KALGOORLIE GOLDFIELDS, IN AUSTRALIA, AND DIED PENNILESS ALTHOUGH HIS FIND YIELDED $600,000,000 IN GOLD, IS COMMEMORATED BY A MEMORIAL TO HIS GENEROSITY - *A FOUNTAIN DEPICTING HIM SHARING THE PRECIOUS CONTENTS OF HIS WATER BAG*

Over-oared

At the age of 63, Mr William Cluff rowed a boat along four Australian rivers. The journey, from the Queensland border to Narrandera (Vic.), taking in the Namoi, the Darling, the Murray and the Murrumbidgee, took three years!

Caveman

Bill Penman, aged 37, broke the record for the longest solo underground endurance test when he remained in a cave at Katherine in the Northern Territory for 64 days, 16 hours and 45 minutes in 1962.

Trapped in Mine

Hole-in-one at 91

A week before his 91st birthday, Cyril Winser walked out on to the golf course at Barwon Heads (Vic.) in 1975 and hit a hole-in-one at the 146 yard (133 m) 8th!

Man of Class

The longest serving teacher in Australia was Mr Christopher Carroll who maintained a continuous career of 55 years. He died in his classroom at Melbourne's St Thomas' Christian Brothers College.

After spending nine days trapped in a mine shaft by flash floods near Coolgardie (WA) in 1907, Modesto Varischetti, who had tapped messages to his rescuers through a pipe, was brought in a collapsed state to the surface, spent a few days in bed and went straight back to work!

Bodyline

During the great 'bodyline' bowling controversy in the early 1930s—when a batsman was left with little option but to defend his body or step away from the wicket—Australian Bill Woodfull was struck over the heart by a ball from Englishman Harold Larwood. Woodfull said afterwards: 'There are two teams out there—and only one of them is playing cricket!'

Battle of Britain Heroes

Of the 22 Australian pilots who took part in the 1940 Battle of Britain, 14 were killed, a 63 per cent death rate which exceeded pilot casualties from 13 other nations fighting with the Allies.

Quickest K.O.

Just 25 seconds after heavyweight boxer Billy Britt came out of his corner to face Herb Narvo at Newcastle (NSW) in 1943, he was lying unconscious, victim of the fastest knockout in an Australian title fight!

44 Off Over

During a picnic cricket match at Toowomba (Qld) in 1921, the umpire became so engrossed with the magnificent batting of Mr P. Barbour, a grammar school headmaster, that he inadvertently allowed nine balls in one over. Barbour used it to advantage, scoring 6 sixes, a four and 2 twos—a total of forty-four!

Grain of Truth

Captain James Kelly, who circumnavigated Tasmania in an open boat in 1815, was so large that when he made a bet that his trousers would hold five bushels of wheat he won—with room to spare!

Double Hat Trick

In a 1920s cricket match between Camden and Campbelltown NSW, bowler H. Longley took six wickets with six balls, two catches being taken by his 73-year-old father!

Cycle Star's Death

Russell Mockridge achieved fame as the most successful Australian cyclist in Commonwealth and Olympic Games even though his eyesight was poor—wearing glasses, he could see no further than 10 m!

After setting a variety of cycling records in Australia he won the Paris Open Grand Prix in 1953. As many feared, his death came in an accident during a race, when he ran into a car.

Mass Escape

Decapitated Japanese POWs who suicided at Cowra

The biggest prison camp break out in modern military history occurred at Cowra (NSW) when, at 2 a.m. on 5 August 1944, more than 900 Japanese prisoners of war used blankets and clothing to scale barbed wire fences.

More than 230 Japanese and four Australians died in the bid but no pictures, dramatic that they were, appeared in Australian newspapers at the time in case reprisals were taken against Australian prisoners in Japanese camps.

Heroine on $5 Note

Caroline Chisholm, who devoted her life to the improvement of conditions for immigrants to Australia until her death in 1877, is remembered by her portrait on the Australian $5 note!

Landed Two Planes

In September, 1940, Pilot Officer L. G. Fuller took off from Wagga Wagga (NSW) in a light training bomber—AND LANDED IN TWO!

During a practice flight his plane and another touched and became locked together, one on top of the other. Two men in the lower plane parachuted to safety, as did Fuller's observer, but Fuller remained at the controls and, with only his engines operating, brought both planes down.

Although they were badly damaged, he escaped injury!

Axes At Two Paces

An Australian wood-chopping champion who went to Paris on holiday became involved with a French lady, the result of which was a slap in the face by the woman's lover.

'Choose your weapon', challenged the Frenchman.

'Axes', said the Australian.

The duel was cancelled.

Turkish Uprising

Two drug-doped Turks who fired on a train of picnickers at Broken Hill (NSW) on New Year's Day, 1915, had managed to get the train to slow down by placing beside the railway line an ice cream cart from which flew the Turkish flag!

Flying Pieman

Pastry cook Billy King (1807–74) earned himself the name of 'The Flying Pieman' after he walked 1634 miles in 39 days, paced it out from Sydney to Parramatta and back (30 miles) for six consecutive days and fairly galloped the 33 miles from Campbelltown to Sydney in 8 hours 20 minutes carrying a 70 lb dog! He also carted a live goat weighing 80 lb over a distance of a mile and a half in 12 minutes.

The Kiss Off

During the 1978 Rugby League grand final in Sydney, schoolboy Brett Sheargold tried to break the world record held by a Californian youth by kissing 3225 girls. He didn't have many takers and was finally forced to kiss the idea goodbye.

Pedal Power

When Australia's Flying Doctor Service began operations in May, 1928, through the influence of Rev. John Flynn—'Flynn of the Inland'—radio contact was made by a transmitter and receiver maintained by pedal power!

Break Through

During an 1800s cricket match in northern Victoria, bowler W. Collins disposed of four men with one ball. The first was badly injured when his thumb snapped, a batsman fainted when he saw the injury, the other batsman said he wasn't going to face such a 'wild cat' and there was no partner for the last man!

Marvellous Milk

Five injured people lying beside their crumpled, burning car were in danger as the vehicle threatened to explode—until a passing truck driver put the flames out with milk!

Mr Chic Anderson was driving his 2300-gallon milk tanker on the Princes Highway near Bairnsdale (Vic.) when he was asked by a motorist if he had a fire extinguisher. Chic didn't—but went one better by turning the milk pump on the burning car, extinguishing the flames within minutes.

★★★★★★★★★★★★★★★

PLAYING BALL WITH THE ENEMY!

LANCE CORPORAL *LEONARD KEYSOR*
-FIRST BAT., AUSTRALIAN IMPERIAL FORCE

SINGLEHANDEDLY DEFENDED HIS TRENCH AND SAVED THE LIVES OF HIS COMRADES BY THROWING BACK LIVE TURKISH HAND GRENADES AND BOMBS FOR *50* HOURS

First Flight

The first man to become airborne in Australia was Lawrence Hargrave who, before his death in 1915, managed to elevate himself to a height of 16 ft at Stanwell Park (NSW)—using four large box kites!

Healthy Night

While working in a Melbourne food store in 1935, 20-year-old Arthur Venville was accidentally locked in a big freezer. Dressed only in a shirt and light trousers, he remained there for ELEVEN hours—yet when he was finally rescued he was in good health apart from a few goose bumps. The secret, he revealed, was running on the spot!

No Croc

His thigh in the grip of a huge crocodile's jaws as he was being dragged deeper into a New Guinea river, Kalipa, a native worker with a reputation for being the district strong man, picked the monster up and with it still hanging on to his leg carried it out of the river, up the beach and back to his village, where others came to his aid and killed it!

Moon Messages

Determined to obtain clear signals with fellow 'hams' in the Northern Hemisphere, amateur radio operator Ray Naughton worked out a method of bouncing his messages off the moon. Ray, of Birchip (Vic.), became the first amateur operator in the world to achieve this.

Man of Action

Up to his death in 1971, Frank Clune had been a paperboy, farmhand, seaman, gold-miner, ship's steward, salesman, opera singer, a United States cavalryman, an Australian soldier at Gallipoli and an accountant. Yet he still managed to publish more than FIFTY books on subjects including biography, geography and history!

On a Bender

Veteran diver Ted Louis of Hurstville, near Sydney, was examining a vintage bottle in the wreck of the 18th-century frigate *Pandora* off the east coast in 1977 when he was attacked by a large tiger shark. His only weapon was the bottle, which he used to prod the shark's nose.

Having got out of that difficulty 68-year-old Ted shot to the surface still clutching the bottle and promptly suffered the bends. He was rushed to hospital, where he recovered.

Crippled Hero

When a Brisbane woman and her young son fell into Breakfast Creek they were rescued by Willie Hopkirk, who plunged in, brought the struggling, drowning boy ashore, then returned to the water to save the mother. Willie was a cripple, aged eight!

1081 Good Turns

A team of Sydney scouts set a world record by helping 1081 old ladies across the road in five hours 30 minutes in 1976.

Fuzzywuzzy Angels

After heavy fighting against the Japanese around the Kokoda airstrip in Papua-New Guinea in July, 1942, wounded Australians were carried from the danger zone by native carriers endearingly referred to as 'Fuzzywuzzy Angels'!

No Retirement

Writer Dame Mary Gilmore believed in working to the very end—her final book, *Fourteen-Men* was published on her EIGHTY-NINTH birthday and at the age of NINETY-SEVEN she was still sending articles to the communist newspaper the *Tribune*.

Back in Form

The power of Tuhoto Ariki, a famous, elderly Maori sorcerer was beginning to wane until 1886 when he was buried by rubble during an eruption of Mount Tarawera and dug out alive four days later. Business then boomed!

Stool Pigeons

During a Rugby League match between two public service teams in Sydney in 1950 a player kicked wide of the uprights but a flock of pigeons flying past deflected the ball through the goal and the referee allowed it!

New Zealand Cross

On of the rarest awards for bravery in the world is the New Zealand Cross, created in 1869 for members of the Militia, armed constabulary and volunteers who had served in the Maori Wars. Struck in silver with a gold crown, only 23 medals were awarded before the Militia was disbanded in 1911.

Potent Protest

Production of a new anti-venom serum against bites from the deadly Funnel Web Spider was held up in Melbourne in 1981 after Dr Struan Sutherland, who developed the potion, was suspended for seven weeks for throwing paper clips at a superior and tipping a bowl of pins over his head.

Great Sculler

Because he had a withered hand, Mervyn Wood had to adopt an unusual style of rowing yet he represented Australia in the Olympic Games four times, winning gold in the single skulls in London in 1948! At home, he held the national skulling title for seven consecutive years and after losing it he retrieved the championship in 1958 at the age of forty-one.

Off Course

Searching for a continent rich in slaves and gold, as painted in a Peruvian legend, Portuguese explorer Pedro Fernandes de Quiros stepped onto a sandy shore after a long sea journey and declared that he had found the elusive Terra Australis. In fact, he had landed in the New Hebrides, now Vanuatu.

Footsore Martyr

To protect his feet while sinking post holes, part of his punishment in Australia for trying to form an illegal trade union in England, James Brine, one of the famous Tolpuddle Martyrs, tied rusty horseshoes under his heels.

Burning with Rage

After rescuing an old man from a house fire and returning into the flames to lead others to safety, a Melbourne motorist found he had been booked for parking on a clearway!

Golden Reception

When opera singer Nellie Melba made a triumphant return to Australia in 1902 and announced she would visit Lilydale (Vic.) where her father operated limestone quarries, the editor of the local paper was so delighted that he printed his paper in gold on blue paper!

Flag Carrier

The Dutch flag was planted on what is now Tasmanian soil by Abel Tasman's carpenter who volunteered to swim through raging surf after his vessel failed to find a safe landing spot in December 1642.

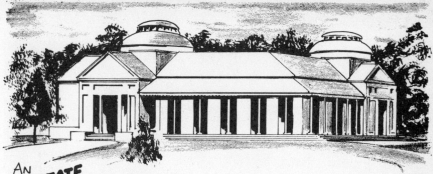

AN **ESTATE** OF 190 ACRES IN WHAT IS NOW THE CITY OF SYDNEY, AUSTRALIA, WAS GRANTED IN 1815 TO CAPT. JOHN PIPER BY THE GOVERNOR BECAUSE *HE WAS GALLANT ENOUGH TO LEAVE THE BEACH WHEN HE FOUND THAT THE GOVERNOR'S WIFE WAS BATHING THERE*

Lucky Horseshoe

A horseshoe, struck by the back wheel of Ned Hayfield's bicycle as he rode along a country lane near Brisbane in the early 1920s, flipped up and landed on his handlebars. A mile further on, confronted by a huge black snake which took up the whole lane, Ned threw the horseshoe, hit the reptile on the head and killed it!

Tired of Doing Nothing

After Wolfgang Kreuzer set a world record for sitting still and doing absolutely nothing for seven hours and two minutes following months of training on the park benches of Sydney, he was so tired he went straight home to bed for a rest!

★★★★★★★★★★★★★★

Warm Walker

When four-year-old Queenslander Nichol Frousheger wandered from his home near Charleville he wasn't expected to be found alive after the first cold night. He was found on the sixth day 90 miles away—and still going strong!

Uncoached Runner

Driving the mail coach between Collarenebri (NSW) and Moggill (Qld) Mr H. Hanson realised smoke was coming from underneath. As the coach proceeded, he stood up for a better look, overbalanced and fell over the dashboard, two wheels passing over him. Although the horses galloped on, Hanson picked himself up, dusted himself off, ran after the coach, caught it and brought it in to Moggill!

Great Grain Race

Carrying a 63.5 kg sack of wheat on his shoulders, Mr Greg Dax, 20, from Donald (Vic.), ran 1 km to the top of Mount Wycheproof in 6 min 15 sec to claim the $1250 prize in a sponsored race. Wycheproof, 43 m high, is the world's SMALLEST mountain!

Goose Chase

When Prince George, later King George, and Prince Albert were guests at a picnic at Botany Bay during their visit to Australia in 1881 a stray dog made off with the centrepiece, a fattened, stuffed goose. The two young Princes, with a little help from their friends, gave chase and retrieved the bird, making sure they cut out the bite marks!

Left it to Cook

Australia would have come under French rule if Louis Antoine de Bougainville, who came to the Pacific in 1678, had managed to find a route through the coral reefs off what is now Queensland. But he decided it was an impossible task and it was left to Captain James Cook to find a way almost a century later.

Backwards to Fame

Pie-maker Vince Lester went to his local football club in the Queensland town of Clermont to ask them to pay up for all the pies they had ordered from him. When he discovered the club was broke Vince walked backwards for 20 km to raise money through sponsorships and, accompanied by the school band at the end of the walk, was such a hero that he was elected to the State Parliament!

Picked Wrong Woman

Freeing herself from the wheel of a dray to which a gang of bushrangers had tied her in 1840 in order to steal £60 from her, Isabella Kelly, known as the 'Iron Woman' of New South Wales' Manning River district, chased after the robbers with a pistol, shot one in the shoulder after a five mile chase and forced the others at gunpoint to hand over all the money they had in their possession!

Too Early

When Mr Charles Goodwin, who migrated to Australia after World War II following service on minesweepers, returned to his home town in England he found his name deeply etched on a memorial to those killed in the war!

Little Perisher

At the end of the Perisher Cup skiing competition at New South Wales' Perisher Valley in 1962 the winner, who beat the leader of the men's section by one second, stepped forward shyly to be congratulated—eight-year-old Glenda McGregor!

Snake Charmer

Bernice Koppler, who nearly fainted when a snake hissed at her while she was picking blackberries in Scotland, won a series of beauty contests on arrival in Australia in 1951. Her picture was spotted by the owner of an Adelaide zoo and she was given the job of washing 20 pythons daily in a pool!

Can't Keep a Secret

Mrs Petrov and Soviet officials

A 15-year-old Melbourne high school student was visited by two agents from the Australian Security Intelligence Organisation following an essay he wrote in September, 1982, about the defection of Russian diplomat Vladimir Petrov in 1954. The boy had written to a government office in Canberra and was supplied with secret information. His essay was confiscated then returned with large sections removed.

Simpson and the Donkey

Every day Private Simpson ate his breakfast amongst the other Australian soldiers at Gallipoli then led his donkey between the beach and the firing line carrying wounded men to safety. On 19 May for the first time, his breakfast wasn't ready and he told the cook he would have a good feed when he came back. HE NEVER RETURNED. A statue of Simpson and his donkey now stands at the Shrine of Remembrance in Melbourne.

Tinned Snake

Confronted by a snake when returning home from a shopping expedition, Mrs L. Stephens of Beaufort (Vic.) stunned it with a tin of fish!

Sign Language

A certain man wandered the streets of Melbourne wearing a sandwich board proclaiming a message to one and all. 'Jesus is Coming and Boy, is He—Off!' said the sign. 'Cast that aside', was a traffic officer's response, or words to that effect. But David McKay remained steadfast and verily he was booked for displaying an indecent word.

McKay bore witness in court that he used the offensive word to reach young people. Magistrate Brian Clothier felt the word was odd and strange when used in a religious context but felt it was not indecent. And lo, McKay walked free and that night there was much rejoicing and merriment in the house of a friend.

Plucky Peta

Peta Lynn Mann was only 12 when she jumped from her boat into a swamp in 1981 to help her ranger friend Hilton Graham whose arm had been grabbed by a crocodile. She siezed Hilton's other arm and tugged until the crocodile let go. As she helped him up the bank the crocodile attacked again and once more she pulled her friend free.

Finally she helped the badly bleeding Hilton into his car and drove him 30 miles to get assistance. The Royal Humane Society later presented her with a gold medal. Said Peta: 'Hilton is my friend and I love him very much. I wasn't going to let him die.'

Australian Crawl

With his hands and knees padded with foam, Kevin Tyerman, 19, of Coonamble (NSW) crawled 22.4 km for a bet!

Fighting Parson

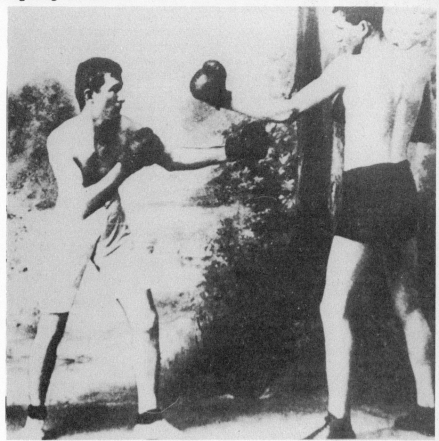

The small English parson who arrived at a camp in the outback near Longreach (Qld) was a figure of fun for the big tough navvies who worked there—until the Rev. Frederick Sams opened his black bag, pulled out two pairs of boxing gloves, fitted on one pair and looked for a challenger. He became known as the fighting parson but it was the fight against the enemy in France in July 1915, that finally killed him.

Light Relief

Five Army paratroopers lifted up in a helicopter for practice near Perth had to jump out, like it or not, when the chopper developed engine trouble. As soon as they left, the aircraft recovered!

Play It Again, Dave

After playing the piano for 22 hours a day over a period of seven weeks to break the world record in 1982, David Scott, 37, was horrified to hear the crowd at the Wagga Leagues Club (NSW) shout for an encore!

Chinese Morrison

Fixing a false pigtail inside his hat and dressing like a Chinese, Australian doctor George Morrison travelled across China from Shanghai to the Burmese border in 1894 and, being widely accepted as a local, avoided the high prices usually charged to European travellers. The journey took 100 days, cost him £20 and earned him the title of Chinese Morrison.

Heroic Career

When Roden Cutler, who was to be knighted and become Governor of New South Wales, swam through the Sydney surf at the age of 18 to help a mate during a shark attack, he began a career of great heroism.

While serving as an artillery lieutenant in Syria during World War II, he leapt from his trench and raced towards three enemy machine gun emplacements. Two crews surrendered when he jumped into their posts and he knocked out a third with a grenade before returning with eight prisoners.

After this deed, for which he was awarded the Victoria Cross, he was involved in another battle in which he was badly wounded.

He later enjoyed a distinguished diplomatic career.

Tasman's Circle

Dutchman Abel Janszoon Tasman was the first man to circumnavigate Australia—but due to his wide course the only parts he saw were the west, the south and Van Diemen's Land (Tasmania).

Aerial Funeral

After Prime Minister John Curtin died in July, 1945, he was given an aerial funeral.

Parliamentary colleagues travelled in two DC 3 planes to Western Australia following the plane carrying Curtin's body which, as it passed over Parliament House, dipped low in a final salute.

Lost Ball

During an Australian Rules football match at Brighton (Vic.) in the early 1920s, Arthur Hando, who later played for the South Melbourne league, produced a mighty kick which sent the ball high out of the ground and straight in through the open window of a passing railway carriage. It was never returned, despite frequent checks with the Lost Property Office!

Life-saver

Lying seriously ill in bed, 70-year-old Otto Starick of Gosnells (WA) wrote a note asking for help, attached it to his dog's collar and whispered the name of a neighbour who always gave the dog biscuits.

The dog ran two miles through the bush to the neighbour and Mr Starick's life was saved!

Police have Seizure over Painting

Six months after the magazine *Art in Australia* brought out a special edition containing etchings and drawings by Norman Lindsay, police seized the plates, claiming that the works were obscene. The main cause for concern was a picture of a gentleman nervously putting his hand inside a lady's dress to fondle her ample bosom. And the lady appeared to be enjoying it!

Diplomatic Poser

Lillian Gasinskaya escaped to the West in January 1979 from the Russian cruise ship she had been working on by crawling through a porthole in a red bikini and swimming to a wharf in Sydney Harbour. Her English was very limited but she did manage to say 'I want to be a model'. Within a few months she had given up bikinis. In fact she had given up clothes altogether to pose for a girlie magazine.

Daylight Bathing

In the interests of decency, daylight surf bathing was banned in most parts of Australia at the turn of the century until a Manly newspaper editor defied the law and bathed publicly at midday on three successive Sundays. After a long talk with the police, he made his point and from then on bathers were not obliged to leave the water at 8 a.m.

Hello Sunshine

After travelling 3000 miles across Australia from Perth in a car powered by sunlight, adventurer Hans Tholstrup reached Sydney and was asked to hand over his first and only travelling expense—20 cents to the tollkeeper on the Sydney Harbour Bridge!

Extra Passenger

When their passenger ship, the *White Squall*, was wrecked on rocks after leaving Port Phillip for Sydney in 1851, the eight members of the Keyes family—father, mother and six children—headed in a lifeboat for a lighthouse on an island. When they put ashore there were NINE members, Mrs Keyes having given birth to another child in the boat! The new-born baby was fed goat's milk until help arrived!

Discernment

While Victoria's former Minister for Police, Mr Lindsay Thompson, was opening the annual 'peace keeping' road blitz in Melbourne an angry dog ran up and bit him on the leg!

Horse v. Shark

Printer George Pritchard pulled a man from a shark's jaws off Hobson's Bay—ON HORSEBACK!

Hearing the shouts of the victim as he rode along the beach, Pritchard rode into the surf and grabbed the man from the shark and brought him to shore.

Despite his bizarre rescue, in the mid 1800s, the injured man died, but the shark was later captured by men using the side of a pig as bait.

Gloom City

Actor John Barrymore, arrested in Melbourne in 1906 for being drunk, complained the city was the only place on earth where it was a crime to be happy!

Fat Cricketer's Game

Australian Rules football, which regularly attracts over 100 000 spectators to big games in Victoria, began in 1858 after Mr Tom Wills suggested that cricketers who were 'inclined to become stout from having their joints encased in useless, super-abundant flesh' should do something to occupy themselves in the winter months!

Battered Businessman

One of Sydney's best known businessmen in the 1940s, Mr Norman MacDonald, had 11 bullet holes in his body, five graze marks on his head and a wound caused by an iron bar—injuries received on separate occasions when trying to help others in trouble.

After forcing his paralysed legs to move during one hospital stint, he was produced as a star exhibit at a national surgeons' conference in Sydney!

Moody Blues

Flying over the Indian Ocean *en route* to Australia in 1982, a British jumbo jet suddenly lost power when ALL FOUR ENGINES FAILED! It had flown into a cloud of volcanic ash which clogged the engines and for 13 minutes, as New Zealand and Australian passengers hugged their loved ones, the aircraft was on a death glide! Then, miraculously, the flight crew managed to restart the engines and pull the plane out of danger!

On the aircraft was Mrs Billie Walker, whose maiden name was Moody—the same as the captain. When she was transferred to another flight later she learned that the pilot was called Walker!

Once Too Often

Billy Hughes, Prime Minister of Australia during World War I, decided to 'settle' and enter politics after his 150th appearance as an extra in the cast of *Henry V*, making his entry on stage at the cue: 'Once more unto the breach, Dear Friends!'

Short War

Frank Crozier The Beach at Anzac

The first Australian legislator to enlist for World War I was Lieut-Col George Braund who became the second man to die on duty! A little deaf, he did not hear a sentry's challenge when returning to brigade headquarters at Gallipoli AND WAS SHOT DEAD!

Horse Trial

Charles Campbell, a Scottish settler in South Australia, claimed he was one of the fastest and strongest men to migrate from England. To prove it, he ran against a male challenger and carried a small pony on his shoulders! HE WON!

Birthday Suits

To celebrate the state of Western Australia's 150th birthday in 1979, freelance photographer Fiona Girvan-Brown stripped and took a photo of 150 male volunteers in their birthday suits!

Slipway

At the end of an incident-free voyage over 1450 km in the Great Circle Yacht Race, crewman John Taylor slipped and fell overboard while being taken to Flinders (Vic.) pier by coastguard boat!

The Perfect Buyer

Leading 19th-century politician William Charles Wentworth, in purchasing the estate on which his one time home 'Vaucluse House' stands and discovering he had paid too cheap a price for it, insisted on paying extra—far above the agreed amount!

Have Shawl, Will Travel

Famous Australian explorer, Robert O'Hara Burke—a member of the Burke and Wills team who perished on a journey of exploration to the country's interior—had a devoted childhood nurse, elderly Ellen Doherty. As she could not 'die happy without seeing him again' she saved enough from her meagre earnings to follow him to Australia from England, but arrived too late. He had already set off on that fated expedition!

Public sympathy was so aroused by Ellen's story and the exhibition of her devotion that the Government of Victoria undertook her support for the remaining years of her life.

Keg of Cheer

On the way to his son's wedding in 1951, Mr Peter Roper spotted a barnacle-encrusted keg of beer lying in the mud at Moreton Bay, where it had lain submerged by water after falling from a jetty. The keg was retrieved. The reception was deemed a great success.

Time for Bath

For three years in a row in the 1940s, Queensland farmers were blessed with much needed rain when Divisional Meteorologist Richards took his holidays and his deputy, MR BATH took over!

CLARA CROSBIE

A GIRL 12 YEARS OF AGE, WAS LOST IN THE AUSTRALIAN WILDERNESS, NEAR LILYDALE, FOR 20 DAYS IN THE MIDDLE OF WINTER WITHOUT FOOD OR SHELTER —YET SUFFERED NO ILL EFFECTS FROM EITHER EXPOSURE OR HER FAST

Deadline Headline

Phar Lap was so famous that when the great racehorse died in the United States newspaper headlines in Australia simply said: 'HE'S DEAD!'

Using his Loaf

When the ferry steamer *Pearl* sank in the Brisbane River in 1896, Charley Briggs jumped overboard with an umbrella and the loaf of bread he was taking home for supper in a bag. Treading water, he opened the umbrella, turned it upside down, put the bag in it and 'floated' it downstream for a quarter of a mile until he was rescued. The bread remained perfectly dry.

Parachuting Upwards

Instead of drifting down to earth during rehearsals for a colourful sky drop for the opening of the 1982 Commonwealth Games in Brisbane, parachutist Rick Collins went up, up and away. Caught in a freak updraught he rose from 6000 ft to 12 500 ft and, still rising, cut himself free from his main 'chute. He was then tossed around in a thunder cloud and battered by hailstones 'as big as cricket balls'. After free falling down to 1500 ft he opened his reserve 'chute and landed five miles from his target!

Nellie's Walkabout

Although in her eighties, Nellie Flynn of Rum Jungle, near Darwin, never missed the annual 15½ mile walkabout, one year finishing the race at an average speed of 3 mph.

Kindly Canon

The kind deeds of Canon Begbie of Willoughby, Sydney, earned him the nickname 'The Considerate Canon'. One wet Sunday in 1930 he placed his car and his son as chauffeur at the disposal of his congregation. It took 22 trips before the entire flock were all home and dry!

Hairy Hide

The only man known to have escaped with his money after being held up by bushranger Ben Hall was a local Forbes (NSW) personality known as Red Jack. Having been stripped and searched by the outlaw, the farmer was allowed to dress and continue his journey to town where he pulled his purse out from under his bushy red beard!

Paste with Taste

While Mr Andrew Peacock, Australia's former Minister for Foreign Affairs, was escorting American actress Shirley McLaine, she revealed he was the only man she knew who used a Gucci toothbrush, adding: 'I'll give him a Foreign Affair he won't forget!'

Sticky Finger

Despite losing his right hand in a gun accident in 1918, 15-year-old pianist Roger Cavanagh continued to play the piano at local dances in Queensland, playing bass with his left hand and picking out the melody with a stick tied to his right forearm!

Well Placed

A Japanese officer, Lieut-Gen. Fukuye, who gave orders to kill two Australians and two British soldiers, was later executed by firing squad on the EXACT SPOT on Changi Beach, Singapore, where the deaths occurred!

One-Legged Golf

John Zoch of Melbourne plays better golf at 55 than most do at twenty-five. His handicap is having only one leg. He doesn't use crutches or an artificial limb and, steadying himself on his one leg, can hit the ball 200 m.

Final Order

The last message sent out by Commander Hay of HMS *Harrier* was a recommendation that a seaman on his ship, Sam Mitchell, should receive an award for bravery. For Hay sent his message as he lay dying after Mitchell had carried him mortally wounded from a battle area at Tauranga (NZ) in 1864. Mitchell became the first Australian to receive the Victoria Cross.

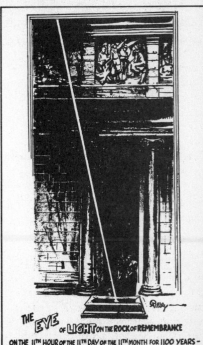

THE **EYE** OF LIGHT ON THE ROCK OF REMEMBRANCE
ON THE 11TH HOUR OF THE 11TH DAY OF THE 11TH MONTH FOR 1100 YEARS—
A SHAFT OF LIGHT WILL CROSS THE CENTER OF THE AUSTRALIAN
WAR MEMORIAL IN MELBOURNE

Lost Heroine

When the two sons and the seven-year-old daughter of a Goroke (Vic.) station worker became lost in wild bush country in 1864, Isaac (aged nine) and Frank (four) were kept alive through the freezing nights by young Jane who used most of her clothing to protect her brothers.

The Duff children were found nine days later and Jane's courage became a household tale.

Quick Cook

The world's fastest Chinese food cook is Australian Ron Coe who, on 5 July 1980, cooked five dishes—steak in black bean sauce, sweet and sour fish, garlic prawns, lemon chicken and Cantonese beef—in 5 min 40 sec!

Practical Reward

As a reward for playing his 300th game for the Perth football team of Melville in 1981, amateur footballer Len Glamuzina was treated by his club to an all-expenses-paid stay in hospital to have his nose, battered during matches, reshaped!

Holes-in-One

When Mr W.P. Ralph hit a hole-in-one at Auckland's Remuera Golf Club in the late 1940s, he set up an amazing family record—his mother, father and brother had also achieved the same golfer's dream!

One-Armed Hero

While being interviewed by reporters about his dramatic rescue of three men from pounding seas near Sydney the day before, Basil Amm, who had the use of only one arm, dashed back into the sea to save a girl being carried out by a treacherous undercurrent!

Rider in the Sky

When James Skulthorpe, one of Australia's greatest horsemen, died in 1958, he took some mementoes with him. Buried with him at the foot of the Blue Mountains were a small silver horse, a bullock bell—and his stock whip!

Fastest Barber

The fastest barber in the West, the Southern Hemisphere and the world is Mr Albert di Lallo of Midland (WA) who, in June, 1978, cut, set and styled hair at an amazing pace over a period of 256 hours, 35 minutes!

Bogus Review

Famed Australian novelist Marcus Clarke entered the realms of freelancing and writing books after being sacked from a Melbourne newspaper in the late 1860s for handing in a review of a theatre show he never attended. He didn't know the performance had been cancelled!

Milkmaid's Hands

Eileen Joyce aged thirteen

Famous Australian pianist Eileen Joyce rejected all hand creams and lotions, believing the best thing was to exercise her fingers milking cows!

Heart Starter

Riding his bicycle to a school sports meeting at Coffs Harbour (NSW) in 1982, 14-year-old Neil Scobie was struck by lightning. His teacher, who spotted the boy's predicament, felt his heart and found that it had stopped. He got the heart started after mouth-to-mouth resuscitation but Neil 'died' twice before he revived.

Tom's Tenacious Teeth

Nineteen-year-old Eviline Carmichael was rescued from wild seas by Tom Pearce, also 19, who swam through the surf to her aid and seized her dress with his teeth!

The youngsters were the only survivors of the clipper ship *Loch Ard* which went down with 15 passengers and 35 crew at Cape Moonlight (Vic.), in 1878.

Tom was washed ashore into a small opening in the rocks and as he lay gasping he heard faint cries from the sinking vessel. Swimming back to the ship, he found Eviline, whose parents, brother and three sisters had drowned, clinging to a mast.

After using his teeth to drag her ashore he became a national hero and a waxworks figure was made of him. Would he marry the girl he rescued? everyone wanted to know. Alas, it was not to be. Eviline sailed away on another vessel.

★★★★★★★★★★★★★★★★★★★★★★★★★★★★★★★★★★★★★★

Flaming Taxi

Finding the back seat of his car ablaze in 1953, a Newcastle (NSW) taxi driver stepped on the accelerator and drove half a mile to the fire brigade headquarters, delivering the outbreak onto their doorstep! They saved his cab.

Great Boxing Record

Jim Sharman, one of 13 children born on a New South Wales dairy farm in the 19th century, became a lightweight boxer who recorded 83 knockout victories in 84 fights, losing the other on a foul. He became the successful owner of a boxing tent show.

Two Outers

During action in Europe in the First World War, Private Jack Hagan of the 16th Battallion decided to put an enemy sniper out of action and, despite attempts to stop him, crawled into no man's land.

After a shot was heard he returned to the trench with a missing left ear lobe. Shortly afterwards, Jack tried again, returning this time with a hole in his helmet and a missing right ear lobe.

He decided against a third effort, saying the next shot might strike home in the middle!

Gritty Granny

A New Zealand great-grandmother, Mrs Kitty O'Sullivan, setting out to walk the 667 miles from Brisbane to Sydney in size 7½ US Navy boots, said her next adventure would be a visit to the United States to challenge grandmothers to a head-standing competition.

Loser Wins

Losing his line and tackle landing a crocodile on the banks of Queensland's Lower Tully River, Mr N. Dixon opened the creature up and found a neatly folded £1 savings certificate in the stomach. He used it to buy new fishing equipment!

Biting Remark

As he was about to be hanged in Rabaul for war crimes against Australian, British and Indian prisoners, a Japanese officer shouted 'Long Live the Emperor' and sank his teeth into the hangman's hand, causing it to bleed profusely!

Sign Him Up!

When Arthur Gilligan, skipper of the England cricket X1, took risks and hammered up 138 in a match against Western Australia in 1924, he was dropped no fewer than six times. But when he slammed a ball over the fence into the crowd, a 12-year-old boy jumped up and caught the ball WITH ONE HAND!

Double Winner

E. W. Cole

During public debate on the issue of Australian Federation, Mr E. W. Cole, a colourful Melbourne character, offered £100 for the best essay in favour of Federation and a similar prize for a work opposing it. James Edmond, an associate editor on the *Bulletin* magazine, entered both using his own name and a pseudonym—and was successful in both! But he received only one of the prizes, Cole claiming Edmond had behaved against the spirit of the competition.

Crime Fighter

Hugh Buggy (left) and Stanley Bruce

Ace crime reporter Hugh Buggy, who covered scores of murder investigations in the 1940s and 1950s and helped police with new theories, was asked by a Victorian police commissioner to give up journalism and join the Melbourne Criminal Investigation Bureau!

Villains Misfire

In an attempt to persuade Rev. John Garvan to hand over his cash after breaking into his house in New South Wales in 1841, bushrangers Henry Stede and Charles Vaut forced his wife to sit on a log fire. Before she went up in smoke the clergyman charged at the robbers, pulled his singed wife free and struggled with their attackers until visitors turned up. Vaut and Stede fled but were caught by police and sentenced for life.

No Voters

During elections in South Australia in the early 1900s Police Inspector John Kelly of Blinman received an urgent message that the keys of the polling booth at Sliding Rock had been sent to Blinman by mistake.

Inspector Kelly set off with the keys into a blinding storm across 40 miles of country he hardly knew. Arriving battered, bruised and bleeding at 6 a.m. the following day, he opened the polling booth—but not a single person came to vote!

Lifeboat Hero

Chief Officer Edward Condon helped crew members into the lifeboat of the sinking ship *Lake Illawarra* after it collided with the pylons of the Tasman Bridge at Hobart (Tas.) in 1975.

However, the lifeboat wouldn't release and Condon went under the water with the ship, wondering how the men in the lifeboat would fare. When he swam to the surface he saw that the boat had inexplicably freed itself at the last minute! The men in the boat hauled him aboard.

Saved by Lace

A shoe-lace saved the life of 18-year-old Brian Steele, chopping logs alone in the bush in Western Australia.

When part of the axe splintered and severed an artery in his thigh, Brian managed to pull a string from his boot and tie a tourniquet before he passed out. He was found two hours later and rushed to hospital. Doctors said he would have died had he not used the shoe-lace.

Gordon's Leap

Poet Adam Lindsay Gordon, a morose fellow, galloped his horse at a high guard fence beyond which was a tiny area of land before a 350 ft drop on to jagged rocks around the Blue Lake, Mount Gambier. Some said it was a bizarre suicide attempt, but his horse refused to participate. At the height of the jump, the animal turned sideways, landing parallel to the fence, thereby saving its rider's life and its own!

Ill Omen

When penniless writer Adam Lindsay Gordon met a group of broke writers at Melbourne's Yorick Club in the 1860s, he could not help noticing the skull with a pipe between its teeth sitting on the club hat rack. The following day HE COMMITTED SUICIDE.

From Gumboots to Glory

In May 1983 Cliff Young, a 61-year-old potato farmer who musters cattle on his rugged Otway Ranges (Vic.) farm in gumboots, became Australia's newest hero as he stormed home in the Sydney-Melbourne marathon, a gruelling distance of 875 km.

Battling headwinds, driving rain, badly lit roads, a dislocated shoulder, blistered feet and only 15 hours sleep in five days, Cliff complained only of the waving to the crowds that lined the roads, claiming it was the most tiring aspect of the race!

Wearing plastic trousers to protect himself against skin cancer, Cliff ate tinned spaghetti throughout the five day 15 hour spectacle. Averaging 10 kph, he arrived way ahead of schedule at Doncaster, slicing 42 hours off the previous record and finishing 50 km (or two days) ahead of his nearest competitor. Winning the hearts of all Australians, this amazing long-distance runner divided his well-earned prize of $10 000 between the other competitors and members of the back-up team.

After standing ovations on national television shows; being asked to do a lap of honour at Victoria's most salubrious sporting event, the VFL Grand Final; having a song ('From Gumboots to Glory') written about him, and receiving a civic reception in Melbourne's City Square which 8000 fans attended it was back to the farm for Cliff where he donned his gumboots to begin training for his next race—the 1000 km world record!

Cliff started running at the age of 57 ... beginning with the occasional round trip of 80 km to Colac JUST TO GET HIS HAIR CUT!!!

TWELVE

Victims
Death and Destruction

We are all victims. Victims of circumstance and fate. We can suffer at any moment from the actions of a person or forces beyond our control. We are victims of storms and heatwaves, victims of disease—even when we catch the common cold we become victims of bacteria we cannot even see.

Soldiers go to war and become victims of the enemy. The troops even sang to victims during the 1914–1918 war, one of their favourites being:

> She was poor but she was
> honest,
> Victim of the squire's whim:
> First he loved her, then he left
> her,
> And she lost her honest name.

Many believe they are masters of their own fate. But is that really so? No matter how carefully we tread, can we really dictate our destiny? Sometimes the very things we see can turn us into victims of fear, like the small New Zealand boy who had been raised on a lighthouse and screamed with terror

when he sighted his first train on the mainland.

In this chapter you will meet scores of victims of the elements, of deceit, of fate, accidents and freaks of birth. Freaks of birth? In Wanganui, New Zealand, a man died as a result of being born with an extra rib!

But there are others who are examples of how little control we have over destiny or, in fact, what can happen in a matter of seconds. Take the lady who was walking through Sydney when suddenly her hair burst into flames! Or the spectator at an old gentlemen's bowls match who was knocked unconscious when a ball flew into the air and landed on his head!

They say we 'live and learn'. But how can we learn about fate, except to acknowledge that it is there? We cannot avoid it as the following stories will portray.

Let us look, then, at:

> The death tractor with a mind
> of its own.
> The man who was knocked

down by a train after he spent a lifetime avoiding travelling on them as he feared they would be the death of him!

The cricketer who was stabbed to death by a flying stump.

The fatal game of ping-pong.

The groom who had to get married in his pyjamas.

The girl who ate her hair.

Fool's Duel

Victoria's first duel, a challenge between argumentative New Year revellers Peter Snodgrass and William Ryrie, came to a sudden end in 1840 when, lifting his pistol to fire first, Snodgrass shot himself in the foot!

When Ryrie fired his pistol in the air the disappointed crowd shouted for blood but were finally satisfied with taking potshots at a second's top hat!

Badly Trained

Working for the early railways was a dangerous business. Employed at the Newcastle (NSW) Railway Goods Shed at one time was a man with no legs and six men with only one leg, all results of accidents with trains!

Barbaric Punishment

Two English soldiers in the early settlement of Sydney deliberately got themselves arrested for stealing in order to get out of the army and remain in Australia after their sentences. They were given seven years jail, a condition being that they would wear heavy leg irons and iron spiked collars for the whole period. The collars made lying down to sleep almost impossible.

But they succeeded in remaining in Australia—one died from heat stroke, the other went mad and was put in an asylum.

Hot Seat

Four labourers were travelling home in the front seat of a truck after landscape gardening when a box of dynamite under the seat blew up flinging them out through the doors and the roof. They escaped with only scratches!

Hot Evidence

'Excuse me, your worship, but the witness is on fire', said a police sergeant in the Dannevirke Court (NZ) 50 years ago. Smoke was billowing from the man's pocket after he had hurriedly put his pipe there when called from the corridor to give evidence. The court business was held up while the burning witness was extinguished.

Soon Parted

James Hunt, who discovered the Thames (NZ) gold-field, made himself £100 000 and as a wedding present bought his wife the carriage used by the Duke of Edinburgh in Sydney. He ended up in Coolgardie (WA) in 1894, stony-broke!

In the Neck

While washing his neck in 1930, a Waverley (NSW) tram guard was surprised when a small round object popped out through the skin. On examination, he found it was a bullet that had entered the calf of his right leg while he was fighting at Gallipoli.

Doctors worked out that the continual bending motion of neck and shoulders during the man's work had forced the bullet, which had travelled through his body, through the skin!

The Quiet Boy

When three-year-old John Bliss was taken to Dunedin, (NZ) in April 1948 he screamed with terror when he saw a train, shrank from other children and ran from cats and dogs. As he had been born and raised on his father's lighthouse on Dog Island, south of New Zealand, he had never come in contact with civilisation!

Tasty Dish

Correction in a New Zealand newspaper: 'Mai Thai Finn is one of the students in the programme and was in the centre of the photo. We incorrectly listed her name as one of the items on the menu.'

Airport Abuzz

Australia has very strict quarantine laws. Among items confiscated by Department of Agriculture officials at Sydney Airport in 1978 were 26 pigeons, four hedgehogs, two tortoises, a snake, 7.35 kg of snails, 60 clams—and a BUMBLE BEE!

One Call Does It All

As Mr Paul Simpson, of Thornleigh, Sydney, picked up his telephone in January, 1938, a flash of lightning shot from the instrument, entered his left ear and came out through his feet, setting the house alight.

Despite a torn muscle in his leg, Mr Simpson dashed upstairs and rescued his 11-week-old daughter, Karina.

The lightning had struck a telegraph pole in the street and travelled along the wire into the telephone. Mr Simpson's wife, Narelle, who had just finished using the phone, said her husband lit up like a neon light and had almost exploded.

Mighty Mouse

Af 1978 after Wayne Purkiss of Nambucca Heads (NSW) ran off the road, mounted an embankment and smashed into a telegraph pole, dislodging lines, he explained to police he had been distracted by a mouse running up his trouser leg!

Corpse's Guardian

When a schooner containing the coffin of a Chinese sank in Torres Strait in the mid 1800s, the man's relatives begged for his body to be recovered so it could be buried in China.

A diver who went down to the wreck never returned. Weeks later, a second diver disappeared. A third, more experienced, had a theory and, on reaching the wrecked schooner, threw two charges of dynamite into a porthole before ascending. The charges were fired and when he went down again he found what he had expected—the mangled body of a giant octopus which had claimed the divers and which had been guarding the coffin!

Plane v. Camel

Lieutenant Heppingstone of the Australian Light Horse Regiment was riding a camel in Egypt during World War I when he was knocked off the mount by a low flying aeroplane! He was taken to hospital and survived.

Ricochet

Waiting for a tram in Redfern, Sydney, 60-year-old Claude McNamara was knocked over by a bullet which had been fired by a policeman into a poisoned, dying dog 150 yards away, had passed through the animal, bounced off a pipe and hit Claude in the leg!

Fire-Bug

Climbing up a tree with a magnifying glass to study bees near Albury (NSW) in the late 1940s, 12-year-old Peter Ash accidentally directed the sun's rays onto the dry bark and started a major bushfire.

Short Fall

S. T. Gill Unlucky digger that never returned

John Cunningham, of Kondinin district (WA), perished in the bush from exhaustion after walking for days without food or drink. If he had walked another TWENTY YARDS he would have come in sight of three homesteads!

Truro Story

Ten years after the bodies of four women were found in shallow graves at Truro, Massachusetts (USA) four female bodies were found in shallow graves ... at TRURO (SA).

Was He Stewed?

A painter who fell into a vat of boiling water at an early Sydney brewery was officially described by a doctor to have been STEAMED TO DEATH!

Finger of Fate

When ship's bosun Patrick Henricks arrived in Sydney he told reporters that a hoodoo was plaguing him. His ship had been torpedoed in the war, the crew had walked off another of his ships at Newcastle after a huge brawl and shortly after that incident he heard from England that his daughter had died suddenly.

'The finger is upon me', he lamented. Three weeks after that declaration he fell down the stairs of a lodging house and died!

Travelling Needle

For 30 years, a needle which entered Mrs Sam Watson's finger in 1919 travelled around her body, passed through HER HEART and was eventually removed from her thigh by a doctor!

The needle pierced Mrs Watson's finger when she was putting on her coat and over the years she had felt sharp pains in various parts of her body. After it was removed by Dr F. L. Nance, Mrs Watson, of Colac (Vic.), CONTINUED TO USE THE NEEDLE!

Wheeled Out

On the night, in 1918, Percy Budd was arrested for the murder of his taxi driver, Harold Jacques, Mrs Jacques gave birth to a baby son. Like his murdered father, the young Sidney Jacques became a taxi driver—and 40 years almost to the day of Budd's arrest, Sidney was murdered in his cab by a gunshot to the head!

Desperation

Walking on a beach near Fremantle (WA) in September, 1887, five boys found a dead albatross with a message, scratched in French on a piece of tin, around its neck. Translated, it read:

'Thirteen shipwrecked sailors are taking refuge on the Crozet Islands. 4th August, 1887.'

The islands were in the southern Indian Ocean, near the Antarctic ice—3200 miles away!

French authorities established one of their vessels was indeed missing and when a search party landed on the Crozet Islands they found a message saying that the men had sailed on by long boat for the Possession Islands.

Despite an extensive search of the islands and the surrounding sea, the men were never found.

Authorities believed if they had waited for a day or two longer on the Crozet Islands their desperate attempt to get help by using the albatross would have worked!

Quick Splint

When jockey Jim Williams broke his arm in a fall at Mudgee (NSW) a policeman and another jockey ran to his aid. The policeman had a baton, the second jockey a whip. The two items were used to make a splint.

Prominent Politician

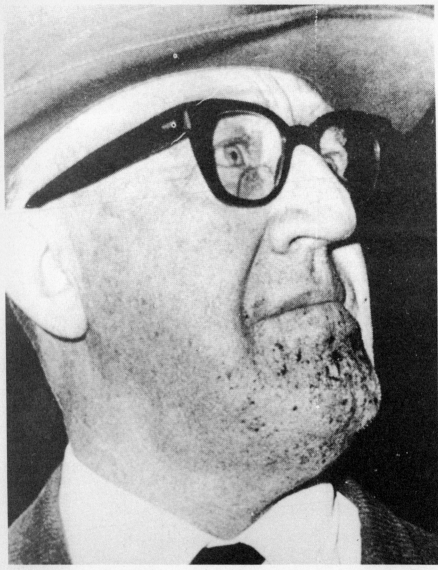

Arthur Calwell, leader of the opposition in Federal Parliament, in 1966, became known for his prominent chin. When a young man took a shot at him after a political meeting in Sydney the only thing that suffered was that chin, which was showered with glass. Mr Calwell was unable to shave for some time!

Eight Lives

Determined to end her life, 20-year-old Roma Powell of Melbourne threw herself in front of a truck in 1946, but it swerved around her. She managed to clamber on to the back and then jumped off but when she failed to destroy herself she ran to the nearby St Kilda beach, stripped and ran into the sea. But she was washed ashore and dragged by two policeman to their car.

Twice on the way to the police station she tried to jump out and then in a police cell she tried to hang herself with a strip of blanket and then choke herself with a strip off her dress, recovered from the beach. When police removed the dress she tried to choke herself with a strap from her petticoat. After police took the straps away she gave up and went to sleep.

Tipped Out

Driving at night through Summer Hill (NSW) confectioner Donald Bates was dealt a glancing blow by the wing of an Avenger aircraft being transported in the opposite direction.

Leaping from his car, he shouted 'I've lost my arm; I'm going to die'. He did, that night, from shock.

The coroner, finding death was accidental, said it would be advisable to place lights on the wing tips of planes travelling along the road at night.

Waterlogged

Bathing in the Wanganui River (NZ) a swimmer was killed by a tree felled half a mile away. It had been cut on a plateau above but fell the wrong way, rolled down a slope, toppled over a cliff and hit the swimmer!

Fiery Locks

Walking through Sydney's Martin Place on a sunny day in October, 1946, Miss Ann Anderson thought a bee had become caught in her hair when she heard a faint buzzing from above—until someone said they saw smoke coming from her head! When the glowing locks were cooled a cigarette end, believed to have been tossed from the window of the Australia Hotel, was pulled from her hair!

Rib Tickler

A man in Wanganui (NZ) died in 1921 because he carried a spare rib!

Instead of having 24 ribs, he had 25, the extra bone standing vertically inside those on the right hand side. A pathologist said pressure caused by the rib had been the ultimate cause of death!

Snakes Alive!

While eating a lollipop in the early 1900s, an Adelaide schoolgirl felt a tickling in her throat, coughed—and brought up A SMALL SNAKE!

A doctor worked out that while eating watercress several weeks earlier, she had swallowed an egg which had miraculously developed!

Lacey Luck

The strength of a shoelace saved a man from certain death in a motor cycle accident!

Thrown from the machine into the path of a tram in Auckland (NZ) Mr Ronald Porter was suspended just in front of the tram's front wheels after his shoelace caught on a bolt, leaving him dangling until the tram stopped!

Naval Disaster

The worst peace-time disaster in the history of the Australian services occurred when the aircraft carrier HMAS *Melbourne* slammed into the destroyer HMAS *Voyager* off Jervis Bay (NSW) in February 1964, with the loss of 82 men, including Captain Duncan Stevens.

Babe to Gallows

Convicted of manslaughter in 1855, 22-year-old Mary Brownlow took her new-born baby to the hanging platform and breast-fed her while final adjustments were made to the rope.

Then she handed the child to a warder and the baby's cries were the last thing she heard...

Bowled Over

In a 1920s bowls match for the championship of New Zealand on the Canterbury Club's green, Mr W. F. Raphael drove a ball which missed the head it was intended for, smashed into the ditch, jumped up and landed heavily on the toe of a spectator, then bounced high to land on the head of another watcher, who was knocked out!

Intractorble

Two days after two-year-old John Ciappara was crushed to death under the wheel of a tractor on a property near Dubbo (NSW) in December, 1982, the man who loaned the machine to John's father, Mr John Storck, used it to try to free a cow trapped in mud. The tractor tumbled over an embankment and Mr Storck was also crushed to death.

Hair Today...Here Tomorrow

A New South Wales man living on the banks of the Murrumbidgee River tried to commit suicide by drinking a glass of water and strychnine but failed because his thick bushy moustache held back the undissolved crystals.

Police who found him lying sick recovered enough poison from the bristles to have killed 20 men!

Scratch Caused Death

While she stood on a hedge at Port Macquarie (NSW) in 1921, Mary Borthwick's foot was pierced by a thorn. She used a pin to remove it and died in hospital of tetanus.

Lousy Verdict

A jury locked away to consider a verdict at the end of a trial in the Brisbane Supreme Court in 1950 began to scratch their heads—but it had nothing to do with indecision. Bird lice had infested the room and the jury had to be moved to other quarters while insect sprays were used!

Hard Cake

After a customer complained he had found a rusty nail in a walnut cake, an Adelaide baking company started checking others with a metal detector!

Hurt by Hose

Mr Samuel Kirk is the only man to go down in history for being injured by a runaway hose pipe.

While operating the hose at a dredging works near Adelong (NSW) it jumped from his hands when enormous pressure built up and then, gushing a powerful jet, 'snaked' after him. The hose pipe finally caught him and threw him against a wall, resulting in bruised ribs and a broken leg!

Bondi Chaos

One of the most extraordinary beach tragedies occurred at Bondi, Sydney, in February, 1938—'Black Sunday' as it is now known. The rip from three huge waves in succession swept more than 300 bathers hundreds of yards out to sea. More than 70 lifesavers brought them all back, but five had drowned.

No Heroics

NSW troops off to the Sudan

The first Australian to die on active service in an Australian uniform was Private Robert Weir of the 4th Infantry Company who went to the Sudan in 1885 and who died not by sword or musket—but illness.

Strong Soda

Hearing that his wife was going into hospital to give birth to another man's child, soldier Richard Simpson put himself in hospital by drinking caustic soda.

She was out within days, but he remained at death's door for two years. On his release, he decided to call on his in-laws and found his wife living in a tent in the back garden with the baby and its father. Simpson had no trouble in having his divorce application granted.

Accident and Prone

Swimming in the Brisbane River in the early 1900s, Mr P. Jones was attacked by a shark and rescued with badly injured legs by his elder brother. Doctors managed to save his legs and he went to France to fight in the war, during which he was badly wounded in the legs by shrapnel. Once again doctors managed to save his legs. Returning home to Brisbane, he slipped while crossing in front of a tram and both legs were severed. This time, doctors could not help him.

Finally Got Him

Mr John Lane, a Tenterfield (NSW) pioneer who refused to travel on trains because he believed the new contraptions would be the death of him, was killed at the age of 84 when he was knocked down by the Brisbane mail express.

Stumped

Two batsmen were stabbed in the throat by stumps in two extraordinary incidents at cricket matches in New South Wales.

Playing at Toxteth Park, Glebe, in the 1870s Mr H. Webster was running for the crease when he tripped and fell just as the ball, thrown in by a fielder, struck a stump and knocked it out. Mr Webster fell on the pointed end, was stabbed in the throat and died instantly.

In 1921, during a match between Moree and Welbon, a similar misfortune befell Mr John Hallman. As he ran for the crease the wicket keeper hit the stumps, knocking one out so that it spun and stood on end just as Mr Hallman tripped and fell. With a deep wound in his throat, he was taken to hospital and recovered.

Had to Rehearse

When Patrick O'Connor died in Lismore (NSW) the front part of the hearse had to be removed to accommodate his coffin. He was 7ft 4in tall.

Fateful Day

A woman's gravestone in Kew cemetery, Melbourne, says she was born on 26 January 1867, was married on 26 January 1887, and died 26 January 1897.

Maori's Farewell

After a young Maori chief, working as a crew member on the English ship *Boyd*, had been flogged for disobedience in 1809 a shore party from the vessel were attacked by angry Maoris at Whangaroa (NZ), killed and eaten. The Maoris boarded the ship and massacred the rest of the crew, the only survivors being two children.

Mayday

Up to 1922, the May family who emigrated to Australia from England in 1852 had lost only five of its 146 members through *natural* causes. Apart from the many who were killed in World War I, the original Mr May and one son, along with a brother-in-law, were drowned in a flood on the Clarence River in 1862; one of the two surviving sons was drowned in the Clarence 50 years later; a daughter was killed in a driving accident; and two grandsons died in riding accidents. The original Mrs May remarried and the only son of that marriage was killed in a mining accident.

HEART DISEASE in Australia, IS RESPONSIBLE EACH YEAR FOR *OVER 54 PERCENT OF ITS DEATHS*

Final Record

With only one burial to go, John England, grave digger at Bathurst (NSW) would have created a record by covering his 2110th coffin. But before the chance came, John died in April 1922. The body which would have given him the record was his own!

Kicked to Death

A young man claimed £1000 compensation from the YMCA in Wanganui (NZ) in 1930 because his foster father had been accidentally kicked to death after a friendly game of ping-pong!

Mr D. Milligan said his foster father was secretary of the YMCA where it was customary for the winner of a game of ping-pong to kick the loser, giving one kick for each losing point. Milligan played and lost by 13 points to 10 and the winning boy was invited to hand out the usual punishment. One kick was fatal!

Fatal Attraction

Although its light beamed out strongly into the night, the Wonga Shoal lighthouse off the South Australian coast was hit by the S. S. *Dimsdale* in 1912 and the two keepers were drowned when the tower sank.

Masking Red Tape

Although everyone was instructed to wear a gauze mask during a post-war influenza epidemic there were some odd exceptions—a New South Wales clergyman was told he could keep his mask off if his outdoor service lasted only 30 minutes and the worshippers stood 3 ft apart; and men playing musical instruments were allowed to remain unmasked, as were horse riders!

Ready to Eat

Riding on a bush track in Queensland with a turkey under his arm during the early 1920s, young Dave Williamson's pony stepped into a hole and did a somersault, landing heavily and tossing the boy several yards onto jagged stones. The boy and his mount were completely unhurt—but the turkey's neck was broken!

Knotty Problem

When doctors operated on a Western Australian girl who had been complaining of internal troubles they removed a pound of hair from her stomach—and told her to get out of the habit of chewing the ends of her long tresses!

Narrow Squeak

During a Punch and Judy Show at Young (NSW) Punch was dealt a nasty blow by the policeman and with a loud shriek fell down.

A crowd of children waited impatiently for him to get up but it was to be a long wait. The magician operating the puppets had swallowed his 'squeaker' and while Punch lay unconscious on the stage above, the magician's wife was in the process of removing the squeaker from his throat.

Both Punch and the magician finally recovered to continue the show!

Elevenses

After young Jim Winter set off from his Victorian farm on a horse he had been warned to be careful of, he was found dead beneath a tree. He was 11 years, 11 months and 11 days old and his body was discovered at 11 o'clock on the 11th day of the 11th month!

Broken Journey

Bringing his younger son home from the doctor after the boy had broken his arm in March, 1922, Mr G. Thomas of Wellington (NSW) found his other son waiting for medical help—he had broken his arm, too!

Ready for Bed

A groom injured in a car accident was married in his pyjamas at a Sydney hospital in the 1920s because the bride believed that to postpone their wedding a third time after two cancellations through unavoidable circumstances would be unlucky!

Toothy Tale

An Australian Serviceman who complained of a persistent sore throat for more than a month was told by his doctor that he had swallowed his false teeth!

Dr C. Rosefield of Melbourne's Alfred Hospital explained to the soldier that earlier X-rays had failed to detect the metal clasp of his upper dentures which had lodged themselves in his throat.

The soldier lost his teeth after a fainting attack at a camp and his mates had searched unsuccessfully for them while he was in hospital being treated for 'tonsilitis'.

THE SWIMMER WHO ESCAPED FROM THE VERY MOUTH OF A MAN-EATING SHARK!

TREACLE, A PEARL FISHERMAN IN TORRES STRAIT, OFF AUSTRALIA, ESCAPED AND SWAM SAFELY TO SHORE. AFTER A DEADLY MAKO SHARK THAT HAD BITTEN ALMOST THROUGH HIS NECK *ATTEMPTED TO SWALLOW HIS HEAD.*
WHEN THE SHARK OPENED ITS MOUTH WIDER TO BITE DOWN ON THE SWIMMER'S HEAD TREACLE WRIGGLED FREE AND RACED TO THE BEACH. HE RECOVERED COMPLETELY AFTER A MONTH IN THE HOSPITAL

A **WHALE** HARPOONED OFF THE COAST OF AUSTRALIA, WAS LANDED ON THE WHALER "JOHN and WINTHROP" **ONLY AFTER IT HAD BITTEN IN HALF 2 WHALEBOATS** (1886)

★★★★★★★★★★

Brought House Down

Unaware that her bricklayer husband had put 12 sticks of gelignite into the kitchen stove to warm it before using it to blow up stumps for firewood, Mrs J. McAuley, 25, of Warrandyte (Vic.) closed the door of the oven...

The explosion shattered the stove, blasted her out through the back door and brought the house down. Although parts of the house were found half a mile away, Mrs McAuley received only a SCRATCH on her leg and did not even have to call a doctor!

Unlucky Break

Travelling home from hospital with his arm in plaster after breaking it in a football match between Gellibrand River and Johanna (Vic.) Peter Robe broke it in a different place when the car he was travelling in overturned.

Safer in Bank

After keeping £470 in notes left by her late police inspector husband hidden at her Coogee (NSW) home, 70-year-old Mrs C. Cowle decided to deposit the money in a bank.

While stepping from a tram on the way to the bank in December, 1935, with the money in a cardboard shoe box she was knocked breathless by a man who accidentally hit her in the back with a suitcase. When she recovered from the blow, the money she had kept for years was missing.

Lethal Chimney

While trying to catch a parrot on the roof of his home, 29-year-old Max Goldstone, of Melbourne, slipped, made a grab for the chimney and fell off. The fall only stunned him, but he was killed by the chimney which tumbled on him!

Lost Four Legs

Geordie Gill, a former Broken Hill (NSW) identity, is the only man to have his legs amputated twice.

The first time was when he fell from the platform of a moving train while on his way to a Labour Day picnic and had both legs taken off. Several years later he fell under a steam tram, the wheels of which chopped of Geordie's artificial feet.

He sat in the road roaring with laughter at the fact that he had lost four legs!

Helpful Ducks

Crossing a river near Wagga Wagga (NSW) with a one-legged corpse that had been found on the bank, a boat carrying a party of policemen overturned, casting them all in. The police swam ashore and watched in amazement as a flock of ducks herded the body to the bank.

Second Aid

Running to aid a football player lying unconscious under a tree after a mid-field collision at Sydney's Moore Park in 1923, ambulanceman Jim McPherson dropped his bag, tripped over it and knocked himself out on the tree. When he came round the player was back on the field and McPherson found himself being attended to by one of his mates!

Two Chapters on Page

Joshua Page, found dead with his neck broken after falling from a horse at Coonamble (NSW), was the brother of W. H. Page who two years earlier had been found dead 100 yards away with his neck broken after falling from a sulky!

Warm, Clean and Bored

A former World War I soldier, Trooper Rolfe, had such a sensitive skin after being gassed it burned even in the coldest weather, so a doctor designed a special zinc bath filled with luke warm water for him to live in at Randwick Hospital (NSW).

Reward Saved

A man who lost an ear in a car accident in Adelaide in the 1930s was on the point of offering a reward for its return from his hospital bed when a cyclist arrived with the missing piece wrapped up in a newspaper in which the victim was going to advertise. The ear was grafted back on.

Fateful Trees

Within the space of two weeks, three Catholic priests were killed and a fourth seriously injured in freak accidents with trees in the 1930s.

In New South Wales, Father O'Looney of Culcairn was standing at the roadside when a falling tree struck the branch of another and the limb fell on the priest and killed him.

Just two week later three priests, Father Tehan, Father O'Sullivan and Father O'Connor were returning from a conference in Victoria when their car left the road and hit the only tree standing at the roadside!

EVERY SHIP

IN THE HARBOR OF BROOME, ON THE WEST COAST OF AUSTRALIA,

IS STRANDED HIGH AND DRY BY A TIDE THAT DROPS 30 FEET

Bad Shepherd

Wayne Orpwood of Christchurch (NZ) volunteered to collect donations for the Society for the Prevention of Cruelty to Animals in 1982. When he entered one house with his collecting tin he was attacked by a German Shepherd dog and ended up in Christchurch Hospital for treatment for bites to his arm and buttocks.

In the Lion's Mouth

Jostling for a look at a lion tied to a post in a circus complex in Queensland, schoolchildren accidently pushed six-year-old Alice Passi within reach of the animal. It grabbed Alice in its claws, then clamped its mouth around her head. Circus workers managed to pull the lion's jaws apart and Alice was taken to hospital for stitches. Circus workers said her survival was a true miracle.

Beaten by a Blow

Ivy Bazley, 27, suffered a blow during her bid to set a new pole-sitting record. During a vigorous exercise program to get herself in shape she fell over and broke her right arm.

Too Tempting

For two years Peter Fuller of Wirth's Circus had been training Philip the lion but on the day he believed the animal was at last completely under his control he had his finger bitten off when he passed Philip a bowl of water!

Death Stone

A falling stone which killed two men in McBride's Tunnel at the Victorian State Coal Mine, Wonthaggi, was in the shape of a coffin. On the top was the outline of a white cross.

White Tribeswoman

A white woman who, as a child, had been rescued by Aborigines from a shipwreck was taken from the tribe when she was discovered in 1886 at the age of 35 and placed in an institution in Cooktown (Qld). For three days the woman, who had been found naked, cried and moaned for her tribal friends. And on the fourth day she died.

Under Water 30 mins

When Reginald Daniels, aged eight, fell into Cudgen Creek (NSW) on Boxing Day, 1930, he remained under water for more than 30 minutes before rescue. A doctor injected arsenic as treatment into the unconscious boy— and he survived!

Living Corpse

Fifty years later, on Thursday Island, north of Australia, they are still talking about the corpse that lived!

An islander, badly mauled while pearl diving, was considered dead by his friends when they pulled his bloody body from the sea. They dutifully wrapped him in canvas for burial.

The canvas was sewn so tight that it stopped the flow of blood and just as the 'dead body' was about to be lowered into a grave it sat up in its wrapping and emitted a loud groan. Those who didn't run away in terror released the man, nursed him back to health and six months later he was diving for pearls again!

THE STRANGEST SHIPWRECK IN ALL HISTORY
THE "GEM" A CUTTER CARRYING 6 CREWMEN, 4 PASSENGERS AND 500 BAGS OF WHEAT · SAILED SERENELY INTO SHELTERED SOUTH BAY, AT ROTTNEST ISLAND, AUSTRALIA, ON MAY 17, 1876, *AND SUDDENLY VANISHED!*
DIVERS LOCATED THE WRECKAGE, WITH ALL SAILS STILL SET, BUT COULD DISCOVER NO REASON FOR THE SHIP'S SINKING -*AND NO TRACE OF THE CREW AND PASSENGERS HAS EVER BEEN FOUND*

THIRTEEN

Wonders
Nature's Strange Designs

Man was guilty of a gross miscalculation when he stopped at 'Seven Wonders of the World'.

For a start, he forgot an eighth wonder. Himself! 'Wonders are many,' said Sophocles, 400 years BC, 'and none is more wonderful than man'.

If we pause a moment, is it not a wonder that we can walk on a spherical ball that spins in space? Is it not a wonder that there is night and day, winter and summer?

Look at the tides, the harvests, the deserts, the forests. Are these not, in themselves, wonders? Yet it is the quirks of nature that fascinate us, perhaps because we only glimpse them. The other wonders we take for granted—our days and nights and seasons. The world holds countless wonders. Extraordinary occurrences which take place when and where we least expect them to happen. Take, for example, the pearl found inside a coconut instead of in an oyster. Can you believe that really was so? Preposterous though it may sound, it is perfectly true.

Oddities abound in man, animals and 'still life'. How did a frog live encased in rock 870 ft down a Victorian mine shaft? How did a small gum-tree find the strength to split a granite rock? We can only wonder...wonder about:

The rock which rings like a bell.
The amazing exploding tree.
Fish that fall into a trance.
The man with a horn in his head.
The chicken that laid a boomerang!

Heavily-Laden Tree

Significantly, one of the most flourishing apple trees ever known in Victoria was brought from Tasmania by Mr John Batman, Melbourne's founder, in 1838. Planted at Heidelberg, now a Melbourne suburb, it grew to 20 ft with a girth of 5 ft and became so heavily laden that in 1910 huge branches snapped off under the weight of the fruit!

Hopping Mad

Mrs Fiona Grey, hearing that frogs always returned to their territory, painted a ring on the back of one that had been in the habit of hopping into her bathroom sink in Northern Queensland.

She then took it by train to Halifax, seven miles away and released it near a creek. Six days later it was back in the wash basin!

Ringed Fish

Fishing off Sydney's South Head in 1923, an angler pulled in a trevally fish which had a small nickel ring through its bottom lip. The ring bore the letter 'J' and was stamped 1912.

Wood Beats Stone

At Palmer Hill, near Mannum (SA), a small gum-tree which grew through a crack in a huge granite rock attained full size, splitting the stone in half!

Handy at Market

Mr Albert Fox of Port Campbell (Vic.) is 7 ft 3 in tall and can hold a dozen hen's eggs in one hand. But the tallest man to live in Australia is believed to be Mr Denis O'Duffy, who died in 1957—he was 7 ft 5 ¼ in!

Tree Hits Back

While felling an old, dry tree in Queensland Mr Jim Cross was knocked backwards by an explosion which was followed by loud hissing from the tree. The hollow trunk had filled with decaying vegetation and the gas had been sealed in until Mr Cross's axe hit home. The axe head was blown 40 ft and was buried blade-deep in another tree!

A Flying Oyster

Opening a coconut presented to him from Sabai Island, Torres Strait, Sir William McGregor, Governor of Queensland, found a small pearl! It was later worn by a lady at a court function in London but she couldn't convince anyone about its origin!

Heavyweights

Mr Barney Worth who was born in Cooktown (Qld) in 1916, was a 15½ lb baby who grew up to weigh 42 stone! His wife Joy, who was born in the same town, weighed nearly 38 stone. Ironically, they both died in the same year, 1955, in Bristol, England.

Medical History

On 6 March 1935, quads were born in a Dunedin hospital creating medical history in New Zealand while on the same day triplets were born in Sydney, the first for eight years!

Brilliant Aurora

Every year on certain nights a display of coloured lights illuminates the night sky and can be observed from southern Australia and New Zealand. Known as Aurora Australis, the lights are caused by sun spots which send out charged particles that fly around the earth beyond the atmosphere.

What a Lark

Two elderly sisters on a picnic at Cataract Dam (NSW) in 1920 found a lone lark's egg and decided to take it home. Carrying it in her hand, one of the women felt it crack and when she arrived home she was carrying a young lark!

Thanks a Million

Sending a motor mechanic for trial on a charge of assaulting two sailors who were attacking a woman, a Melbourne magistrate said he should be thanked by the court on behalf of the community for aiding a woman who had cried for help!

Maple Apple

A resident at Otatara, near Invercargill (NZ), was puzzled to find a pile of apples lying in his garden under a MAPLE tree in the late 1940s. Looking up, he saw clusters of apples growing from the branches. That was the only season they grew.

"LONDON BRIDGE"
Port Campbell, Australia
NATURAL STONE FORMATION

Disappearing Lake

Lake George, 35 km from Canberra has emptied four times since its discovery in 1820—but nobody knows why. Scientists agree that the disappearance of the water is not due to evaporation!

Boo-meringue

A few days after watching Aborigines throw boomerangs—one of which was lost in the vicinity of her farm's hen house—Mrs W. Rowe of Bowraville (NSW) was surprised to find that one of her fowls had laid an egg in the exact shape of a boomerang. Neighbours suggested that the bird had been struck by the missing boomerang and its shape had been printed in its mind!

Sorry Catch

A party of Queensland government officials, taking a week-end break from politics in 1930, pulled in their heavily-laden fishing net at Moreton Bay and found it full of State Hansards!

Best Blankets

Scientists with the Commonwealth Scientific and Industrial Research Organisation boiled Army blankets 150 TIMES and found no harm came to them!

Raining Fish

During a heavy rainstorm at Longreach (Qld), located hundreds of miles inland, thousands of fresh whiting fell on the district. It was thought a whirlwind had pulled the fish from the sea and deposited them in the storm clouds.

Glassy Rock

At Ashton, near Bombala (NSW), a 5-ft-high rock resembling a mass of glass that has been melted by heat rings like a bell when struck with metal. The sound can be heard hundreds of yards away. Many theories have been put forward about the rock's origin, the most likely being that it is the remains of a meteor.

Deep Frog

While working 870 ft down a gold mine at Bendigo (Vic.) in 1936, miners found a live white frog in an aperture in the reef. Jelly-like and semi-transparent, it was brought to the surface but died as soon as it was exposed to the sun. There was no opening in the reef before it was broken open!

The Big Eye

One of the largest optical telescopes in the world is located at Siding Springs in New South Wales' Warrumbungle Ranges. It weighs 326 tonnes and has a 16 tonne mirror!

Horned Man

A six-inch-long horn which had curled from the forehead of a man was displayed at the Australasian Medical Congress in Melbourne following its removal by Dr G. A. Syme. The conference, in 1923, was told that a few centuries earlier the 67-year-old man who had grown the horn would have been killed as 'a child of the devil'.

THE **GRASS TREES** OF AUSTRALIA, GROW AT THE RATE OF ONE FOOT EVERY *120 YEARS*

Glasshouse Mountains

When James Cook saw a mountain range made up of volcanic cores north of Brisbane in 1770 they reminded him of glass furnaces he had seen in England. So he called them the Glasshouse Mountains!

The Devil's Marbles

A large granite outcrop near the Stuart Highway south of Tennant Creek in the Northern Territory has been so worn and weathered that it looks like huge stones have been piled on top of one another.

White settlers called the phenomenon The Devil's Marbles, but Aborigines believed the rocks were the eggs of the Rainbow Serpent!

Ball of Light

Supernatural forces or the work of nature? Both theories have been put forward to explain a hovering ball of light that has been seen and photographed over the years in the Boulia district of Queensland.

Because it was first seen near the Min Min Hotel, the glow is now known as the Min Min Light. Scientists say it is possibly caused by the spontaneous combustion of escaping natural gases but those who believe in the supernatural have a variety of other explanations!

Hollow Tree

Fancy garaging your car in a tree? A hollow Tingle Tingle tree near Walpole (WA) is so large that it is possible to drive a car into it!

Hot Well

Water from an artesian well at Tinneburra, near Cunnamulla (Qld), is hot enough to scald—yet a pan of it takes longer to boil than cold water!

Maori Canoes

Large spherical rocks on New Zealand's Koekohe Beach, near Oamaru, are believed by Maoris to symbolise the petrified remains of a sailing canoe that brought their ancestors to the New Land.

Lasting Lightning

Residents of early Sydney were amazed during a violent storm to see a fork of lightning remain stationary for five minutes! The freak, observed in 1793, has not been equalled.

THE **STANDLEY** CHASM IN THE MacDonnell Mountains of Australia, **20** FEET WIDE AND **500** FEET DEEP, IS A CLEFT SO DARK THAT A MAN STANDING AT THE BOTTOM OF IT *CAN SEE STARS IN THE DAYTIME*

Glacial Power

A hydro-electric power station in New Zealand is powered by a glacier! The Tasman glacier, the longest in the country, is moving down the eastern slopes of Mount Cook at the rate of about 30 cm a day and its melting waters, flowing into Lake Pukaki, have been dammed to derive power for the hydro-electric plant at Lake Waitaki.

ELLEN MATTHEWS of Collingwood, Australia WHO LOST THE USE OF HER VOICE IN AN ACCIDENT—RECOVERED IT 7½ YEARS LATER *—BUT SHE SPEAKS WITH A SCOTTISH ACCENT*

Glow-Worm Grotto

In New Zealand's Waitomo Caves, south-west of Hamilton, visitors are greeted by a myriad pinpricks of light. They are the luminous glow of tiny insect larvae hanging from sticky threads and one cave is so 'bright' that it is known as the 'Glow-Worm Grotto'!

Biggest Rock

The world's largest rock sits in the desert 320 km east of Carnarvon (WA). Mount Augustus is 8 km long, 5 km wide and 377 m high. The more popular rock among tourists is Ayers Rock, in the heart of Australia, and although it is almost as high (335 m) it is only half the size.

Explorer W. C. Gosse, the first white man to see Ayers Rock, in 1873, described it as 'an immense pebble' rising abruptly from the plain!

THE **BOUNCING** FALLS ON AYER'S ROCK - Australia
A SERIES OF ROCK BASINS INTO WHICH WATER FROM DEW-PONDS ON THE SUMMIT FALLS IN SUCCESSIVE CASCADES - EACH 90 FT. FORMING PERMANENT WELLS AT THE BASE

ONCE **A BLUE MOON** APPEARED IN AUSTRALIA
IT WAS CAUSED BY A TREMENDOUS DUST STORM CONTAINING MYRIADS OF SPECKS OF SILICA OXIDE WHICH CUT OUT THE RED AND YELLOW RAYS - LEAVING ONLY THE BLUE

Worm Cover

An army of millions of worms which appeared at night in December 1932 and covered a road at Kenmore (NSW) for a distance of 500 yards caused a car being driven by Mr L. Kelly to skid and crash into a pole. They had all gone by morning.

Entranced Fish

Shoals of fish are caught every year throughout the Pacific—thanks to the efforts of local medicine-men! Wading out from the beach they make a special call which attracts fish and puts them into a trance. They are then easy pickings for villagers.

Napoleonic Tree

The memory of Napoleon lives on at the Old Farm, near Albany (WA), where a willow tree flourishes, having grown from a cutting taken from a tree at Napoleon's grave.

Wave Rock

A giant ocean wave, frozen in stone! That is the appearance of Wave Rock, near Hyden (WA). Made of solid granite, the spectacular rock formation was formed by weathering and erosion during its 2700 million year lifespan. To add to its effect, chemical deposits helped by rain water have left bright bands of colour.

Bird Catchers

On islands of Australia's Great Barrier Reef are trees that CATCH BIRDS! Ocean birds choose the bird-catching tree for their nests but the young become entangled in the sticky fruits which bind their feathers and make them immobile.

Golf Hazards

The golf course with the worst hazards is at Rotorua (NZ) where hot springs spout steam and gurgle mud in the middle of the fairways!

Chocolate Snow

As a result of a dust storm in the Mallee district of Victoria and a snowstorm over the Victorian Alps CHOCOLATE-COLOURED SNOW fell at Mount Hotham in July, 1935!

THE THICKEST BRUSH IN THE WORLD

THE HORIZONTAL SHRUB OF TASMANIA STARTS ITS GROWTH AS A SLENDER SAPLING, BUT WHEN IT REACHES A HEIGHT OF 20 FEET IT *FALLS OF ITS OWN WEIGHT—* THE TANGLED MASS OF BOUGHS WHICH GROW FROM THE PRONE TRUNK ARE SO THICK A TRAVELER CAN WALK ON TOP OF THEM *AS IF HE WERE ON A PLATFORM*

Blue Lake

Every
November a lake at
Mount Gambier (SA)
mysteriously changes colour
from a murky grey to a
splendid deep blue!

Scientists have not been able to
satisfactorily explain the sudden
transformation. One of four lakes in
the crater of an extinct volcano, it was
known by pioneers as the Devil's
Inkbottle but today it is referred to as
the Blue Lake.

Strange Craters

For more than 10 years, scientists and geologists have been baffled by the discovery of some 30 strange craters between Bundaberg and Gin Gin (Qld). Made of sandstone, siltstone and red ochre and at least 25 million years old, the craters contain unidentifiable markings which could be man-made!

The holes were discovered by a farmer clearing his land and they have now been opened to the public who offer a multitude of theories about their origin ranging from natural formations—although the craters are not of volcanic origin—to the work of visitors from outer space!

Meteorite

A meteorite weighing more than five tons crashed near Cranbourne (Vic.) and was discovered in pieces in 1854. One chunk, weighing three tons, was sent to the British Museum while a smaller piece was put on display in Melbourne.

Cave Dwellers

Even in 1983 residents of Coober Pedy (SA) and White Cliffs (NSW) are living in underground 'caves'! The unique homes have been set up in disused opal mines and residents say they are much better than conventional houses—the dugouts are warm in winter and cool in summer!

Salt and Pure

Lake Gallilee, near Aramac (Qld), is the strangest stretch of waterway in the world—for it is two lakes in one! Half of the 70 square miles is salt, the other part fresh water and apart from a few yards of 'overlap' the two types of water do not mix!

Tenacious Tree

During a heavy rainstorm on the New South Wales south coast in 1919, a 15 ft coral tree slid down the side of a steep hill, landed upright in a hole at the side of the road and continued to grow!

Underground Wheat

Miners who entered an unused level of a Broken Hill (NSW) mine in 1901 found a crop of wheat growing, 2 ft high, at a depth of 700 ft!

Gum and Pine

A seed blown in the wind landed in the fork of a gum-tree in South Parklands, Adelaide, at the end of the 1940s. Within three years the eucalyptus had a pine tree growing from it!

Salt Lake

When Lake Eyre (SA) dries up, the compact surface of the salt is strong enough to support a helicopter!

LAKE EYRE
AUSTRALIA'S LARGEST DRY LAKE, COVERING AN AREA OF 5,000 SQ. MILES, *HAS HELD WATER ONLY TWICE IN HISTORY*

FOURTEEN

Madland

Beyond the Fringe

They made a film once, called *It's a Mad, Mad, Mad, Mad World.* Now read the book—or at least this chapter which proves that you don't have to be a Hollywood scriptwriter to show what a crazy world we live in. It's all out there, beyond your window pane!

We hear of an unusual event. 'But that's crazy!' we cry. Perhaps it is crazy. Perhaps it is utter madness. But it intrigues us... and makes us laugh. Sometimes we are driven to doing crazy things by some powerful impulse. On a mad whim. Like playing golf in a thunderstorm to try out a new set of irons (and inadvertently test their qualities as lightning conductors). More often than not someone will exclaim: 'How mad!'

On the subject of golfers—one club captain in South Australia set off for a quiet round and came back to the clubhouse with a human skull in his bag, unearthed when he took a deep divot. 'That's really weird', said the club president. But let's face it, it was downright crazy!

Sometimes the cogs of Madland grind on under their own impetus but more often than not it is the antics of we humans that keep them oiled and running. Belly-bashing contests in Yanko, Queensland, are pretty crazy, but there's also the man who ended up with a severe crick in his neck after driving his car backwards over a distance of 570 miles. To say nothing of the Alice Springs water carnival, held on the dried-up bed of the Todd River.

It is the happenings of Madland that keep us occupied for hours. Take for example, the bullet that you'll read about in this chapter which failed to penetrate a sheet of brown paper. Was the bullet defective, the gun weak, or the paper the strongest sheet known to man?

To contemplate the possibilities is in itself, quite mad. However, if you haven't a foot in Madland, you might like to step into its intriguing realm and consider:

The girl whose hair grows twice as fast on the right side

of her head as on the left!
The people who sit on rocks
for hours at a time.
The entries in the Great
Australian Animal Imitation
Championships.
The Archdeacon who made a
seaman's superstitions come
true.
The statue of a horse which
talked to tourists.

Not Accurate

Although there is a town in Tasmania
called Nowhere Else there is somewhere
else in the same state called Nowhere
Else!

Named by Dutch

The first time the words 'Australia'
and 'Australian' were used was in 1693
in the English translation of a Dutch
novel!

Dry Regatta

One of the world's strangest regattas is
held every year at Alice Springs—
although it is held on a river, no
water is involved. The Todd River
is dry for most of the year, so
competitors take the bottoms out of
their various sailing vessels and—run!

Talking Horse

A statue of a horse talks to tourists at the country town of Nhill (Vic.)! When a coin is inserted into the monument a taped message points out that the statue is in memory of the draught horses who helped pioneers shape their land.

Star Boarder

In Australia's early days scores of places were named Weatherboard after the first building of a community was erected. Almost always, it was made of planks of wood, so nailed that one overlapped another in order to prevent rain from penetrating.

Finally, so many small towns were called Weatherboard that the names were changed. A beauty spot known as Weatherboard Falls (NSW) had its name changed to Wentworth Falls.

The Great Grafter

After being split down the middle by lightning, a navel orange tree in Queensland's Yalleroi district was bound together by a station owner and continued to bear fruit—navel oranges on one side, St Michael oranges on the other!

Flustered Judge

The sixth running of the Melbourne Cup in 1866 had such a thrilling finish, with The Barb heading for the line neck and neck with Exile, that the judge forgot to announce the third horse and there was speculation that he didn't even know. Punters demanded a pay out on Falcon, which stewards decided was third, but the bookies refused to hand over any money pointing out the judge was the only person who could officially place the horse!

Good Testimonial

A portable ice chest, twisted and charred by intense heat during a fire which completely destroyed a Perth garage and its contents, was found to contain a large block of ice which had not shed a drop of water!

Tramtastic

At Lightning Ridge (NSW) old Melbourne trams, still showing their route numbers, have been converted into motel units for tourists arriving to inspect the opal-mining areas.

Parsons Not Wanted

As Archdeacon Oakes of Bathurst (NSW) was boarding a ship for Queensland, a crew member told him that one parson meant a late arrival, two meant a troublesome voyage and three meant disaster—and there were now three on board!

During the voyage, the ship ran into a 50-mile gale, a steam pipe blew out and the skipper was rushed to the bridge in his pyjamas.

Two parsons left at the next port and Archdeacon Oakes noted that the sea was calm for the rest of the passage. However, as the crew member had predicted, the ship arrived late!

Misinformed

Dr Roger Wiseman, lecturer at the South Australian College of Advanced Education, decided many children had a deplorable lack of knowledge about their country when he conducted a survey in 1982 asking youngsters the names of some famous Australians. Their answers included Elvis Presley, tennis star Bjorn Borg, British comedian Benny Hill, the pop group Abba, the Queen, Bing Crosby and John Wayne.

Asked to name symbols reminding them of Australia, answers included the Statue of Liberty, the Queen and cowboy boots and hats. When asked what changes they thought would make Australia a better place, some replied 'Get rid of the Pommies'.

The Right Stuff

One hundred and thirty-four American millionaires who called at Darwin in 1951 during a cruise on the luxury ship *Stella Polaris* bought up almost every stuffed lizard, turtle and crocodile in town.

NATIVES of Queensland, Aus. BECOME SO FRENZIED DURING THEIR "DANCE OF THE FORKED STICK" THAT *THEY THRUST THEIR FEET INTO FLAMES WITHOUT FEELING PAIN*

Ship in Gardens

During the great flood at Brisbane in 1893, the gunboat *Paluma* was raised 35 ft from its anchorage and carried to the Botanic Gardens where it rested among the trees. A salvage firm contracted to get the vessel back to the water was wondering how it could be done when another flood occurred—and carried the *Paluma* back to its anchor point!

Coals to Newcastle?

Lot 231 at a customs auction in Melbourne in September 1982: three pallets of sheep manure from New Zealand.

Skull Duggery

Taking a deep divot on the Kooyonga golf links, Adelaide, Mr R. L. Rymill, the 1923 captain of the club, unearthed a human skull, believed to be that of an Aboriginal!

Needs a Breeze

Johnson River hardwood, found only in the Innisfail district of northern Queensland will burn fiercely when soaking wet. But it won't burn unless there is a draught—even when it is tinder dry!

Longest Name

The longest place name in Australia is Lake Cadibarrawirracanna, 95 km from Lake Eyre (SA).

Capital Name

Suggestions for a name for Australia's capital in 1913 included a composite of the major cities, Sydney, Melbourne, Adelaide, Perth, Brisbane and Hobart—Sydmeladperbrisho!

Letter Games

Glenelg (SA) is spelled the same backwards. Faulconbridge, in the Blue Mountains of New South Wales, uses exactly half the letters in the alphabet including a straight seven from A to G. Woolloomooloo is of equal length, but only four letters are used.

Belly Whammy

A pub in Yanko (Qld) was the origin of whammying!

Whammying, for the uninitiated, is the art of growing a rotund beer stomach and then attempting to knock an opponent, similarly blessed, to the floor. Using only the belly, of course!

Brick Throwers

There are four Strouds around the world—in New South Wales; in Ontario, Canada; in Gloucestershire, England; and Oklahoma, USA—and each year they hold similar contests. Brick throwing!

When the American and English Strouds found they were each brick-making areas they decided to hold brick throwing competitions and the Australian and Canadian namesakes followed.

Contestants have to toss a 2.26 kilogram brick, made in Oklahoma. Just to keep the womenfolk happy, there's a rolling pin throwing competition, using a 900-gram roller made in Australia from hardwood!

Angel Place

The World Evangelism Centre in Sydney is located at 1, Angel Place.

In Remembrance

A pendulum clock hanging on the wall of an office in Port Fairy (Vic.) stopped at exactly 11 a.m. on Wednesday, April 25, 1923—Anzac Day—and having observed two minutes silence started without help at 11.02 a.m. It had been wound only three hours earlier!

Rocksitters

Once a week members of Darwin's Rocksitters Club meet to drink a few cans of beer and... sit on a rock or two. Club members set a world record for rock sitting in 1980 when they remained on a rock for 12 days.

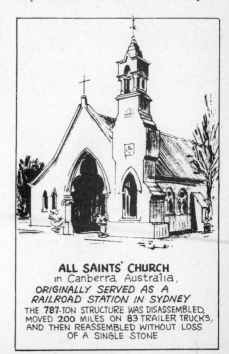

ALL SAINTS' CHURCH
in Canberra, Australia,
*ORIGINALLY SERVED AS A
RAILROAD STATION IN SYDNEY*
THE **787**-TON STRUCTURE WAS DISASSEMBLED,
MOVED **200** MILES ON **83** TRAILER TRUCKS,
AND THEN REASSEMBLED WITHOUT LOSS
OF A SINGLE STONE

Farmer's Princedom

The Hutt River Province is a state within a state, established by a Western Australian farmer, Leonard Casley, who decided to break away from local government rule because of a dispute over taxes and concessions.

Now Prince Leonard, who has 'ruled' his 7486-ha property since 1970, issues his own postage stamps and his 30 'subjects' carry their own passports and use their own local currency. The money can only be spent in the Hutt River Province—neither the State nor Federal governments recognise the principality.

Rock Lifters

Rock lifting is a peculiar form of entertainment at Trebonne (Qld) where the town's 300 Basque residents uphold the sport of Arijaso, using rocks specially imported from the Pyrenees.

Participants in the sport, on which wagers are laid, have to lift a 100 kilogram rock onto their shoulders as many times as possible in one minute!

Fancy Animals

A human fly, a human toad, a human cockerel and a human lion have all made their appearances at Bungendore, near Canberra, where every year the Australian Animal Imitation Championships are held!

Those taking part dress appropriately— it helps to guess what they are when the imitations are poor!

Whistling Ship

We've all heard of a ship's whistle, but what about a whistling ship? There's one at Emu Park, near Yeppoon (Qld). Tall musical pipes form the masts of the ship and play tunes when the wind blows to commemorate Captain James Cook's discovery of the Capricorn coast in May, 1770.

Mediaeval

Hangings, whippings and jousting tournaments are realistically re-enacted at a copy of a 16th-century castle near Ballarat (Vic.). Some of the acting is so life-like that tourists have fainted.

Kryal Castle also has a replica of the Crown Jewels and anyone caught stealing them may be sentenced to the Bloody Tower!

Countrymen

Four families, all friends, who arrived at Perth from the United Kingdom in 1923 were named England, Ireland, Wales and Scotland!

Time Wasting

Fred Baker of Melbourne, editor of an educational magazine, concluded that if we live to be 70, we will have slept away 23 years, worked for nine years, commuted for about one and a half years and have spent 7.3 years eating, washing and shopping. It took him six months to work it all out.

Weak Bullet

Lieutenant Peter Galloway, of the 19th Battalion Citizen Forces, kept on his mantlepiece the only bullet that failed to penetrate BROWN PAPER. During shooting practice at Anzac Range, Liverpool (NSW) a rifle was fired at a target 200 yards away and the bullet stuck fast in the paper.

Rear Vision

Sitting behind the wheel of a 1968 Holden Kingswood, Mr Barry Stewart, 35, drove backwards over a distance of 570 miles in 24 hours 17 minutes at Broadbeach (Qld) in 1980. He averaged 23.77 mph and, not surprisingly, no-one has equalled him!

Mighty Stamp

Because a fourpence stamp, printed in Western Australia in 1854, had an inverted frame it became a greatly sought-after specimen for collectors. Fifteen were known to have been used and one was auctioned in Melbourne in 1977 for no less than $22 000!

Times Change

The South Esk River (Tas.) was the first Australian waterway to be used to generate electric power and the settlers of the late 1890s welcomed the operation. By the end of 1982 thousands were protesting about a new hydro-electric project which involved the damming of the Franklin River and scores of conservationists were arrested while demonstrating.

Useful Stamp

Issued in 1855, the five pence green stamp of New South Wales remained in use until 1913 to create a world record for continuous use.

Foundation Town

The only name that stuck for the region when Captain James Cook stepped ashore on what is now the Queensland coast was Seventeen Seventy, the year he landed. In 1953 Seventeen Seventy was officially approved as the place name.

Doo Town

'Welcome Doo Town, Doo Drive Slowly', says the sign outside the Tasmanian village, founded in the 1930s. The names of all the houses make use of the word Doo in pun fashion—including 'How Doo you Doo', 'Doo Us 2', 'Av Ta Doo', 'Thistle Doo' and 'Didgeridoo'!

Witless Clock

The town hall clock at Gawler (SA) cannot count!

When the hands move around to the 6 o'clock position they indicate that it is 4 o'clock again! A manufacturer's mistake in the 1860s resulted in the Roman numeral IV being placed on the face instead of VI!

Princely Yacht

The Queensland Government yacht *Lucinda*, which carried the King and Queen in the early 1900s, as well as Field Marshal Lord Kitchener and numerous other dignitaries, was built for an East Indian Prince who could not afford to keep up the payments and sold it to Brisbane!

Short Address

The man with the world's shortest address is Mr A. Ey, Ayr, Queensland. That's all correspondents need write on their letters for Allan's mail to get through to his nature display in northern Queensland.

Fast Growing

The hair of Lilon, a village girl in Vanuatu, grows twice as fast on the right-hand side of her head and has to be cut four times a year while the hair on the left side is cut only once!

Tea Reviver

'Waltzing Matilda', regarded by many as Australia's national song, was helped towards fame after its first public performance in 1895 when it was adopted by a tea company to help promote its product!

Big Dragon

The largest Chinese dragon in the world lives in Bendigo (Vic.). The 90 m creature, made of embroidered silk, is brought out annually for Bendigo's Easter fair which has been held since 1871. 'Sun Loong' is more than 80 years old.

Dangerous Driving

Drivers who exceed 15 mph (24 kmh) on Lord Howe Island, off the New South Wales coast, are likely to be booked for speeding! The New South Wales Government, which administers the tiny island, decided that anything above 15 mph was dangerous.

FIFTEEN

Stars

Living in the Limelight

Where would we be without our stars to gaze upon?

A star is whomsoever we would make. An entertainer, a politician, a sportsman or sportswoman. They shine in a world often filled with disaster and gloom. We watch them on television, admire them on the stage, read of them in our magazines.

They range from the Queen of England to the man who plays the mouth organ in the local pub. They are in the limelight and they are to be admired. Like those that shine in the heavens, there are great and lesser stars—each admirer to his own taste.

Some place themselves on a pedestal for the purpose of public admiration. Others become stars through none of their own making. Fate, which takes us all by the hand at one time or another, catapults some to stardom when they do not ask for it, like the Australian miner who won the admiration of his mates when he escaped death three times.

As Olivia's steward, Malvolia said in *Twelfth Night*: 'Some are born great; others have greatness thrust upon them.' New South Wales cricketer Arthur Mailey, for example, became a star among the opposition when he allowed them to hit 362 runs off his bowling. And who could not idolise the dance band whose members answered to the names of Field, Marshall, Wellington and called themselves the Waterloo Orchestra?

Step onto the launch pad and be on standby for lift-off to the stars. Among those who shine in this section are:

The Australian cricket team who tossed Winston Churchill in a blanket.

The British ambassador's butler who attended a long-distance runner on a bicycle.

Chloe, the naked lady of Young and Jackson's Hotel.

The parachutist who landed *on* Sydney.

Wally French, the champion gum-leaf blower.

Broken Man

The rise to fame of Albert Namatjira, the first Aboriginal artist to be widely recognised in Australia, also led to his destruction. Tribal custom demanded that he shared the profits from his colourful paintings with his people and he was eventually charged under laws prohibiting the distribution of alcohol among Aborigines. After a spell in prison, he was released before serving out his sentence and died shortly afterwards. Those who knew him say he lost the will to live.

Solid Start

Bob Hawke, who became Prime Minister of Australia in 1983, made a name for himself—and earned a place in the record books—for his drinking exploits 30 years earlier.

In 1952, he won a university speed drinking competition by downing three schooners of beer in 9.3 seconds and at Oxford University he drank 2½ pints of beer in 12 seconds! Years later he declared himself to be 'on the wagon'!

Too Slow

The first Melbourne Cup, one of the world's great horse-races, was run in 1861 and was won by a Sydney horse, Archer. The following year Archer won again. But the horse's owners were not so fast off the mark and in the third year Archer was rejected because the telegram including him in the race arrived too late!

King Don

After a clairvoyant predicted that Adelaide would be destroyed by a tidal wave in 1977, hundreds of people drove to the hills. But Premier Don Dunstan played King Canute to put people's minds at rest. On the day the big wave was expected he walked to the end of a jetty at Glenelg where he grinned at the calm sea. After waiting 15 minutes, he returned to a nearby hotel where he was cheered by a large crowd.

Piercing Peter

Mr Peter Van de Vooren can whistle to an amazing 112 decibels . . . and he proved it on Sydney's Radio 2SM in February 1980.

Mouths to Mouth Recitation

After staring into thousands of mouths as a dentist in the early 1900s, Melbourne-born Horace Stevens decided to open up his own and take singing lessons. Up to the time of his death in 1950 he sang the bass part for Mendelssohn's 'Elijah' 500 times and was hailed as one of the greatest singers of his time.

Tunes of Glory

A dance band in a Melbourne suburb in the early 1930s was known as the Waterloo Orchestra. The players answered to the names of Field, Marshall, and Wellington!

Mixed Grill

Fearing that actress Nellie Stewart might be overcome by heat in a country town, organisers of a show she was appearing in during the 1880s gave her a large meat cooler to sleep in!

Reluctant Playwright

It was suggested to Australian actor/playwright Ray Lawler when he was director of the Melbourne Repertory Theatre that he stage his play *Summer of the Seventeenth Doll*. He reacted with horror and hostility. Anything Australian was guaranteed to fail and even Lawler had fallen prey to the attitude of knocking things Australian. Weeks passed before he reluctantly capitulated.

The play was not only a domestic hit but became something of an international sensation and earned Lawler a fortune!

Bird Pool

A swimming pool at the residence of the New Zealand High Commissioner in Suva, Fiji, is in the shape of a kiwi!

What a Critic

In 1966, when artist Charles Blackman returned from overseas, he found eight of his paintings nailed to a garage wall. 'Put there', said the owner of the property, 'to get them out of the way. They've been rubbish around the place for years'. Blackman's paintings were fetching $2000.

The Wild One

Australian rock star Johnny O'Keefe, who earned the nickname 'The Wild One' after a song of that title, lived up to his name with his brashness and a hectic life leading to drug dependency, nervous breakdowns, a failed marriage and a car crash which almost killed him. He idolised Elvis Presley and died in October 1978, a year and two months after Elvis' death.

BOONARGA CACTOBLASTIS MEMORIAL HALL

BOONARGA, Australia

MEMORIAL HALL
ERECTED IN HONOR OF A BUG!
THE *CACTOBLASTIS BUG* ATE ITS WAY THROUGH VAST AREAS OF PRICKLY PEAR IN QUEENSLAND - MAKING IT POSSIBLE TO TURN VAST WASTELAND INTO RICH AGRICULTURAL LAND.

Melba's Mad Scenes

Whenever the famous Australian colaratura soprano Nellie Melba sang the opera *Lucia Di Lammermoor* life took a dramatic turn.

In Milan, on her first visit, everything was done to break her nerve before the performance because she was considered a foreign intruder. She was told her food would be poisoned, that the building would be set fire to and that the hotel lifts would be tampered with. Despite the threats, she stayed on. When the performance began the audience turned its back on the stage, but at the end of the first recitation the house sat foward and took notice and by the end of the 'Mad Scene' she was given a standing ovation!

* * * * *

During another performance of *Lucia,* this time in the United States, the theatre caught fire. Melba stepped out of the middle of her aria and into the screams of hysteria and panic to reassure the public, who settled down.

But the conductor lost his nerve and scrambled excitedly onto the stage, panting and yelping. Nellie, with Australian aplomb, gave him a resounding crack on the head with her fist and he fell to the stage senseless!

After that, there was no more panic.

Dented Diva

Nellie Melba's first public performance earned her what she described as the 'most devastating criticism' of her life, when a playmate, asked how she enjoyed the song, replied in disgust: 'Nellie Mitchell, I could see your drawers showing!'

Holy Roller

Northern Territory Government officials were delighted that the Queen would be visiting Darwin in October 1982. There was only one problem—they didn't have a Rolls Royce to drive her around in. So they hired one from a local businessman who usually leased it out for weddings.

A Short Snort

When a 4 ft 3 in midget actor asked for a drink in a Sydney pub in 1946, barmaid Maisie Tilley refused because she thought he looked like a nine-year-old child. Actor Raymond Hartley, 19, sued the hotel licensee for calling him a 'dirty little lout' and the hotel keeper was fined £2!

Saved by a Skirt

When former Australian Prime Minister William McMahon made a world tour in November, 1971, his trip spawned only two newsworthy events.

Mr Nixon, then President of the United States, knew so little about him he could not even pronounce his name and Sonia McMahon, his wife, created a sensation when she wore a revealing dress with side-splits almost up to her waist!

Titter Totter

Unable to stand the continual giggling of a group of girls in the audience during the stage production of *The Willow Tree* at Sydney's Criterion Theatre in 1918, actress Kathleen Macdonnell suddenly threw a mirror into the footlights, ran off the stage—and fainted in the arms of her manager!

The Juke's on Her

Olivia Newton-John, one of the world's most successful singing stars, whose hits included a song about a girl who doesn't want to hear a record on a juke box, began her career in a Melbourne coffee bar which used her solo talents to replace a juke box!

The Long Drop

Baritone Fred Baker, playing Mephistopheles in Gounod's opera *Faust* at Melbourne's Princess Theatre in 1888, threw his cape around Faust and the two disappeared through a trap door to give the impression they were descending into Hell.

When the platform reached the cellar, Baker had a heart attack and died shortly afterwards!

Immortal Poem

Tom Burlinson and Sigrid Thornton in the film

Despite the passing of decades, Banjo Paterson's poem 'The Man from Snowy River' has been a constant inspiration to Australians. The volume of verse was a best seller in Australia up to World War I and in 1982 a film of the same name and based on the poem was a box office hit!

Fallen Idols

Eight of the world's most beautiful women were up-ended when a stage collapsed in the 1979 Miss Universe contest in Perth. It happened just after Miss Venezuela received the crown when dozens of photographers rushed onto the platform to get pictures. Most of the 75 girls managed to avoid falling through the hole but eight went straight through! None was badly hurt and all, except two, were able to tuck in to the official lunch later.

"Whiskey" A FOX
TERRIER LOST BY
DRIVER GEOFF HANCOCK
AT HAYS CREEK,
AUSTRALIA, REJOINED
HIS OWNER AT A TRUCK
STOP AT MAMBREY CREEK
8 MONTHS LATER --
HAVING TRAVELED
1,800 MILES
OVER SOME OF
AUSTRALIA'S ROUGHEST
OUTBACK AREA

Hot Bass

After buying a double bass that had
been used in the film *Some Like it
Hot*, classical musician Chris Roberts
strapped it to his back and trudged
through the jungles of Papua-New
Guinea with it, stopping in villages to
play Bach to the tribespeople.

'I became bored with playing in
concerts in New York', said the
American, who made his journey in
1982. 'There was little response during
the performances in America, but in
the villages people clap and stamp
their feet all the way through.'

Slow Company

Sorry End

Bennelong, an Aboriginal who died in
1813, was one of the first of his
people to live among settlers at Port
Jackson after being captured in 1789
by Governor Arthur Phillip. Later
Bennelong and another Aboriginal
sailed with Phillip to England and,
being the first Aboriginals to be seen
there, were introduced to King
George III.

However, when he was brought back
to Australia by Governor Hunter he
became an outcast, began to drink and
fight and was killed in a skirmish by
other Aboriginals.

When actress Sarah Bernhardt toured
Australia in 1891 she refused to live in
a hotel in Melbourne and took a villa
in the beachside suburb of St Kilda,
sharing it with four companions—a
woman, a kangaroo, a lapdog and a
tortoise.

Jack the Trouper

Plugged in

Thirteen members of the European Parliament were among passengers stranded in Australia by an airline strike in March 1981. Anxious to get to their destination in New Zealand they agreed to fly on an Air Force Hercules provided they were given ear plugs. The air force duly obliged.

What a Racket

Tennis star Vitas Gerulaitis always has a date lined up when he travels to Melbourne. He plays his guitar with a local pop group called—The Racket.

Carry the Banner

Playing principal boy in a Melbourne production of *Jack and the Beanstalk* in 1883, Nellie Stewart, one of the famous stage personalities of the 19th century, fell off the beanstalk and broke her arm!

She hurried backstage, had the arm bound up, then returned to the stage to do battle with the giant!

All Blacks

Two origins have been suggested for the name of New Zealand's rugby team, the All Blacks. One theory is based on the fact that Maoris have been included in the team since the first overseas tour in the late 1880s.

The other suggested origin goes back to 1905 when an English journalist cabled that the team played like 'all backs' and a transmission error resulted in the letter L being inserted!

Australian batsman Charles Bannerman achieved some notable 'firsts' in the 1870s. He scored the first run and the first century in the first Test between Australia and England in the 1876–1877 season in Australia and the following year he became the first Australian to score a century in England!

Shark Liked Brass

Asked if they would like to try out a surf-ski at Manly beach, Sydney, in the late 1940s, Lord Brabourne and Maj. Gen. Kimmons, members of Lord Louis Mountbatten's staff, readily accepted. While they were out beyond the breakers, the shark warning bell sounded and a shark swam directly under their ski. They came in faster than they went out!

Ear Champion

Schoolboy Jim Fitzpatrick of Melbourne won national fame in 1975 when he demonstrated he could move his right ear 18 mm while keeping his head as steady as a rock!

Timely Reward

Called to the front of her class at Perth Girls High School in 1952, 13-year-old Robin Tocher wondered what she had done wrong. She held out her hand as instructed and waited for the swish of the cane.

Instead, the teacher fitted an inscribed wrist watch, donated by rail commuters who travelled with her every morning and who were highly impressed by her impeccable behaviour and manners!

Bumptious Colonials

Winston Churchill had a distaste for Australians from the moment he boarded a homeward-bound mail steamer containing an Australian cricket team in the 1890s. When he complained about their 'unruly' behaviour they tossed him in a blanket. He left the ship at Port Said, expressing strong opinions about the people Down Under!

Moving Target

American golf star Ben Crenshaw was feeling a little shirty after dropping four shots in the first four holes in the Australian PGA tournament at Victoria's Royal Melbourne course in November 1982. But he thought things had gone a little too far when his ball bounced high off the fairway and landed in a spectator's shirt pocket. The man dropped the ball onto a good 'lie' and commented, 'I think he owes me a beer'.

Starting Early

Winnifred Roberts, aged five, and her three-year-old sister Betty were Australia's youngest violinists, each able to play the major scales on instruments specially made for them!

AUSTRALIAN MERINO RAM SOLD FOR $25,000

Gin Required

An official in charge of food and liquor laid on to celebrate the 1901 visit to Australia of the Duke and Duchess of Cornwall and York—known to Sydney schoolchildren as 'corned beef and pork'—jotted on a form that one case of dry gin had been acquired 'for the Duchess'!

Lindrum's Mastery

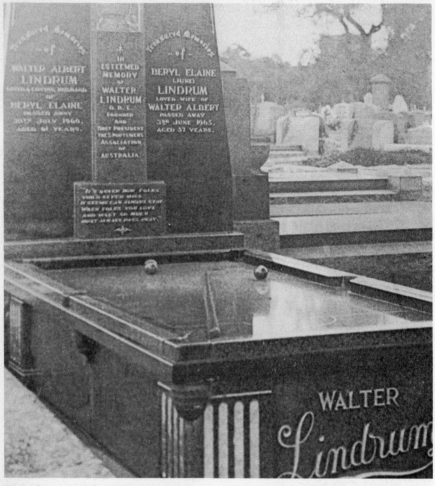

One of the world's strangest tombstones, in Melbourne Cemetery, is a marble billiard table with flower vases as pockets! It commemorates former world professional billiard champion Walter Lindrum who died in 1960. Alongside his grave is that of his wife, Beryl, who died five years later.

Billiard player Walter Lindrum created a world record break of 4137 points in 175 minutes in 1932. His great-grandfather, grandfather and father were all billiards champions of Australia, his brother Horace was world snooker champion and another brother, Fred, was billiards champion of the world!

Mighty 'Smith

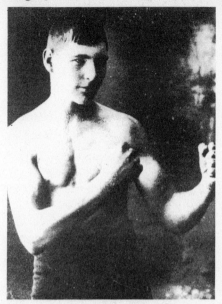

The bulging muscles which helped Les Darcy to 40 wins in 44 fights were developed when he worked at an anvil at an East Maitland forge where he was a boy apprentice in the early 1900s. The anvil has been preserved for posterity and is on display at a museum near Scone (NSW)!

Brooms to Axes

Anne Humphries, Australia's champion broom thrower, decided to change implements, entered the country's first annual axe-tossing contest at Ulong (NSW) threw the 2.75 kg axe a distance of 22.365 m and claimed the women's title!

Crackers

Gary Crocker, of Hay (NSW), ate TWENTY-THREE dry cracker biscuits in 10 minutes in a local contest, beating his nearest rival by 11 biscuits!

Instant Success

A fictitious part-Aboriginal detective known as Napoleon Bonaparte was an instant success for his creator, writer Arthur Upfield, whose books were translated into many languages and formed the basis of 'Boney', a popular Australian television series!

Prefers Work

Gina Hayward, Australia's richest woman, is sole heiress to a mining empire worth more than $600 million. She could spend months in the south of France, drink champagne beside the swimming pool or laze on a yacht—yet she prefers to work up to 17 hours a day for the mining empire owned by her father, Mr Lang Hancock, of Western Australia.

Whizz Kids

'The Konrad Kids'—Jon and his sister Ilsa—were taught to swim at a migrant camp in New South Wales after their arrival from Latvia in 1949 and by the 1960s the youngsters had jointly recorded THIRTY-SEVEN world swimming records!

Indecent

Annette Kellerman, an Australian distance swimmer who, in Hollywood in 1915 starred in *Neptune's Daughter* in which she created a high-diving record, had been arrested eight years earlier and accused of indecent exposure when she wore a one-piece bathing costume!

Bolt to Safety

For Fred Ridley, Australia's most accident-prone miner, it was third time lucky.

First, he blew himself up in New South Wales when his drill went into a forgotten gelignite charge; then he was knocked flying in Western Australia in 1895 by a runaway mine truck; and finally he fell into the opening of a mine shaft. But providence beamed on Fred this time—his belt caught on a protruding bolt as he fell and after dangling between life and death for a time he was lifted free by fellow workers!

HUBERT OPPERMAN-Australian cyclist
RODE 860 MILES IN 24 HOURS
1932

One-Legged Affair

In a boxing contest staged at Brisbane Stadium in 1924 C. Olsen and E. Holmes fought to decide 'The One-Legged Championship of Queensland'. When both fell down in the fourth round a draw was declared.

Royal Testimonial

A Christchurch (NZ) factory sent the Duke of Edinburgh two new pairs of swimming trunks in December, 1981, after he wrote to tell them that a pair the factory presented to him in 1954 had finally worn out!

Well Performed

Englishman George Seth Coppin
eloped to Sydney with an American
actress in 1842 when he was twenty-
three. When he wasn't acting and
running a pub he was prospecting for
gold, building theatres and sitting in
the Victorian Parliament which he
brought alive with impromptu songs.
He also declared that MPs should not
be paid and donated his salary to
charity. Among his other claims was
the introduction of the thrush and the
camel to Australia.

Cowchip Tossers

The sport of cowchip tossing is
growing—having originated in Beaver
County, Oklahoma (USA) in 1970, the
art of tossing a piece of dried cow
manure measuring 15 cm in diameter,
is now tested by competitors at
Edgeworth, near Newcastle (NSW).

Gum-leaf Solos

Pinching the leaf of a eucalyptus
tree between his thumbs, Mr Wally
French, aged 82, became the first
winner of the Australian Gum-leaf
Blowing Championships and paved the
way for other contestants who
provided such renderings as 'Love Me
Tender', 'Home on the Range', 'It's
Been a Hard Day's Night' and 'A Pub
with No Beer'.

Only fresh gum-leaves are allowed
following the revelation that
Queenslander Les Hawthorne had
played a beautiful tune on a 34-year-
old leaf!

Message Clear

Sir Donald Bradman

Relations between Australia and
England were strained when England's
cricket captain, D.R. Jardine, brought
bodyline bowling to Australia and even
managed to get the magnificent Don
Bradman dismissed for a duck,
resulting in one newspaper poster
saying nothing more than: DON.

Sports Freak

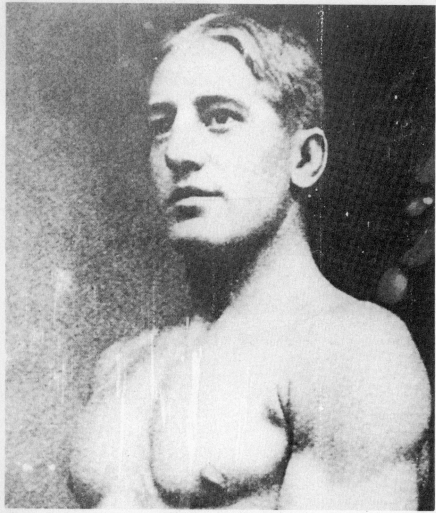

As an all-round sportsman, Reginald 'Snowy' Baker took a lot of beating. Up to his death at the age of 69 Snowy participated in TWENTY-SIX sports and excelled at most!

He became open swimming champion of New South Wales at the age of 13, played Rugby Union for Australia against Great Britain when he was 16, beat most opponents at diving and became heavyweight boxing champion of Australasia when he was 18.

When he wasn't taking part in sports, he was acting in Australia's early films! He later became an actor and stuntman in Hollywood.

Bad Luck

After creating a record by having the highest number of runs knocked off his bowling in a match—362—New South Wales cricketer Arthur Mailey commented: 'I had bad luck, you know. A man in a bowler hat in the pavilion missed four catches off my bowling'!

Wrong Country

Arthur Benjamin, who gave his first public performance as a pianist at the age of seven, became one of Australia's greatest pianists, conductors and composers of serious music—yet since his death in 1960 he is best remembered for his 1937 composition 'Jamaican Rumba'!

NICHOLSON
Australia

↓

RODE
44000
MILES
IN
ONE
YEAR
=

All Black

After a cricket team made up of Aborigines toured England in 1868 under the name The Aboriginal Blacks of Australia many English residents believed most Australians were of Aboriginal descent.

In a break between play the Australian team gave a demonstration of boomerang throwing but one of the weapons went astray and hit a woman who was almost knocked off her seat!

Rope Trick

Mr H. L'Estrange, Australia's answer to Blondin, set out on a rope stretched across Middle Harbour, Sydney, in April 1877. Half-way over he stood on one leg, waved a handkerchief, lay on his back and finally sat down to survey the spectators through a telescope.

Cockroach Country

When Mark Twain came to Australia as part of a world lecture tour to pay off a debt incurred when he backed a type-setting invention he took note of the cities and the people. But his daughter noticed the insects, particularly the cockroaches as large as tarantulas and she commented: 'In the bath, in bed, on the coach and at the table, one's eyes were constantly meeting the gaze of this repulsive creation.'

Famous Dance

The haka, a Maori ceremonial dance, became known throughout the world after the All Blacks, the New Zealand rugby union team, began performing it in 1889 at the start of each game.

Top Booter

The Australian record for throwing a gumboot is held by Roland Doom, who at Pakenham (Vic.) in 1978 threw one a distance of 44.2 m!

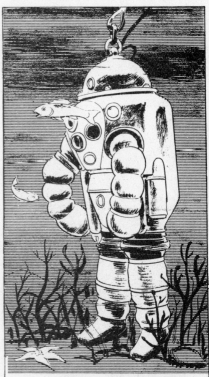

JOHN JOHNSTONE a professional diver CHECKING A CABLE AT THE BOTTOM OF BASS STRAIT WALKED FROM VICTORIA TO TASMANIA - A DISTANCE OF 27 MILES - ON THE FLOOR OF THE OCEAN September, 1948

General Caught in Oil

Sir Howard Smith of Queensland is the owner of the world's most valuable toilet door—on the front is a painting of General Douglas MacArthur, Supreme Allied Commander in the Pacific during World War II, as he would have been observed had someone opened the door of the closet and found him inside!

It was executed by the celebrated Australian artist Sir William Dargie during his stint in the Australian Army. After purchasing it from a vicar at a church fete, Sir Howard asked a local coffin maker to build a special box to transport it to its new domicile. General MacArthur then travelled down the main highway, his feet sticking from the box which protruded from the back of the car!

Nick of Time

Explorer Matthew Flinders pacified a group of warlike Aborigines in 1796 by whipping out a pair of scissors and trimming their hair and beards.

Royal Riot

Before the Duke of Edinburgh, Queen Victoria's second son, left for Australia—the country's first Royal visitor—in 1867 he was told that an enthusiastic crowd was waiting for him. THAT WAS THE UNDERSTATEMENT OF THE CENTURY!

More than 60 000 people who waited in vain for him beside the Yarra River—he had been advised not to appear because of the crowd—rioted, smashing down tables laden with food and helping themselves to vats of wine. In a second riot a boy was killed and two men injured; three boys were burned to death when a model of the *Galatea* caught fire; a specially-built ballroom burned down; and at a picnic in Sydney the Duke was wounded in the back by a pistol-wielding man who was later hanged for attempted murder!

Off the Track

Former motor racing champion Alan Jones, who escaped serious injury throughout his brilliant career, ended up in hospital when he fell off a small motor bike at his farm in northern Victoria after a collision with a farm worker on another bike.

Battle Cry

Not Cricket

Would the gentlemen of Lords, accustomed to the sweet smack of leather against willow have put up with it?

A new cricket bat designed by fast bowler Dennis Lillee was bright yellow and made of ALUMINIUM! He tried to use it in Perth in the summer of 1979–1980 in an Australia-England Test match but England and the umpires had their way and the crowd were denied a new sound in cricket—BOINGGGGGG!

Roy Cazaly, who played Australian Rules football for South Melbourne from 1921 to 1926, was able to leap so high to take a mark that the crowds began a catch cry whenever he raced for a high ball—'Up There, Cazaly!' It caught on so well that Australian troops took it to battle with them in the Middle East. In the 1970s Mike Brady immortalised the cry in a football song of the same name.

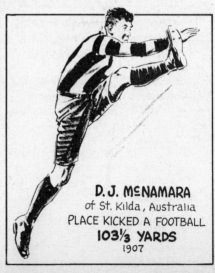

D. J. McNAMARA
of St. Kilda, Australia
PLACE KICKED A FOOTBALL
103⅓ YARDS
1907

Crazy Jump

'Everyone does something crazy in their life', said 28-year-old electrician Wayne Allwood to explain why he sailed by parachute to the 1000-foot-high Centrepoint Tower, Sydney's tallest building, before jumping with a smaller 'chute to nearby Hyde Park in February 1982.

Hands of Fame

Every year at the National Country Music Awards weekend at Tamworth (NSW) a star is asked to slap his or her hand into a square of wet concrete! The handprints of some 50 musicians are now preserved at the Hands of Fame Corner Stone in the city centre.

No Fun

A report by the Hunter Valley Research Foundation revealed that Australia had lost its image as a sporting fun-loving nation. The findings were issued the day after the country's star entertainer, Rolf Harris, was hit on the head by a Fosters beer can during a performance at the Sydney Opera House. At least *his* sense of humour was intact. 'It's empty', he remarked as he left the stage.

Given a Start

When an English cricket XI played in Australia in 1864 against local teams, the colonials were allowed to field 22 players to even up their disadvantage.

TEX TYRRELL WON A "TALL TALE" CONTEST IN ALICE SPRINGS, AUSTRALIA, BY TELLING INCREDIBLE STORIES *CONTINUOUSLY FOR 8 HOURS*

Tense Cricket

Tension was so high during one Test match in 1882 between England and Australia that one spectator dropped dead with excitement, another collapsed and still another chewed half through his umbrella handle!

Memorable Ham

As the passenger ship *London* sank in the Bay of Biscay in 1866 and actor Gustavus V. Brooke disappeared beneath the waves, he called to survivors: 'Remember me to my friends in Melbourne.' How could they forget him? He was the man who played Hamlet on the billiard table of a pub and who received pocketfuls of nuggets thrown to him by appreciative prospectors.

★★★★★★★★★★★★★★★★★★★★★★★★★★★★★★★★★★★★★

THE MAN WHO OUTRACED 4 HORSES!

WILLIAM FRANCIS KING of SYDNEY, AUSTRALIA, RACED ON FOOT AGAINST A COACH FROM WINDSOR TO SYDNEY – A DISTANCE OF **34** MILES – AND *BEAT THE COACH'S 4-HORSE TEAM BY 7 MINUTES!*

★★★★★★★★★★★★★★★★★★★★★★★★★★★★★★★★★★★★★

Kissing Point

Governor John Hunter, guest at a picnic on the New South Wales coast, was kissed by a daring young lady who then demanded the customary pair of gloves. As a result the area became officially known as Kissing Point!

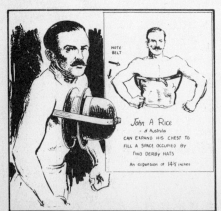

Leader Sprayed

Recovering from a bout of pleurisy and pneumonia, then Prime Minister Malcolm Fraser was lying back on his bed in 1978 when he was hit in the face by a jet of water.

The window cleaner at The Lodge, in Canberra, did not realise the window was open as he aimed his hose pipe. A top-level investigation revealed later that although the windows had been closed in readiness for the cleaner, a maid, concerned that the sick Prime Minister was resting in a stuffy room, had opened them.

The Great Dally

When Dally Messenger, one of the greats of Australian Rugby League, toured England in 1908–1909 with the 1st Kangaroos team he jumped OVER an opposing defender to score a try!

Fighter Turned Actor

When former American bare-knuckle champion John L. Sullivan turned actor he toured Australia in a melodrama called *Honest Hearts and Willing Hands*!

WILLIAM FRANCIS KING
(1807-1874) of Sydney, Australia,
WALKED **28** MILES IN
6 HOURS, 48 MINUTES,
CARRYING A 104-LB. GOAT

Unsung Hero

Captain Arthur Phillip, the first Governor of Australia, severely injured himself falling into a concealed hollow and was later hit in the shoulder by an Aboriginal's spear. He was raised to the rank of Admiral on his return to England. Yet after his death on 13 August 1814, hardly anyone came to his funeral in Bath.

Landmark

One of Melbourne's most famous ladies is known by no other name than Chloe. Naked and framed, she is displayed in the saloon bar of Young and Jackson's Hotel. It is believed the portrait, painted in Paris in 1875 by Chevalier Jules Lefebvre, is of a beautiful French woman called Marie who threw a splendid dinner party for her friends, spent her last remaining sou on a box of matches, boiled the phosphorus from the heads and gained passage to the next world by drinking the water!

JOE KIRKWOOD
Australian Trick Shot Golfer DROVE A BALL OFF THE FACE OF A WATCH AND SCORED A HOLE-IN-ONE

Cedar Rapids, Iowa

Tragedy Beach

Leaving Melbourne in October, 1887, the 1226-ton passenger ship *Cheviot* foundered off Port Phillip Heads with the loss of 35. A beach near Portsea was later named Cheviot Beach after the lost ship—and that was where, 80 years later, Prime Minister Harold Holt was to disappear at sea while swimming!

LANCE SKUTHORPE

famed
Australian horseman

RODE **7** WILD HORSES
IN A PERIOD OF **7**
CONSECUTIVE MINUTES
WITHOUT EVER BEING THROWN

Over Ardent

The first man to greet Queen Elizabeth II at Sydney in 1954—the first time a reigning monarch had ever set foot on Australian soil—was Prime Minister Sir Robert Menzies who once made her blush by quoting:

I did but see her passing by,
And yet I love her till I die!

Double Bite

Bluey the sheepdog and his owner lie side by side in a grave at Pindarra (NSW). Faithful Bluey died from a snake bite and after his owner buried him, he set out to look for the killer snake. But the reptile got him first...

Banjo Queen

Bessie Campbell, who gave numerous concerts for Australian troops during World War I, played the banjo so well that she became known as 'The Banjo Queen' and newspaper critics said she played the instrument with such ability that she rendered it 'almost classical'.

Missing Genius

So many arguments were struck up about the design of the Sydney Opera House that when it was opened amid a blaze of fireworks, Joern Utzon, the original architect, refused to attend.

Miss New Australia

Born in China of White Russian parents, Tania Verstak won the Miss Australia title in October, 1961—the first 'New Australian' to do so.

Hollow Feeling

Governor Sir William Denison and 78 members of the Tasmanian Legislative Assembly got down to the root of politics in 1854 when they invited their relatives and friends to dine in the hollow of the island's largest tree.

To the Top

A young American who came to Australia in 1897 as a mining engineer and lived in a corrugated iron hut under the shadow of Mount Leonora (WA) worked his way to the very top as far as jobs and residences go—his name was Herbert Hoover and later became President of the United States!

Clock Stopper

When Dame Nellie Melba stayed at Bendigo (Vic.), she complained that the post office chimes kept her awake. Although she didn't linger in the town, the clock stopped chiming from 11 o'clock each night for many years to come.

His Biggest Story

The greatest publicity explorer Captain James Cook received was not when he discovered the east coast of Australia—but when he was killed by islanders on Hawaii in 1779.

TOM NORRIS
Noted Australian Athlete
SKIPPED ROPE
FROM SYDNEY TO MELBOURNE
- A DISTANCE OF 590 MILES
472,000 SKIPS -
28 DAYS.

Sporting Gesture

During the third lap of Australia's national mile championship, world mile record holder John Landy stopped to help Ron Clarke, who had fallen. Urged to continue by Clarke, Landy, who had lost seven seconds because of the gesture, bolted around the last lap to win in 4 min 4.2 sec!

A Screamer

Burke and the Actress

Robert O'Hara Burke, the police inspector who lost his life on the Burke and Wills expedition across outback Australia, had been in love with Julia Matthews, a beautiful actress who wore a picture of him in her locket.

After Burke's death, Julia sailed to England where, in 1867, she was widely acclaimed for her part in Offenbach's 'Grand Duchess'.

But ill fortune was to befall her, too. While staying in New Orleans she contracted a fever and died at the age of thirty-four.

During the 1896 cricket Tests, Jones, the Australian bowler, sent down a screamer that went straight through the beard of the famous Dr W. G. Grace. Grace walked down the pitch and said, 'Where the hell are you bowling, Jonah?' to which Jones, embarrassed and stumbling for words, could only reply: 'Sorry doctor, she slipped.'

Canefield Tenor

Aboriginal Harold Blair developed such a fine singing voice while working in canefields in Queensland that he was persuaded to sing for the soprano Marjorie Lawrence and he went on to become the first Aboriginal to win a Diploma of Music!

Flag Waiver

When E. H. Flack of Victoria, Australia's sole representative at the Olympics in Athens in 1896, won both the 800 m and the 1500 m, no Australian flag was available. So officials raised the closest emblem they could find—an AUSTRIAN flag!

Flunkeyed Out

Edwin Flack, Australia's first gold medallist, had to drop out of the 1896 marathon in which he was attended by the British Ambassador's personal butler (fully attired in waistcoat and bowler hat) who rode alongside on a bicycle!

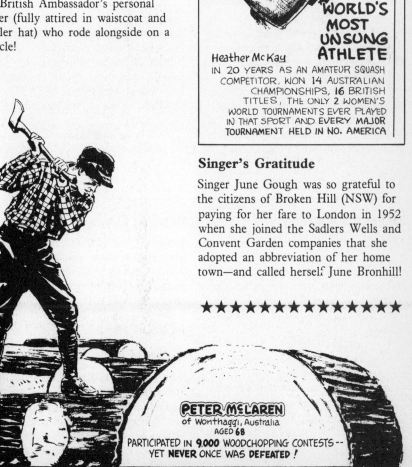

THE WORLD'S MOST UNSUNG ATHLETE

Heather McKay

IN 20 YEARS AS AN AMATEUR SQUASH COMPETITOR, WON 14 AUSTRALIAN CHAMPIONSHIPS, 16 BRITISH TITLES, THE ONLY 2 WOMEN'S WORLD TOURNAMENTS EVER PLAYED IN THAT SPORT AND EVERY MAJOR TOURNAMENT HELD IN NO. AMERICA

PETER McLAREN of Wonthaggi, Australia AGED 68 PARTICIPATED IN 9,000 WOODCHOPPING CONTESTS -- YET NEVER ONCE WAS DEFEATED!

Singer's Gratitude

Singer June Gough was so grateful to the citizens of Broken Hill (NSW) for paying for her fare to London in 1952 when she joined the Sadlers Wells and Convent Garden companies that she adopted an abbreviation of her home town—and called herself June Bronhill!

★★★★★★★★★★★★★★★

Fiery Lola

While Lola Montes, the flamboyant actress, was appearing in a show called 'Asmodeus, or the Little Devil' at Ballarat (Vic.), lightning struck the Critereon Theatre, some of the audience were hit by pieces of flying wood, the scenery caught fire and women screamed in terror.

Amid the confusion, Lola walked up to the footlights and told the audience: 'Previously I have had to put up with theatrical lightning. But it would appear that Bendigo folk must have the genuine stuff.'

Lover of Liszt (the man, not his music) and mistress of King Louis of Bavaria (who made her a Countess), Irish adventuress Dolores Gilbert, alias Lola Montes, arrived in Australia in 1855 where she smoked cigars, drank whisky and presented a stage fantasy of Bavarian history. The editor of the *Ballarat Times*, Erle Seekamp gave her a bad write up and she announced from the stage that he was a little fond of drinking. The controversy between them reached such a pitch that the Countess hit him with a whip in a hotel bar. Seekamp responded by hitting her with a heavier whip. This resulted in a poet writing the following lines in the Melbourne *Punch*:

> Erle Seekamp's face bore bloody trace
> Of Lola Montes' lash;
> Her shoulders fair, if they were bare,
> Would show a crimson gash!

Singing Blacksmith

Franz Natzka started work as a blacksmith's apprentice but his singing voice was so good that while performing with local groups he was 'spotted' by Australian baritone John Brownlee and encouraged to travel overseas.

After his 1938 debut at London's Covent Garden he made several concert tours and during a 10 week season in 1947 sang six new operas, five in different languages.

While singing in 'The Mastersingers' in New York at the age of 39 he collapsed and died from a cerebral haemorrhage.

Puzzling Game

Spectators who watched a baseball game between two visiting American teams, Chicago and All-America, in Sydney in 1888 were so confused about the rules that many did not know who had won until they read the morning papers.

Baldness Cure

When old Ma Edith Evans of Queensland rubbed her knee with a potion made from a recipe given to her by a gypsy in England many years before, hairs sprouted! She later sold the recipe to an Adelaide hair-care company for $1 million.